Soccer in
the Weeds

Soccer in

the Weeds

Bad Hair, Jews, and Chasing the Beautiful Game

DANIEL LILIE

Cover design: Tanja Jeremic/3Tanja@99design
Interior design & book production: John W. Glenn
Text set in Alegreya, a typeface designed by Juan Pablo del Peral
    for Huerta Tipográfica

For my dad, who saved a lumpy soccer ball for me, and the memory of my grandfather Moe Hellman, who knew nothing about soccer, but everything else.

Contents

Acknowledgments

THE MORE YOU WRITE the less you know. Writing a book can seem like an asymptotic journey, the end being infinity that you can approach but never touch. Many talented and generous people helped me in different ways. Fred Cantor, author, attorney, and soccer player, adopted my story and served as reader, advisor, editor, and omniscient arbiter of my occasionally wacky opinions and digressive tendencies. John W. Glenn, agent and publishing advisor, has assisted in the design, presentation, and market development, resulting in a book that has far exceeded my aesthetic expectations. My copy editor, Rich Graham, author and a friend for many years, shaped up the manuscript and provided technical support at a critical juncture in the process. Thanks to Sharon Brinkman's punctilious talents the book is a book, rather than an aggregation of misspellings and grammatical non sequiturs. My old high school friend, Professor Michael Bernhard, is one of the few people I know who has gotten smarter over the years. His critical reading and assessment of the manuscript was a big boost. My cover designer, Tanja Jeremic, working remotely from Serbia, nailed the spirit of the book with a cover that evinces nostalgic grace and sporting elan.

A whole bunch of soccer and sports friends through the years came to visit my memory, and all of them inspired me. Thanks to Ed Gans, David Yolen, Bob Glick, Ernst Buggisch, Maurice Raus, Dave Wentz, Alex Marin, Dan Michaud, Paul Mira, Chris Mira, Bob Fritz, Doug Winshall, Avi Saban, and Jeff Anderson. Two goalkeepers, my sister Jessica, who always pretended she liked getting shot at, and my step-brother Neil Gordon, a real goalkeeper, helped shape my thoughts. My brother-in-law Dave Smiley, a new convert to soccer, keeps me on my toes. And thanks to my wife Melissa and my kids, Ava, Owen, and Derek. Through the everlasting joy they bring to me, I had the peace of mind to finish the book.

I would also like to thank every kid unlucky enough to have not played as much soccer as they could have. There is always the next life.

D.L.
August 2012

PART ONE
Connecticut
1965–1983

ONE

My Strange Soccer Roots

THE FIRST SOCCER BALL I ever saw was a fixture in the trunk of my dad's 1965 VW bug. The bug was compact, black, and the trunk was, of course, in the front. In the early days of the VW, there was a whiff of subterfuge about it, something still too German, maybe a bit subversive. It was not a car you'd take on a hunting or fishing trip, but perhaps to the Strand book store in the Village to paw through the bins looking for a second edition of *Animal Farm*. When he popped open the hood, I'd grab the little hand pump and hope that the needle wasn't broken so I could breathe some life into the old thing. Calling it a "ball" is a stretch. It had none of the characteristics that would be needed for a ball today. Constructed of thick brown leather and smelling like wet wool, it was neither round nor smooth. It was always semideflated. The leather was heavy, baseball-mitt tan. Today that ball might be a prop in some Ralph Lauren nostalgia emporium selling $225 rugby shirts. It harkened back to the dawn of soccer, a muddy affair played in heavy, cleated boots. English soccer in its infancy was not so much the beautiful game that we see today, but exercise designed to exhaust schoolboys. The actual construction of a soccer ball was not as important as the idea of a ball. But in 1966, when I was seven, there was nothing more exciting or beautiful to me than that heavy, moldy, lumpy brown thing in my dad's trunk.

In 1966 England won the World Cup, but on the sporting landscape of Stamford, Connecticut, that news barely caused a ripple and may in fact have gone unreported in our local paper, the *Advocate*. Stamford was a "big three" town: baseball, football, and basketball. Hockey was played in New Canaan and Darien, richer and smaller towns to the north, and soccer in Stamford was played by Italians—mostly immigrants—who lived on the city's west side. Soccer goals, which today are a common fixture pretty much everywhere in America, were an exotic sight in 1966. Usually, they were a part of a modified football goal, with a second, lower crossbar appended to the football crossbar. As a kid in Stamford, I recall that the only soccer goals were in the biggest public park, Scalzi.

Except for my father, I didn't know a single person who played soccer. I had never seen soccer played on TV or in person. Not another kid in my class knew a thing about the sport. My dad played as a kid, as had his father, who came to Queens from Germany in the 1910s. The German-Jewish community had by that time been set up with a social and sporting club—the Prospect Unity Club—that fielded teams that competed successfully with the other immigrant teams in the German-American (now Cosmopolitan) Soccer League. I have a photograph of the

1948 champion Prospect Unity Club, looking fit and prosperous in their floppy shorts and striped jerseys, standing on a field in Queens that probably looked very much like the one their fathers and uncles played on in Germany and Austria twenty years before. My dad was a bit too young to have played on that team, but they were his influence, and he went on to play for the same club and then for Brooklyn Technical High School. So my dad played soccer, and so did his uncles on both his mother and father's side, and so did my grandfather. On my mother's side, both her parents had been born in New York. Their parents emigrated from the Russian/Polish border area sometime around the 1880s, and there was not a whiff of soccer anywhere from my mother's family. Their primary sport once they came to the U.S. seemed to be survival.

In 1966, the relationship between dads, sports, and their children was, of course, very different than the hyperinvolvement of today's parents. It was enough back then to go out in the driveway or the backyard, toss a ball around for ten minutes, and consider your child to have his (or her, but not so much her back then) sporting quota fulfilled. If they wanted more, that's what the neighborhood kids were for.

Although he was a mere twenty-two years older than me—making him a virtual twenty-nine-year-old colt when I was seven—grown men were not playing sports back then, unless that sport was one of the old guys' holy trinity of golf, tennis, or sailing. I suppose that there were some committed types playing basketball at the Y, but if you were a white male with a suburban life, you did not run off to play in a sports league in 1966. What was clear to me even at seven, as soon as I caught the soccer bug, was that the ball in the trunk was as symbolic as it was practical. For my dad, the brown leather oversized meatball was a small connection to his adolescent life, more of a prop than anything. But it would only be much later when I understood the psychic value of carrying a ball in your trunk: that at any time, any place, there is a chance to get a game.

I did manage to get him to take the ball out of the trunk, but it was an annual, perhaps semiannual event. Since our yard was too small and hilly for soccer, the only place to play was in the park. In the hierarchy of importance for doing things on the weekend, going to the park and kicking a soccer ball around was pretty low. One Saturday my dad must have run out of things to fix, and he asked me if I felt like going to the park to play soccer. To me this was the call of the wild. We went to Cummings Park, near the water, with Stamford's only public beach. I remember a large grassy clearing ringed by large shade trees. My dad got the ball out of the VW, and we kicked it around. And that was it. I was hooked. Hooked at the wrong time and the wrong place by the wrong sport. As I kicked the ball back and forth with my dad, my sense was that there was something simpler about it than the other sports I had started to play. Not using your hands was liberating. You moved and the ball moved. You didn't have a mitt or a stick or have to think too hard about where that big lump of ball was. I noticed that even with that lumpy excuse for a ball, my dad could impart a little English on the ball that caused it to spin and swerve, its path starting outside of me, looking like it would fly right past but then gently settling at my feet. That was my first soccer nibble, a bucolic kick-around with my dad in a quiet suburban beach park. Except for maybe some of the Italians new to Stamford, there is little doubt that we were the only father and son kicking a soccer ball that day. It would be somewhat like going to a typical suburban park today and setting up a cricket wicket and bowling a few overs with your kid. In the Stamford of 1966, I was unaware that I had been blooded into the world's largest fraternal organization—that of the soccer player.

What was it about soccer? Eduardo Galeano, in his anthology *Soccer in Sun and Shadow*, describes the ascendancy of the sport in Argentina:

> The process was unstoppable. Like the Tango, soccer blossomed in the slums. It required no money and could be played with nothing more than sheer desire. In fields, in alleys and on beaches, native-born kids and young immigrants improvised games using balls made of old socks filled with rags or paper, and a couple of stones for a goal. Thanks to the language of the game, which soon became universal, workers driven out of the countryside could communicate perfectly well with workers driven out of Europe. The Esperanto of the ball connected poor Creoles with peons who had crossed the sea from Vigo, Lisbon, Beirut, or Besarabia with their dreams of "hacer la America"—making a new world by building, carrying, baking, or sweeping. Soccer had made a lovely voyage; first organized in the colleges and universities of England, it brought joys to the lives of South Americans who had never set foot in school.

That my dad's dad had made his way over here from a little German town, Selinginstat, not far from Frankfurt, was a part of the Esperanto equation. He and a bunch more relatives on my father's side smelled something in the water earlier than a lot of Jews and made their way out of Germany in the 1920s. My grandfather and father were both members of the Prospect

1986. In 1989, Verebes was called a "dirty Gypsy" by an editor of *Nepsport*, a national Hungarian sports publication. When MTK visited Ferencvaros and other stadiums around Hungary between 1987 and 1989, the chants "Bones! Soap!" and "Dirty Jews!" could be heard on a regular basis.

Whether real or perceived, certain European teams have become linked with "Jewishness." I say "Jewishness" as opposed to Jews, because in the two most prominent cases, Ajax and Tottenham, the link is far more abstract than real. Neither team today has a single Jewish player. Both teams play in parts of their cities where Jews are perhaps more represented than in other parts of those cities, but hardly in exclusively Jewish areas. Both teams are flash points for anti-Semitic behavior, with Ajax's Jewish associations bordering on the bizarre. Ajax, which in the 1970s would catalyze my love for soccer and for many fans become the iconic representation of the sport, has adopted the six-pointed star and imprimatur of Judaism, without any true association with Judaism. This paradox has been widely chronicled, but it is perhaps the only instance in the world where the fans of a major sports team have coopted a religion—a religion that in fact most of the fans probably do not believe in—to unite them in battle against their rivals.

As ignorant as I was about soccer history, I sensed a connection with the sport that day: my dad, pretty phlegmatic by nature, seemed alive kicking that ball around. It occurred to me that I had never seen him run before; dads did not run in the '60s. He was a bit stiff-legged, but if I sprayed a pass, he could step it up a bit, a fair bit of spring left in his step. Our energy fed off each other, and I started to get a little bolder, striking the ball harder, taking aim at our improvised goal. Soccer, a universal language, the dominion of rich and poor, the Esperanto of all mankind (music and math be damned) became my friend that day.

*   *   *

It's crazy to think that you can be demonized for playing any sport, but that's what it was like in the late '60s in the provincial city/town of Stamford. With a shade over 100,000 people—the official census I recall placed the city's population at 102,000 for years—Stamford had all of the problems of a small city with none of the virtues of a large town. It was not, per se, a bad place; it's that it had multiple identities and therefore no common identity. Stamford was less a community than a commuter town dotted with a few ethnic enclaves. Southern Connecticut as a region was full of towns and cities with real identity and community pride. Fairfield County contains dramatic cultural, ethnic, and economic contrasts within a small geographic area. Bucolic and wealthy Westport is moments from the biting poverty of South Norwalk and minutes from radically poor Bridgeport. The smaller towns are insular, generally with one high school, while the cities—Stamford, Norwalk, Bridgeport, and Danbury—are, of course, more ethnic and fragmented. In this mix, Stamford was represented by all classes, races, and income levels. The ethnic enclaves tended to stay that way; "soft" segregation was the order of the day, and there were still parts of the city with redlining and real segregation. In the postindustrial, preurban renewal time circa the late 1960s, the city's downtown was sort of a DMZ: un- and underdeveloped with nothing to recommend it save for the Ferguson Library, a Caldor's discount store, and a couple of Chinese and Italian restaurants.

My grammar school was the parochial Bi-Cultural Day School, the "Bi" alluding not towards an enlightened view of sexual orientation, but to the melding of English and Hebrew cultures. In practical terms, this meant that for us little chosen people, we were in school a couple of hours longer than our Gentile brethren because of the need to get in the full complement of both English and Hebrew studies. The demand for cramming in a schedule that included English, social studies, math, science, Hebrew language, and Bible studies left precious little time for gym or recess. Forty or so years ago, Jews were not yet part of the sporting fraternity in America. The Jewish athlete was an aberration, someone so talented that he could not be ignored. The cataclysm of World War II affected not only European Jews and survivors but also the "lucky" ones in America whose ancestors had already made it here. With Jews restricted from elite American universities and by lingering anti-Semitism after the war, sports and recreation were secondary concerns for Jewish families. What mattered was that you mastered your studies and presented unimpeachable credentials—ideally as an independent professional—to ensure your security in America. Sports, an area where Jews actually flourished in the 1920s and 1930s, were swiftly swept under the rug.

For a seven-year-old at Bi-Cultural Day School, this translated into a form of juvenile incarceration. The school had no gym or gym teacher and consequently no sports at all. Recess, a twice-a-day staple at every school today, was given once a week—on Wednesday. Why Wednesday was chosen was a mystery. I suppose that even our wizened rabbis and antisports school administration realized that confining several hundred schoolchildren for forty consecutive hours a week just might not be the best idea and that by midweek they needed to run around. So there it was, every Wednesday at about eleven, the doors would open and we were free to play for a half hour.

You would be right to think that a school that granted a half hour of recess once a week would not be stocked with sporting equipment. The entirety of our gear boiled down to three or four standard issue red rubber playground balls. These were the bouncy ones—still in production today, designed for playing on pavement, in games like four square, dodge ball, and kick ball. One day we were playing four square, and I had a bit of inspiration: why not take the red ball and tell the other kids about that exotic sport that I discovered with my dad at Cummings Park, that thing called soccer? Out of sixteen kids in our class, twelve were boys, and out of those only about half had any athletic talent. So the six or so of the boys took one of the red balls down to the field.

The "field" was just that, a real field, with reeds and big grass plants with giant wheat shafts that looked like they would yield tasty bread. Apparently, the rabbis had not provided for a mower or landscape service in the annual budget. The field must have been used for sports at one point because there was a hulking chain-link backstop at the edge. This was uncharted territory, and for us seven-year-olds, an adventure that Ernest Shackleton would have been proud of. I told the other kids about not using your hands, about how the object of the game was to score a goal, about passing and shooting. I think we put down jackets or sweaters for the goals, which sat up high on the lofted grass plants. The red ball, lightweight as it was, did not completely touch the ground but hung at shin height supported by the vegetation like a little hovercraft. We were all in long pants and lace-up shoes in keeping with the strict dress code, which was not to be broken even on the unholy recess day of Wednesday. We did have the benefit of not having our skullcaps on—the rabbis let us put them in a wood box by the exit, figuring that they would just blow off and get lost if we wore them outside.

I was the self-designated captain, a legend in my own mind. After all, I was the experienced one, having played once, for twenty minutes with one other person, my dad, at a park. But it was evident that I was better than the other little, pasty, over-clothed kids thrashing around that overgrown field. Relative to them, I was Pele, a master of deft touch, control, and power. I was able to dribble down field, eluding my would-be tacklers with either speed or sudden cuts, and score almost at will. If I also had endurance as part of the package, I never could have told, because that first game lasted a total of maybe seven minutes. What mattered to me that day was that I ran rampant on the not-so-verdant playing fields of Bi-Cultural Day School, not exactly Eton or St. Paul's, but one of the most difficult pitches in the world (if not the most difficult opposition). It was also my first day of soccer in the park (that is to say, a real game, where scoring counted and not just a kick-around). There was purpose and drama, a victor and a loser, and, in a radical departure from one of the great objectives of Hebrew educators in 1966, there was sweat that came from an activity besides studying for an exam.

From that point on, soccer started to occupy my thoughts. It was more abstract than anything: I would think about kicking a ball, about moving past the other kids, about how exhilarating it felt to be in control and doing something that was flat out more fun than anything I had done before. Like walking or breathing or waving your hand, soccer can feel just a tiny step removed from anything else that you do naturally. It is you plus one other thing, a ball. Cooped up in the classroom, usually starving (in addition to rationing recess and gym, there was just a meager milk and cookie snack before lunch at almost one o'clock), I started to spend my days staring out the window, dreaming of the following Wednesday.

For me, this became the start of a rebellion. As strange as it sounds, being a sports-minded Jewish kid at a Hebrew day school and with a mother who wanted one thing only from her son—to become a doctor—wanting to go out and play soccer was heretical. My destiny was clearly mapped out for me: be a star math and science pupil, cruise through public high school, and get accepted at an elite university, preferably MIT, where my dad went. I was supposed to be a charter member of the pale and pasty society, sitting with a book cracked open while snacking on a bowl of Fritos. With the exception of my dad, it was clear to me that every other adult in my life thought that sports was a waste of time and a needless diversion from academics. There wasn't a whole lot of love coming from the other kids either. While a couple of them were OK athletes, scrappy and game, no one else in my class seemed to really get the zeitgeist of soccer. Looking back, I must have seemed like a curiosity, a kid all amped up about running around a weedy field and kicking a ball between a couple of cardigans strewn on the ground.

The movement, like all grassroots movements with great purpose, could not be denied. Slowly, I gained converts. The games got a bit longer; instead of waiting until our thirty or forty minutes of recess was half over, we would take the ball and immediately run to play soccer. Perhaps by coincidence, the rabbis managed to get the field mowed so it seemed less like playing in the Everglades and more like a soccer field. By sixth grade the soccer bug was biting harder. The manifestation of this was five minutes of schoolroom frenzy between classes (and teacher changes) that comprised (1) moving all of the desks and chairs to the edges of the class, (2) the construction of a tightly wadded improvised paper soccer ball about the size of a softball, and (3) all the boys playing until the next teacher came in the room. Absent gym or after school-sports programs, we created our own pitch, ball, and rules. You would be surprised at how much of a workout you can get playing five up-tempo minutes of classroom futbol. The four girls in our class were rendered helpless bystanders—our day school sense of moral and religious justice was fine with this—as the boys scrapped on the linoleum. Although the teachers were obviously pissed off, there wasn't a whole lot they could do. We had it timed pretty well so that the classroom would be back in order by the time they came back. It seems that they had a sense that little boys needed to run around, and wasn't it better to let them work it out in five-minute intervals between classes rather than letting them out for structured playtime.

But instead of slaking my thirst for soccer, my condition got worse. The more I played, the more I pined for just one more game. At home, in my cul-de-sac development, we played football and softball after school. Those were the two seasons: football from September to March, baseball from April to August. The other kids were all white, Irish, German, or Italian Catholics. I don't think a single one of them would have been able to recognize a soccer ball. I vaguely recall that my friend Ernie's dad made some allusion to soccer in his German-tinted English, but soccer was never to be uttered again within the cozy confines of Buckingham Drive. I didn't take it too badly, since that other "exotic" sport, hockey, also had pariah status. My dad played hockey as a kid and some in college, and we used to play on the driveway—shooter and goalie. Connecticut was a cold place in the '60s, enough that the ponds froze with decent regularity. The New York Rangers and Boston Bruins were both good by the late '60s, and it would have seemed natural that kids would have been into hockey. But hockey was also considered offbeat. Maybe it was that it was a Canadian thing, or that it wasn't played in schools, or that you really needed a rink to play it competitively, but I couldn't even get any of my friends to try it, let alone play a game. Later, in high school, when the Philadelphia Flyers brought an element of mixed martial arts to hockey, it started to catch on; Stamford built the Terry Connors Ice Rink, and the city started a street hockey league as a rec program. I came to possess two distinct sporting personalities: my average Joe, Mr. Football and Baseball Guy in the neighborhood, and my secret life involving soccer and hockey.

The big problem with soccer was that it was a mystery shrouded in an enigma. For a little kid in the 'burbs, there was no evidence of it being played anywhere. Sure, I played it and my dad played it, and I got the kids to play it, but there must have been some people somewhere who really played it, and played it a lot better than I did. That England won the World Cup meant nothing to the great sports TV producer Roone Arledge, who, for reasons that elude me to this day, did not consider soccer "worldly" enough to put on his show *Wide World of Sports*. What I did see on *WWS* was a steady diet of stuff like cliff diving, cross-country motorcycle racing, and skiing, amusing all, but not soccer. In fact, if you surveyed the sports landscape in America—all of the newspapers, TV, and radio in America—you would probably have concluded that soccer was about the seventy-sixth most popular sport in the world.

At school, there was a world event taking place that pretty much absorbed the entirety of 1967, at least at Hebrew day schools around the country: the Six Day War, a comprehensive and swift victory for the Israeli military over joint Arab forces. With the benefit of time, I now see that the attention the war received in my classroom was the result of a collective sigh of relief for our Jewish faculty. But there was perhaps a second, baser reason for all of the hullabaloo: that victory may have been the greatest evocation to that point in time of the aspirations of the Zionist Max Nordau, who advocated in the 1890s for a "muscular" form of Judaism, embodied by strength and power. I had zero perception of how close 1945—the end of the Second World War—was to 1967, but two decades is pretty damn close. Without Jewish athletes to speak of, and nothing to root for, the Israeli Army became America's (at least my insular slice of America) team.

As a kid I should have been stoked about this. Our side kicked their ass. Yeah, team. Not only could I have cared less, I was pissed off. I saw the point—how Israel was threatened by its neighbors, how against all odds it rallied its smaller forces against the far greater number of Arabs, and how it was a triumph for Jews all over the world. But what I cared about was soccer. Did the Jews play it and were they any good at it? I was especially intrigued because I gained possession of a fantastic piece of ephemera, a cartoon showing a team with a sign that read 8:0. The piece was in some kind of Israeli magazine, the kind of thing one of the Hebrew teachers subscribed to about Israeli life and culture. When I saw it, I knew there was no choice but to channel my inner felon and rip it out. I managed to squirrel it home and paste it up to my bulletin board. I knew it must have been an Israeli team because there was a Hebrew caption of some sort—two words without vowels. As every Hebrew school student knows, there are two kinds of Hebrew: with vowels and without vowels. The first kind is an adaptation to America, and if it wasn't invented expressly for to-be Bar Mitzvah boys, then it became the de facto standard for them. The second kind of Hebrew, the kind you see in newspapers and when you go to Israel, has no vowels. To the typical American kid haplessly trying to grasp enough Hebrew to limp through his Bar Mitzvah, Hebrew sans vowels might as well be Arabic. Neither my dad nor I could tell whether the simple caption alluded to a team or a score or was some kind of colloquialism. It didn't matter to me. That paper became one of my favorite things. It was tangible evidence that organized, high-quality soccer existed somewhere in the world, and it tickled me that someone cared enough to make a cool cartoon out of it. Not only was soccer cool somewhere, it was cool in Israel, and most importantly, it was cool enough in 1967 to steal some attention away from that stupid war that was being deconstructed in excruciating detail in my classroom.

In truth, the seeds of soccer were starting to germinate—actually regerminate—all over. Soccer neophytes are usually completely in the dark about the sport's high notes in America. For forty years or so, leagues like the United States Football Association, the American Soccer League, and the German-American league flourished with professional and semiprofessional teams. Great European sides, including the Jewish Hakoah teams from Austria, came to America on barnstorming tours that played before crowds of 40,000 or more at the Polo Grounds. And of course, there was the great U.S. World Cup triumph over England in 1950, commonly held to be as much, if not more, of an upset than the U.S. taking the Olympic hockey gold medal in 1980. With the demise of the ASL in the 1950s, there was little effort to cultivate soccer on a professional level in the U.S. But in late 1958, Pele became a sensation as a teenager with

Brazil at the World Cup in Sweden. By 1970, even ABC and Roone Arledge noticed, showing a color broadcast—albeit delayed by six months—of the World Cup final, in which Brazil thrashed Italy 4-1, behind a transcendent Pele. It was a prescient media move, and was critical for the establishment of the NASL. No matter that at first the NASL was really a fat farm for ex-European stars, soccer was now visible again.

About the only blip for soccer in my narrow circles was that there seemed to be a vague awareness about a guy with a funny name—Pele (was it Peelie? Paylay? Or what?)—who played a sport that was for foreigners. Pele was the beginning and end of any conversation you could have with anyone about soccer. My conversation with the kids at school went something like this:

"Hey, did you see the World Cup?"

"Yeah, that Pele is great."

"Yeah. The Mets are on tonight."

I would have to wait until the next World Cup in 1974 to get blooded.

Although in 1970 I wasn't aware of him, there was a coach by the name of Albie Loeffler in Westport, Connecticut, who was hired by Staples High School in 1952 and formed its first soccer team in 1958. I didn't live in Westport, which was twenty minutes north of Stamford on the Merritt Parkway, but Loeffler, through the transitive property of soccer knowledge, had a big influence on me. Of the two types of Fairfield County towns, Stamford and Westport were close to opposites. While the wealthy, northern part of Stamford had demographics and income levels that were close to that of Westport, Stamford lacked several things that made Westport great. Looking at a map, you might conclude that both towns had ample waterfront on Long Island Sound. The difference was that Westport cultivated Compo, its large public beach, with public golf, concessions, play spaces, and an overall air of friendly family fun that made it integral to its city. By contrast, Stamford's Cummings and Cove Beaches were a long trip from affluent north Stamford and had little in the way of family attractions back then. They were also not so big and suffered kind of an image problem before the southern part of the city and downtown started to revive.

Few of my high school friends went to the beach on a regular basis, but the Westport kids did. In part due to the beach and in part due to its long reputation as a community for artists, advertising folks, and other creatives, Westport cultivated the kind of insouciant cool vibe that is typical of small coastal California towns. As was the case with most of the richer towns in Fairfield County in the '60s and '70s, it was also overwhelmingly white. With its towheaded skateboarding kids, boats, and beaches, it could have passed for a town in Orange County. Stamford had more than its share of estates and rich kids, but nothing of the close-knit community (at least in its more affluent sections) that Westport had. For one, there was no center. Downtown was a mess, a victim of urban renewal policy that afflicted many cities in the northeast. The waterfront, cut off by I-95 and dotted with abandoned factories and warehouses, was unappealing and strikingly neglected for a city of its size. It is hard to believe, but the waterfronts in many communities along the east coast were not in favor a generation ago. As manufacturing started to migrate overseas and to cheaper parts of the U.S., many East Coast cities—Stamford and Providence, for example—struggled to come up with ideas about how to revive their waterfronts.

Without a cool beach or a charming village, Stamford was fragmented and lacking in identity. There were the Ys—both a YMCA and a YMHA (Jewish center)—that had youth basketball and baseball, but for a lot of kids in North Stamford, they were way too far to go. This, too, was before the "kid first" culture that we live in today. Most dads worked all day, and the moms stuck close to the house. My mother would have rather gouged out her liver than drive me around to play sports and be entertained, and it was probably much the same for my friends. Unstructured after-school play was the rule, and as a lot of parents are beginning to realize, that was not a bad thing at all.

While I was whiling away the hours staring out the window of a stuffy classroom at Bi-Cultural Day School, Albie Loeffler was busy turning Westport into a soccer machine. Unwittingly, Loeffler was the progenitor of the Soccer Mom. Although it is difficult to confirm the time and place of the first sighting of a Soccer Mom, my estimate would put it somewhere on Main Street in downtown Westport in the fall of 1971. Loeffler, whom I knew little or nothing about as a kid and even in high school when I captained the soccer team that played against him several times, was Westport's own Amos Alonzo Stagg, Vince Lombardi, and Dean Smith rolled into one. He was an educator and coach of three sports—soccer, basketball, and baseball—but most famously of soccer. Little did I know that while I was running the kids ragged on the weed field, there were other kids—more soccer-blessed kids—playing actual organized soccer in Westport.

There was so little soccer on the Stamford landscape that it never occurred to me to even ask my parents about playing it. My job was to get good grades, come home, leave the house to play, come home for dinner, shut up, and go to bed. In frigid weather or rain, TV was the play substitute, a steady diet of *F Troop*, *Gilligan's Island*, *My Three Sons*, and *Batman*. After a point, the kids at school started wanting to play more kickball and less soccer at our once-a-week recess. It was getting kind of pointless for me anyway, since I was the only kid who was decent at it, so I wasn't getting better. My team would win and win by a lot. In Westport I would have been average, but at my little school for pasty Jewish kids, I was unstoppable. With no organized soccer, no interest from the neighborhood kids or kids at school, I lost the soccer plot when I hit fifth and sixth grade. We still played classroom soccer, but that got to be so chaotic that it resembled a food fight more than soccer. At home, with my dad, we had a couple of little plastic balls in the playroom. Using the bottom of the stair riser as the goal, we would kick those little balls around in the basement. Between TV shows, I would force my baby sister to play goal, and she would put up with it until I smacked one off her thigh or shin.

But Albie Loeffler kept plugging along, amassing an impressive number of wins, shutouts, and Connecticut state titles. By the time I entered Westhill High School in the fall of 1972, his Staples High School team was a power. Westhill High School was built in 1971 to accommodate Stamford's expanding population. The construction of Westhill coincided with a major corporate expansion into the northern part of the city. Within a short span of time in the early 1970s, several major corporate and regional headquarters were established, primarily due to Stamford granting very attractive tax incentive packages to these companies. Olin Matheson, General Electric, and Xerox all built comfortable corporate campuses off Long Ridge Road, one of two major north-south spines in the city. Westhill was partly carved out of a flood plain at the "Bull's Head" intersection of three main roads—Roxbury, Westhill, and Long Ridge. The school was designed in a style that could be considered "academic brutalist" vernacular: twin brick and masonry structures with a bilevel concrete courtyard. The school managed to capture neither the countrified charm of Connecticut nor any true spirit of modernism. It was prosaic, blandly executed in browns and grays, and, for its decent sized campus, contained two subpar fields—one for football and one for baseball.

In eighth grade, my final year at Bi-Cultural, my friend Ernie told me a scary story. Ernie was a year ahead of me but was still in middle school because Westhill had a "soft" opening with only tenth through twelfth grades in its first year in 1971. Apparently, there was a stabbing after a big racially motivated brawl in the lunchroom. Ernie, a butcher's son, was not the kind of kid prone to exaggeration, and soon I had heard the same story from other kids as well. For a parochial school kid who had never had more than sixteen kids in his class, all white and all Jewish, this was about as terrifying as it could get. All summer I fretted about the prospect of ninth grade. Westhill had about five hundred students per grade—by the time I graduated, the school had more than 2,300 students. My fate was clear: I would be beaten and stabbed shortly after my first day of class.

But there was a possible way out, although it was a bit of Scylla and Charybdis: Bi-Cultural, in the afterglow of the Six Day War, started a program for ninth graders. The catch was that it consisted of an entire year abroad—in Israel. On a Kibbutz. Having gone through nine grades with more or less the same cast of kids in class, I was pretty attached to a lot of my friends and certainly the musty trappings and outdated facilities of Bi-Cultural had grown familiar. But I did not especially want to go to Israel, and, despite a pretty crappy home life due to a hostile and depressed mother, I did not want to be away from home that long. The stabbing business got me to reconsider. I weighed the options: I could become a human sacrifice at Westhill or be enslaved by pioneer socialists in a country where I knew nobody.

At least they played soccer, based on the evidence I had from that cartoon. I decided that I would lobby to go to Israel.

I had several things working against me. Money for one. To paraphrase George Orwell, my parents were upper-lower-middle class. We had one of everything, but nothing extra. We were the kind of family who rented a tiny cottage in June for a week on Cape Cod, not a ski and beach family. I don't remember how much the year in Israel was, but if it was $10, that was over the family budget. I was also on some kind of modified scholarship, which I never knew about until much later. While the school was willing to give us a little break on tuition, I don't think they would be willing to subsidize an Israel adventure. Second, I had a bipolar mother, by turns smothering and hostile. Much as she began to despise me in adolescence, she equally couldn't bear to have her precious son leave. I was, after all, only thirteen, having had my Bar Mitzvah in the spring of 1972. As a parent now, it doesn't seem that crazy to not want your kid to go halfway around the world to a war-torn region for a whole year. But as the end of eighth grade loomed, I grew terrified of being separated from my merry little band of Jewish classmates. I wasn't at all attached to Judaism—that I could take or leave. Not one of the neighborhood kids was Jewish; it was just that after so many years of being in class with the same group of kids, I couldn't imagine going to a huge high school, especially one with a lot of angry black kids.

But my lobbying went nowhere. After dozens of dinners in our cramped little kitchen with the little round table and turquoise Formica chairs, I realized that I would have a better chance of starting a militia and declaring independence from my family. I resigned myself to being thrown to the wolves at Westhill in the fall.

TWO

Total Football

THE SUBURBAN DEVELOPMENT of southern Connecticut was an exercise in clear-cutting. Tract homes were filled as soon as they were built, and virtually none of the land use, zoning, or design precepts that are used to control suburban growth were in effect in the 1960s. A developer, if he adhered to basic density and utility requirements, could clear-cut woodland or plop houses right next to, and sometimes on top of, a flood plain or wetland area. My neighborhood, Castlewood Park, was built by an MIT architect named Norman Feber. The main street, Buckingham Drive, roller coastered from Long Ridge Road, down across the less than mighty Rippowam River, and back up a hill. The bridge across the river basically trampled a whole bunch of wetlands, something that would have been an absolute deal killer if you had that land in Connecticut today. Even more striking was the absolute lack of family amenities for a project that catered pretty much only to families. There was not a tot lot, sidewalk, or shred of open land in the whole one hundred some-odd home development. Houses were sited on quarter-acre lots with no thought given at all to optimizing the site with regard to light, views, or privacy. Castlewood was the ultimate cookie-cutter development, with one saving grace— cul-de-sacs. Intended not for kids to play but as expedients for traffic and parking, there were two or three slabs of tarmac that laid out well for "fields." They were also kind of public, so the moms could stick their heads out the front door and scream your name when they wanted you home. For some reason, the Gentile moms demurred from this, and I had the pleasure of the daily humiliation of hearing "Daniel! Daniel!" echoing through the 'hood while my friends cringed and snickered.

Staying within eyesight and earshot was the rule until I was about twelve, but in the spring of '72, with my newly bestowed manhood and banana yellow Schwinn Varsity ten speed a part of my arsenal, I started to spread my wings. This was especially the case when my buddies were over. I knew I had Westhill in my future, and I figured that venturing across Long Ridge Road now and then to check out the campus would ease the transition. Better of course to do it with a friend, and especially if there was a fair going on. One day, a Saturday in late spring, my friend Dave and I left my house to hit the annual carnival on the Westhill grounds. My parents gave us each a few bucks, and, looking forward to an afternoon of rides and junk food, we headed down Buckingham Drive. Coming the opposite direction was a pack of three kids, bigger kids, only one of whom I recognized. Dave and I had on the typical summer camp kid outfit—dork shorts with clips and pockets and o-rings, T-shirts, and white Keds. I quickly knew we might be in for it because the other kids wore tough-guy clothes: army jackets, jeans, and dirty sneakers. They also had tough-guy hair—party in the back, bangs in front, while we dorks had buzz cuts.

My plan was to get across the Rippowam Bridge as quickly as possible and cut through the woods. It wouldn't look like we were showing fear—any victim's death knell—because the woods really were a shortcut to Westhill. And besides, the other guys were on the opposite side of the street. I whispered to Dave not to look at them, but before we could get to safety, they intercepted us right at the bridge. The one kid I recognized was the legendary but recondite bully, Eric.

"Yo—where you two going?"

"The fair. How 'bout you?"

"I ain't going nowhere."

"OK—see you, Eric." I nudged Dave to get going, but Eric stepped in front of me, then turned around and grabbed Dave around the waist, picking him up like he was about to throw him in the river. He dangled him over the rail. I tried to distract him, and it occurred to me that he might throw both of us over. It was the first time in my life that I remember time being suspended. I was simultaneously blabbering something to Eric, planning Dave's eulogy, and scheming about how to try to defend myself and pry Dave from Eric's meat hooks. Probably spooked by a car coming down the hill, Eric let Dave down. After a couple of requisite "fuck yous," they took off up the hill.

Dave and I stood there for a minute looking at each other. There was nothing to say. We were alive, but no longer in a party kind of mood. Looking every bit the Boy Scout, Dave took off his thick glasses with the coke bottle lenses and wiped them on his shirt.

My mother was rooted in her usual sentry post on the sofa about four feet from the front door.

"Why are you guys back?"

I explained what had transpired at the river with Eric and his henchmen. My mother grabbed her pack of Merit Ultra Lights, and with a flick of her Zippo, lit a cigarette, bared her teeth, and shouted to my dad, "Let's go."

"Let's go where?" my dad asked.

"To get them, that's where."

"Get who? A couple of teenagers?"

"You got that goddam right."

Dave and I were horrified, especially me. His mom would be picking him up in a few hours and take him back to Port Chester, while I would be left to deal with the fallout from Operation Eric. Not only would I be fending off street thugs at Westhill, I would no longer be able to walk the streets of my own neighborhood without checking my back.

My dad went to the car with us, but I sensed he was as scared as Dave and I were. My mother was possessed, demonic, and was driving using a maneuver I have never seen before or since: cruising at about twenty-five miles an hour with the door open. Holding the wheel with one hand, smoking with the other, and sort of using her foot to keep the door from being flung wide open, my mom was ready to go all Charles Bronson on the bad guys. Little did I know that behind the entitled and mercurial Jewish mother who disdained violent TV, there lurked a maniacal gunslinger. Now that we were pregnant with the chase, I was getting into it. Did she really have the cojones to try to kick the neighborhood bullies' asses?

We drove around for about ten minutes, and then the effect of the nicotine, twelve cups of coffee, and prescription barbiturates started to fade, and we abandoned the chase. My parents asked if we wanted to go to the fair, and we said no, playing around the house seemed like a better idea. My mother went back to her position on the sofa, smoking. My dad went back outside to work on our leaky Mercedes, inherited from my grandmother. It was a magnificent 1962 dove gray 220S with red leather buckets and a wood-and-chrome dashboard. As living room furniture it would have been terrific, but it stank as a car. For my dad, maintaining that car was his weekend routine and antiwife protective device.

After the terror and humiliation of the Eric incident started to fade, I started to fear Westhill High School less and less. I had seen evil and had stared it down. Or this was my revisionist interpretation of it anyway. I also had camp to buffer me and give me one last jolt of confidence before public school. Up to the age of twelve, camp was kind of an adjunct of school—eight weeks of day camp in bucolic New Canaan, on a fifteen-acre campus that was right next to Phillip Johnson's iconic glass house. Camp Playland was friendly enough, and although I played softball there, the camp day was organized around a "well-rounded" experience, including time wasters (as far as I was concerned) like swimming, nature, art, and archery. For the last year before high school, I convinced my parents to send me to the more sports-minded Long Ridge Day Camp.

Right away at Long Ridge, I knew it would be different. A lot of the kids in my group—most of them fourteen—had furry mustaches and defined biceps. At Camp Playland, I was always one of the best athletes in my group, but finally I had real competition. The big sports at Long Ridge were, of course, basketball and softball. I don't think that either day camp I went to, from a span between 1965 and 1972, owned a soccer ball. It wasn't like we were in some kind of soccer-hostile territory like Alabama or North Dakota. New Canaan and Stamford were in spitting distance of Westport, where Albie Loeffler was putting together his dynastic Staples squads.

The entire summer passed without me giving much thought to soccer. I was happy with basketball, and the softball was a lot more competitive than at Camp Playland. A bunch of kids in my camp group were on their middle-school baseball and basketball teams and would go on to be varsity athletes in those sports. Along with the mustaches, I finally started to get some inside baseball on girls, and we had a kid who for a buck or two would produce well-thumbed copies of *Oui* and *Playboy*.

Not a bad summer, but as August approached, I started to go into a funk. I realized that in high school you suddenly needed a wardrobe. From about sixth grade on, my sartorial survival depended on the fashion whims and largesse of my one cool uncle, the only male member of my family who bought clothes more than once a decade. He was my dad's sister's husband, and while we didn't see my aunt and uncle often, when we did he usually had a box of clothes for me. It was a sweet gesture, and to this day I am thankful for it. The problem was that his swinging thirty-something-year-old wardrobe didn't translate so great for a thirteen-year-old. While I was at Bi-Cultural, it didn't matter what you wore. Most kids wore the same poly pants and button-down or polo-shirt ensemble, along with sensible shoes that, as per the school's tacit "no-sweat" policy, encouraged the least amount of exercise possible.

High school was a different matter. My uncle Mark's taste in shirts ran from wildly floral and garish to astoundingly garish and floral. I had just about any kind of shirt as long as (a) it had a giant floral pattern and (b) it was maroon or yellow or maroon and yellow. My pants were strange: I had basically two pairs of striped poly bell-bottoms that were kind of stretchy like a thick pair of girl's tights. The shirts were two sizes too big, so they kind of flopped over my belt, the excess polyester fabric flouncing around my waist like a belly dancer's skirt. My first days of high school passed with me noticing nothing but the kid in front of me at homeroom and how most of the other kids had cool clothes like jean jackets, Pumas, Levis, and Frye boots. In those days I wore my hair "Jewfro," loopy ringlets reaching towards the sky. I would say that overall, I probably looked like a composite of Starsky, Ron Jeremy, and Art Garfunkel, which for the time might actually have been OK.

Westhill, downwind economically from swanky Staples in Westport, apparently had a soccer team. I had pretty much forgotten entirely about soccer by the time high school started, and as a kid who was almost a full year younger than everyone in his class, I was overwhelmed by the sheer size of the school. Everything—class sizes, the impersonal tone of the teachers, the throngs of minority kids (obviously sitting around planning how to knife me), the attractive girls walking around—was distracting and scary. No one from my eighth-grade class was in my freshman class at high school. The friends that were in my district were going to Israel.

With the help of my parents, I decided on my classes, although there wasn't a whole lot of choice. Basically it boiled down to taking advanced, regular, or dummy classes in the core subjects. They insisted on "zero" algebra, "zero" somehow being some school admin's brilliant idea for advanced math. My math teacher, Mr. Hanford, had a drill sergeant buzz cut but a happy demeanor, no matter how fierce a problem he was tackling on the blackboard. It was quickly clear that I couldn't keep up. I was not, in the vernacular, "adjusting" to high school. I had no friends, looked and dressed like shit, had never kissed a girl, and needed to have more fun. In short, I was depressed.

Walking home from school one of those first days in September, I saw a bunch of guys heading towards the far field—the baseball field. It looked like they had soccer uniforms on, so I decided to investigate. The team was out for practice, and it was like no other sports team I had seen up close. Big guys, little guys, skinny guys, muscular guys, black guys, white guys, and all colors in between. The coach, though, was as white bread looking as they come, a big tall blond guy named Scotnick in a purple wind-breaker and carrying a clipboard. I must have looked pathetic in my stretchy bellbottoms and polyester hand-me-down floral shirt. I introduced myself and asked about trying out.

"You're a little late," he said, glancing away. "We've been out here practicing all of August."

Seeing as I had just started school at Westhill a week or two before, I wasn't quite sure how I would have found out about practice in August. This was a quick and brutish introduction to organized sports. I would play for the same coach next fall, and I later found out that he was the swim coach and was coerced into coaching soccer, a sport about which he knew nothing.

That fall, I barely had it in me to get to school. My mother took my first semester grades like a personal indictment of her parenting skills. A "D" from Hanford did not resonate with a mother who dreamed of lording her son the neurosurgeon over her friends one day. For his part, my dad just seemed confused. I cranked along with good grades right through eighth grade, and I don't think he needed another speed bump to deal with. Until then, we bonded mainly through watching the Rangers. I was a huge hockey fan, and the Rangers were on WOR, with only the away games shown on Saturday nights. The broadcast team was Jim Gordon and "The Big Whistle," Bill Chadwick, a half-blind ex-NHL referee whose excitement would spill over quickly into Tourette's-like spasmodic outbursts. We watched hockey in our dreary rec room on whatever TV my dad was fixing that week. Usually the picture would roll or the sound would be garbled, but it was enough for me just to be having a guys' night in.

In the spring of 1972, as the hockey season was winding down, ads starting popping up in the papers about a team called the New York Cosmos. The North American Soccer League had been around since 1969 but had sputtered without a real player pool and committed ownership. But with its huge ethnic population, the Cosmos were surviving on a bumpy pitch in the badlands of Randall's Island. Unknown to the vast majority of New Yorkers, Randall's Island lies in a giant shadow underneath the Triborough Bridge, and its closest neighbor is a maximum-security prison. The field the team played on looked like any public field in New York, that is to say, less of a field and more of a dirt patch. The stands consisted of a couple of rickety-looking grandstands that looked like they were borrowed from a high school. Even today, with a corporate raider makeover, Randall's Island is nearly invisible on the New York City sports landscape. In the afterglow of Brazil's World Cup victory, the NASL had managed to launch as a professional league, but it was far from elite-level soccer. What the 1972 Cosmos lacked in skill, they made up for in flamboyance, particularly with their big Bermudan striker, Randy Horton. Horton, who was about 6'3", but looked about 6'7" with his huge 'fro, was the leading scorer in the NASL for the 1972 season and a telegenic athlete who flung himself about and scored mostly with headers. On the occasional spring and summer evening, WOR would broadcast a Cosmos game. There was no schedule or listing, so finding a game on TV was sheer serendipity. The Cosmos would go on to win the NASL championship that year, building a bit of momentum that would eventually lead them to sign Pele in 1975 in the twilight of his career and temporarily ignite the soccer landscape in New York.

As bad as the overall quality of soccer was, it got me thinking about the sport. The Cosmos were a hoot, and for me it was a terrific, albeit temporary relief, from the onslaught of academic angst that plagued me throughout ninth grade. I did get a bit of what I wished for: after years of living under the pale and pasty edict decreed by the Bi-Cultural Day School, I was finally among the sweating proletariat in public school gym class. Westhill may have been short on fields, but it had a full complement of angry gym teachers, one of every ethnic flavor. The first requirement for teaching gym at Westhill was to be angry. The master of this was Dom L, "Mr. Laz." At about 5'6", 240, Mr. L had stonemason's forearms and massive torso. He was fat enough that he didn't really walk but pivoted around. No need to move when you had a clipboard and whistle. Mr. Laz did not speak; he barked and commanded. He yelled your name for attendance, and you yelled back. He then would bark the command of the day: "Run. Eight laps," and believe me, you ran. Smith, the black gym teacher, aspired to Mr. Laz-dom, but lacking the physique and brute force personality, he came across as pissed off but sheepish. While Laz at least appeared to have been an athlete in his youth—football, I assume, since he was a line coach—Smith seemed to have no athletic ability whatsoever, and no apparent knowledge of any sport. He was actually the tennis coach, and I assume that this was the result of some esoteric affirmative action provision in the Connecticut Public School Charter. Fortunately, the girls and boys took gym separately, with girls getting only the female gym teachers. As scary as Mr. Laz and Smith were, the gender-conflicted female gym teachers seemed like they would have gone medieval on the teenage boys given half a chance.

Despite the nefarious Mr. Laz and his henchman Smith, I liked gym, with one big exception: swimming. Westhill had crappy fields and a tiny weight room, but it did have one big "luxury" item, a regulation swimming pool in the basement of the gym. Known as getting "deep-sixed" (that was what Laz and Smith would gleefully call out when they were making the assignments), swimming was assigned to first period. That was first period as in eight o'clock A.M. In the early 1970s, Connecticut was a cold state, with winter settling in as early as mid-November. With the sun barely up by eight in the winter, swimming in a frigid, dank basement was a terrifying prospect. Unless you were superearly and had time to go to your regular locker, the first problem was having to shove your huge book bag into the sadistically skinny pool lockers. Then there was the funky, dank, chlorine aroma, bad enough at any time of the day, but sickening before breakfast. Boys and girls together would then have to march to the "lineup." Cowering and cold, each kid would step forward to a table manned by Laz or Smith and, in front of everybody, have to announce their suit size to get a standard-issue Speedo. Of course, I had only the male perspective on the special form of psychosexual humiliation that could only come from the potent cocktail of an early winter Connecticut morning mixed with swimming and a tight Speedo bathing suit. But the girls, I can now see, clearly had the worst of it. Huddled together, shivering, not enough hands to cover everything they wanted to cover, the girls were more humiliated being out of the pool, being gawked at, than in the pool where Laz and Smith would be barking, clipboards at the ready. Back in the day, it was incredible that not only did you not have to be competent at a sport to teach it; you barely needed to have heard of it. So it was that those two fat and angry guys, nice and cozy in their Westhill standard-issue purple windbreakers, could teach swimming. Being sheltered for nine years in parochial school hadn't really prepared me academically for high school, and it definitely didn't prepare me for the sight of twenty nearly naked girls first thing in the morning.

One day in late fall of freshman year, Laz and Smith ordered us over to the baseball/soccer field and pulled out a big gray bin. They reached in and threw a bunch of soccer balls on the field. "Soccer!" commanded Laz, and he waddled over to the side to read his clipboard. The guys and girls separated, and we made teams. I hadn't played soccer on a field since my Bi-Cultural days on the weed lot. The last game I played was probably sometime in sixth grade, basketball in the parking lot having stolen soccer's thunder from the eight or so semiathletic boys. What came naturally about soccer in grade school came even easier with the benefit of some added strength and muscle memory. By any "real" standard, I'm sure that I was just an average kid with average talent, but none of the other kids had played soccer at all—at least it didn't appear that way. Like in grade school, I ran rampant in gym soccer, an unstoppable force of nature. It was kind of strange, the other kids looking at me with a combination of admiration and loathing: "Sure he's great at it, but why?" One kid after another kept telling me how great I was. It was like I brought a two-headed puppy to school. That morning, I felt my first pang of adult regret: why didn't I go out for the soccer team?

The rest of that school year I was back in soccer purgatory. I did not follow the goings-on of the varsity, having been too preoccupied with playing defense at home over my crappy grades. It was all I could do to drag myself out to play the usual touch football and softball. We did discover basketball that fall as one of the older kids—Jerry down the block—was bold enough to hop the fence and discover a really nice half-court on the grounds of the "Castle," a twelve-acre estate in the châteauesque style that gave my housing development, Castlewood Park, its name. So now there were kids playing all the team sports except the ones I was really into, hockey and soccer. With the increasing tension about my house over my grades, my dad seemed less inclined to go on park jaunts with me to kick a ball around. My sister was four years younger and not the slightest bit interested.

After spending a summer at the Long Ridge Day Camp being tutored by Herman Alswanger, the camp director, as well as the varsity basketball coach at Stamford High school, I was getting comfortable playing the pivot in our camp league. Having been brushed off by Scotnick for soccer, I thought I had nothing to lose by going out for freshman basketball. Since there was no soccer at Long Ridge Camp, I was more comfortable with basketball at that point.

What Bi-Cultural and my little Jewish day camps in Connecticut had not prepared me for was a whole new phenomenon: urban kids. The first day of practice I showed up, and instead of the usual assortment of underweight, overweight, and under-muscled white kids from the rich part of Stamford, there were about fifteen kids, many of them physical specimens. The first thing Coach Gianotta had us do—Gianotta was a Coach Laz acolyte, not as fat, but aspiring to the same prodigious girth and Stalinesque enmity for humanity—was a layup drill. I noticed right away that for some of these guys, it was more of a lay-in drill, that's how far off the floor they were. There was also a little matter called shooting. Perfecting my position as one of the world's shortest centers, I had neglected to work on my jump shot. My release was horrible. I sort of mangled the ball two-handed and flung the ball more than I shot it. I also never really understood the science of releasing the ball at the top of my jump, so my shot was missing any kind of consistent trajectory. Gianotta, who had a lazy eye and bottle-thick prescription glasses, didn't say much, but it was pretty clear that my basketball career was over before it started.

That summer, 1973, was my first working summer—if you can call being a camp counselor "work." It was not quite work, but more like tedium. I was used to at least having the summers to decompress, and after being cooped up in class all year, I was thrilled to be having any kind of fun outdoors. On the weekends there wasn't a whole lot to do. For some reason, the neighborhood kids weren't around as much; most—all of them actually—were Catholic and went to church on Sunday. Saturdays around my house were tense. My mother would fret about the house being a mess but wouldn't actually lower herself to do any cleaning, and my dad would start fixing things outside to escape the gathering storm clouds. If I was lucky, my parents would have plans to go out, which meant that attention would be diverted away from me and whatever it was that I wasn't doing at the time: housework, schoolwork, work-work, mowing the lawn.

To relieve the tedium, I started to run. First I'd jog up and down Buckingham Drive but grew bored of that. I eventually discovered a route that took me through the same shortcut through the woods that Dave and I tried to take before the banditos intercepted us. From there I'd track along Long Ridge Road and cut across to the back entry of Westhill. From there I'd circle the fields where I could really get a sense of the soccer field. Running laps around it was a psychological breakthrough. In a month, preseason practice would be starting. Until then I had never had a whiff of organized soccer of any type. I started to get familiar with the grass and the part of the field where the baseball infield took over. The pitcher's mound was still there— the school maintenance staff, apparently not soccer fans, would leave just enough of it for soccer season that the bump came into play. More than once, one of us, backpedaling haplessly, would trip over it.

There are two kinds of people in the world: park people and club people. It's the elemental public/private dichotomy. More telling than the division between red and blue states, liberals and conservatives, Jews and Christians, is the rift between those who like to pay to play and those who don't. The social and sports clubs like the Prospect Unity Club were based on the same system in Europe that still exists today. In England in the 1930s, country clubs excluded Jews on the basis that they did not drink enough to be profitable members. Most people in the U.S. don't realize that Barcelona is really a giant organization with camps and leagues and facilities serving thousands of members. Its Spanish Primera team at the apex of world soccer is simply the top of the food chain of Barcelona. New immigrants to the U.S. were attracted to the clubs because of their support network, but as the children of these immigrants started going to college, and migrating all over the U.S., the need and demand started to wane. My dad, if he had any allegiance to any institution at all, regarded his college, MIT, as his club. Not being interested the slightest in golf or tennis or swimming, he saw no reason to join a country club. In fact, both my parents, born and raised in the concrete jungle of Queens, were quick to disparage golf and tennis as sports for other people. The fact was that anything outside of my mother's radar was considered by her to be profligate. For sports, the budget was zero. If I asked for sports equipment, her reply was that she "did not have the money for that."

I knew early on that I was a park guy, and if I wanted to be entertained, it would be on my dime, that is to say free. Running around the Westhill fields didn't feel like being in a public park. For one, I was almost always completely and utterly alone. As cold as the winters used to be, the summers in the northeast were hot and humid. On any typical late afternoon Saturday in July, it would be in the high eighties or low nineties and humid enough that the heat would create that weird haze effect, rising visibly in waves from the soft black tar. At those temperatures, the tar would throw off an acrid diesel odor. After running on a short stretch of Long Ridge Road, I would be in the clear, and quickly the hot tar would yield to the sweet elixir of freshly mowed grass. To this day, I believe that mowed grass is a narcotic. I'd try to get three laps of the field in before continuing around the other side of the school, down Roxbury Road, the home stretch.

The main hazard on Roxbury wasn't the traffic. It was the 150-pound scrofulous mongrel that protected a big rickety farmhouse. The house, obviously ancient based on its proximity to the road (as a rule in the northeast, the older the home, the closer it is to the road), never seemed to have any people around, but it was well protected. The dog looked like a mix between a polar bear and a rat hound. White, curly-haired, with wild black eyes, it favored the all-out ambush to the fair-warning system. You'd be jogging along, and boom, the thing would be on you howling for all get out. In the predawn days of suburbia, there was no such thing as a "leash law." As a dog owner, the idea was to spread your personal dominion over as great an area as possible. A typical setup would be, say, two Dobermans and a pug, the former for aggression, the latter for cuteness. It was yin-yang style of dog ownership. Suck 'em in with the little cutie pie, and tear 'em apart with the Dobies. It was actually OK for big and nasty dogs to roam around seeking prey. Because of that dog, Roxbury Road became my de facto sprint corridor, about 200 yards of breathless dog evasion.

Worse yet was riding your bike through dog territory. If running excited the dogs, bicycles sent them into a primal frenzy. Even the smallest, cutest dogs would start foaming when they saw a banana yellow Schwinn Varsity or electric-blue Peugot ten-speed. It's miraculous that in the days before kids wore helmets, there wasn't a fatality every day from cycling. When I was thirteen and finally got my ten-speed, that yellow Schwinn, it was a form of mini-liberation. At last I could ride to some of my friends who were way out of walking distance. Whoever says that growing up in the suburbs in the '70s was soft and cushy never took a bike ride from Buckingham Drive in Stamford to Caprice Lane, in the Westover section of town. Merely two and one half miles or so, this was a ride that would not have been out of place on one of those Animal Planet Network shows like *Deadly Creatures*, or *Wild by Nature*. The topography of the ride alone was scary. It was 100 percent hill. None of them were that big, but the whole ride required shifting, and the Schwinn, though nominally a "ten-speed," was geared so narrowly that by the time you crunched through the gears, you'd have to start the sequence all over. So you'd be crunching uphill, and crunching downhill, all the while swerving like a thirteen-year-old madman without a helmet. But then, nature would take its course. Picking up my scent, there was an agile Doberman who, like most of his breed, was trained as a stealth hunter. The first time he chased me, I got a surge of adrenaline so big, it is still with me thirty-seven years later. I credit that encounter with making me prematurely bald. It wasn't the big dogs, though, that were the worst—with them I'd just figure out their routines: where they slept, what time of the day it was best to travel, what side of the street to be on. The little dogs, with their feverish barking, ears pinned back and running for blazes, were the ones that really pissed me off. For one, it seemed ridiculous to be scared by a little dog. Was I too much of a weenie to fight it off like a man? They said I was a man at my Bar Mitzvah, and I should have been able to prove it on the mean streets of Stamford. Really humiliating, though, was that the little dogs forced you into the "flying eagle spread-leg formation," where you'd have to pedal in a frenzy and lift your legs up high, out of reach of their snapping jaws. Cars would whoosh by and look at you like you were a Martian: who's the kid on the yellow bike with his legs up in the air? Does he have some kind of crotch rot or something?

But between the biking and running I was getting in shape for the first time in my life. The one thing that hadn't yet occurred to me was to . . . play soccer. I don't know whether it was a sense of wanting to conform or whether there wasn't really a good spot to play, or whether it just plain did not occur to me to take the lumpy leather ball and kick it around myself, but I never even thought about it. Getting a new ball, of course, was out of the question. My family didn't just go out and buy sporting equipment. These days, all my kids have to do is breathe the fact that they want a ball or a stick or a bat, and we motor over to Sports Authority. Back then, I had a stash of sports stuff in the corner of the garage; the difference was that this was a fixed amount of equipment, seemingly acquired for me as a toddler and intended to last until I got out of high school. There was very little addition or subtraction over the years. The basic contents included five hockey sticks that my dad had from college, old Northlands without a curve. They were made of solid ash, weighing about ten pounds each, except for the goalie stick, which was half-again as heavy. There were also a couple of baseball bats, Wiffle balls, and strangely, a football helmet. The last item was strange because football, the American kind anyway, was verboten in my household. If, to my mother, sports was the alien realm, football was truly evil.

From a very early age, it was made clear to me that under no circumstances would I be allowed to play football. I didn't quite get it, since it wasn't like any other sport was being promoted. Baseball couldn't have been her favorite either; when a family friend and Little League coach asked my parents whether I'd want to play, they answered for me: "No, it's too organized." Organized? Translation: back then for "We don't want to have to get off our ass and take you anywhere. You can play in the back yard." Football was vilified, I think, because of it propensity to injure. For a Jewish mother at that time, allowing your kid to play football was akin to dropping them in a vat of boiling acid. You were risking their career as a neurosurgeon, and worse yet, other Jewish mothers would find out that you let your son play football. With that, you would have been consigned to a special place in hell for negligent mothers.

My mother obviously knew that my dad had played soccer as a youth. He managed to survive and become an adult. By that logic, I knew that I would have reason on my side as I planned my assault on Westhill soccer '73. The only tricky thing would be to get my grades up. After a "D" and a brush with math hell in Hanford's class, I was relieved to find out that geometry, not algebra, was on the docket for sophomore year. That was half my problem. The other stuff—French, history, and English—I'd just have to kick up a notch. The wild card was chemistry— what was it?

School started the week of Labor Day. Soccer practice started two weeks before that, in the brutal late August heat. That first day of practice, on a Wednesday at eleven in the morning, was my Camp Pendleton. I did not even have a pair of cleats or real soccer shorts. My ensemble was a pair of cotton gym shorts, the tight kind, a white T-shirt, and low-top Converse basketball shoes. No jock, no shin pads, no nothing. With my big jewfro and white clothes, I must have looked like a reject from the junior Mr. Clean team. To my horror, Scotnick was still the coach. He looked every bit the swim guy with his ubiquitous purple windbreaker and regular tennis shoes instead of cleats. He glanced up from his clipboard, looked me over, and said, "Ready to run?"

The other guys looked older, and for the most part they were older, a lot older. The Westhill team was mostly Italian and Jamaican. I had turned fourteen in April, and most of these guys were juniors and seniors, and a lot of them had to repeat a grade for various reasons: truancy, absenteeism, and academic problems. There were a couple of eighteen-year-olds and a bunch that were sixteen and seventeen. And they were a smelly lot. Before we even started to run, I was stunned by how ripe they smelled. About twenty of us started to take off around the field. Right away I was behind. My jogging was OK, but I quickly realized that my pace was not varsity soccer pace. A couple of Jamaican kids shot up front. One of them—I thought I heard him being called "Clyde," but would soon find out that's what all the Jamaicans called each other—like Randy Horton, was about 6'3" plus another half foot or so of afro. No sport I ever played—at school, in the neighborhood, or at camp—came near to preparing me for training with Jamaican guys, some of whom could turn the 400 in a minute and change or better. As an unknown quantity, Scotnick would surely be checking me out for speed and endurance, and I was failing on both counts. How many laps would we have to go? It was freaking hot, my 100 percent cotton Fruit-of-the-Loom T-shirt doing an excellent job of soaking up fifty times its own weight in sweat. Not that there was any wind, but the self-inflicted wind from running took me past the death-march stench of the guys in the front. They clearly lived in laundry-free homes, I concluded. Or was it possible that in Jamaica and Italy, things just smelled different. And then I realized that I could not have been a bouquet of roses; we all stank.

We were seven or eight laps into it—some of us laggards were almost a full lap behind. Scotnick blew his whistle, thank god for the bell lap—a sprint lap! The Jamaicans kicked it into high gear and made the gap even further. I feebly tried to take it up a gear but didn't have the lungs or legs for it. Soaked and parched, the team—or I should say hopefuls, since cuts were still to come—gathered around Scotnick. Two things were apparent: there were no soccer balls and no water. No water? Unlike "modern" times, water was not considered something essential for health and performance, nor was withholding water from athletes considered to be a dangerous practice. Water then was thought by the genius coaching fraternity to be a training tool, to be withheld to simulate "game" conditions. Not letting your charges drink water was an exercise in toughening them up. Scotnick started in with rules and disciplinary issues: we would be in shape for the season, there is no water at practice, and there will be cuts. Unlike Mr. Laz and Smith, Scotnick was more of a corporate/hatchet-man type. He was quiet and acerbic and possessed an array of smirks and eyebrow tricks that kept you guessing.

So I stood there, not knowing a soul. None of these kids were in any of my classes the year before, and I didn't even recognize any of them. At this point, Westhill had well over 2,200 kids and was kind of like a small community college. The kids in my advanced classes were all white, and all from the north half of Stamford. It was clear that day that there were two separate schools at Westhill: a rich school for advanced kids from north Stamford and a remedial, vocation-oriented one for the minority kids and poorer kids from Stamford's south and west sides. School busing was a hot topic when I was a kid. I heard a lot about it, and a lot of white parents bitching about it but never understood what they were complaining about. Didn't everyone—or at least the kids that lived too far to walk—take a bus to school? Stamford, with its ethnic and income variation was the prototype for school integration. About thirteen miles from north to south and only about five miles across, the busing districts for the city's three public high schools ran the long way. The result was integration, or to be realistic, integrated segregation. A lot of the poorer kids from the south and west side had a forty-five-minute trip just to get to school. The rich kids would drive for the most part, and with two separate curriculums going on—one for college placement and the other for job placement, there wasn't a whole lot of commingling going on. Soccer, the sport of the proletariat, gave me my first sociology lesson. After a lot of head banging with the kids at Bi-Cultural and in the neighborhood about soccer, I was now among my people. Although I had not yet spoken a word to any of these guys—black, brown, and dark-skinned—I was convinced they were my long-lost comrades from the planet soccer.

My excitement was short-lived. I was a soccer minister without portfolio, namely, a soccer ball. Briefly buoyed by a sense of esprit de corps, the reality of the heat and the workout set in. Scotnick ordered us to get into a circle. "Clyde," the biggest of the "Clydes" anyway, got into the center. Without Scotnick saying a word, Clyde started doing jumping jacks. So this was soccer: running, then calisthenics, with a soupçon of dehydration thrown in. After jumping jacks came squat thrusts. In my naiveté, I stood on the baseball infield—dry dirt—so when it came time for squat thrusts, the weight of my palms slapping the ground sent up a cloud of dust that, of course, I would inhale. Squat thrusts were hard enough when you were fresh, let alone after running and calisthenics. So it went for the next twenty minutes—push-ups, jumping jacks, squat thrusts, sit-ups, leg kicks. Torture. The sun was out in noon force, and there was no water in sight. After the calisthenics broke up, Scotnick stood in the middle of the circle. There would be no balls at practice, he explained, until cuts were made the following week. Cuts would be based on effort during our conditioning sessions.

Wow. I was flummoxed. I thought that it would be my dazzling skill that would be the deciding factor for making the squad. The soccer-industrial complex had brought its iron fist of ruthless determinism down on me in the form of one Coach Ben Scotnick. Unlike the freedom and exhilaration of passing the ball around with my dad at Cummings Park, Scotnick made it clear that it was militaristic commitment he was after, and nothing more. I thought I was through the woods at the point. We ran for twenty minutes and did another twenty of calisthenics. But we were halfway through. There wasn't a ball in sight, but there were cones. Clyde and some of the seniors started arranging the cones all over the field. Scotnick broke us up into minigroups. It was agility time, running backwards, sideways, and then sprinting through the cones only to come back around and do it again. By the standards of today's hard-core youth sports, we were doing an OK but nothing special workout. By my 1973 never-played-a-sport standard, I was on the verge of complete physical and mental breakdown. I left my house expecting a quick warm-up and some quality alone time with the coach, when I would tell him about my star exploits on the weed field and how my dad and his dad played soccer and how it was my birthright to win a spot on the varsity. Instead, I got what amounted to an hour and a half of combat maneuvers presided over by a guy who could have just as easily been a prison warden as a soccer coach. Act four was sprints: line up at the goal line, sprint halfway, walk to the other end, and turn around. Everyone in the group was silent. The start of each sprint reminded me of the grunting and moaning of a wildebeest migration. Our feet scraped the infield. My thighs and torso were raging balls of fire and I was beyond thirsty, well into some stage of serious dehydration.

I was through my first practice. In that hour and a half, I worked out more than in the entire previous thirteen years of my short life. I had walked the half mile to school and somehow had to walk back again. My mother was waiting on the sofa. I had to drink. I grabbed the powdered iced tea mix and made a half-gallon of it. I drank it all. Buzzed and bloated, I spent the rest of the day in dreadful state of physical purgatory, caffeinated and dehydrated at the same time. I was sick but euphoric. I didn't care that my mother was bitching at me; there was always some kind of bitching, either a high-level, "you better shape up or I'll break your neck," kind of bitching, or a low-level, "don't leave the knife in the sink," kind of bitching. I didn't care now because I was a soccer player. But there would be cuts. Cuts were part of the real world, the tough grown-up world of public school. Resources were scarce. Unlike parochial school, nobody gave a shit that you were someone's precious little doctor-to-be and should be coddled like a little genius. If you sucked (or in Scotnick's case, didn't run enough) you were cut. The crazy thing was that, shattered as I was, I had to go back tomorrow and do it all over again. There would be a week of this nonsense before I even knew if I could stick around. And there was the matter of shoes and shin pads. My dad came through and found a pair of Adidas boots for me. They were new, but as the economy model they were made of plastic. Not a high-tech, soft-to-the-touch synthetic that you'd find today, but hard, molded plastic, sourced I am guessing, from East Germany. Like the brown ball, my first pair of cleats was more representational than functional. At least now I could start to think like a soccer player.

Hell week did not get any easier. I learned the names of the other guys, but none of them were too friendly. The Italian guys constantly talked about a club in Italy called "Juve" (Juventas of Turin), and the Jamaican guys, whom I could barely understand, pretty much had a two-word vocabulary, consisting of the words "blood" and "Clyde." These two words afforded them a surprising amount of creativity. When combined, the phrase "blood-Clyde" (which sounded to me more like "blodclot") could be used as a curse or a phrase of solidarity. "Clyde" on its own was every Jamaican guy's nickname, or maybe they were all named Clyde, but I couldn't really tell. The Italians were all about "chooch" and, amazingly, when I think about it today, "mouly," which is of course a heinously inappropriate racial slur. But the language gulf was such between the Jamaicans and the Italians that each could curse out the other to their face: blood-clot Italians and mouly Jamaicans, and they had no idea about what the others were saying. In the middle were a handful of white guys and assorted other nationalities: a Chilean, a Honduran, a Swede, and a Dutchman.

To be a white U.S.-born kid playing soccer in a city in 1973 was to suffer some of the most blatant reverse discrimination in the history of mankind. The prevailing assumptions were either that you were (a) not good enough at American sports and chose soccer by default, (b) eccentric, or (c) both. It was also assumed (in most cases correctly) that you could not possibly have any soccer skills at all. Looking back, I'm not really sure how the Italians and Jamaicans looked at me and the other two or three white American kids. They seemed not to notice much, jabbering in "Itanglish" and blood-Clyde talk during the brief moments before Scotnick started us on the conditioning session.

He really was a bastard, that coach. I found nothing inspiring about him. He was cynical and sardonic, never encouraging. That I stuck with it is kind of amazing, and I think it may have been partly because I was starting to get involved in some of the drama between the Italians and the Jamaicans. I wanted to make the team, but I also wanted to see how all this enmity played out on the field. Would they pass to each other? How would they communicate, if at all? Who played what position? My new cleats were heavy and hot, but they made for slightly better running traction. As the week wore on, I gradually edged up in the pack, not quite in the middle, but not noticeably at the back.

A few days in—it may have been the start of the next week, a heat wave hit, sending the temperature into the high nineties with almost 100 percent humidity. For once, the group was allied in a cause: we were scared shitless about practice that day. Everyone lined up at the fountain before practice because of the no-water policy. It was obviously dumb to drink too much and get bloated, but that was what you had to do. Scotnick showed no mercy. Seizing on conditions that would support his bizarre performance theories of deprivation and sadism, he added laps, sprints, and calisthenics. We were in pain, moaning, spitting, and wheezing. Two-thirds of the way through, a couple of the Jamaican guys, including "Clyde" Donovan, literally walked off the field to the fountain in defiance of Scotnick. I heard a bit later that he went to puke, as did a few other guys. I was not a puker, but I was pretty delirious by that point, and I'm sure that it was sheer luck that I didn't have to be hospitalized with dehydration or worse. Scotnick had attained his Summum Bonum, his pinnacle of achievement. What was it that he told his wife over dinner? "Hey honey, I made the guys puke today."

"Wow, dear, you must be a great soccer coach."

The next Tuesday, we were all assembled. No fatalities had occurred. Thursday would be the day that cuts would be posted. There was no JV team that year. The football and band zealots who ran the athletic department were probably not too jazzed about having a soccer team at all; I suspect that the only reason they did it was that every other school in the FCIAC (Fairfield County Interscholastic Athletic Conference) had a team. With no JV coach, and I suspect, a strict budget limit for uniforms and equipment, the squad count had to match up with the number of uniforms they ordered.

Never more nervous, I showed up Thursday morning at the designated time. Taped to the door of the locker room was a piece of yellow ruled notebook paper. The team list was scribbled. Somewhere in the middle, I saw it: Dan Lilie. I made the soccer team without touching a soccer ball. Now what?

The next Monday (Friday was an off day), we had our first real practice. Westhill did own soccer balls! A yellow net bag was brought out with about twenty balls, the black and white panel type, which I had never seen before. The only real ball that I had ever seen to that point was the brown bomber in my dad's trunk. These were the "modern-style" balls, made of sewn leather. I hadn't actually kicked any ball in about a year and a half. Scotnick emptied the bag and matched us up with a partner and had us kick the balls back and forth. The balls were astonishingly heavy. They were so heavy that if you didn't get it absolutely dead center—I hesitate to use the phrase "sweet spot," because there was none—your foot stung like a bitch. If I really tried to air it out, I could maybe kick it thirty yards. After a bit, he had us form large groups and we started to scrimmage. Because I was American and pretty big, Scotnick told me to hang back and play defense. With that edict, I began my soccer life as a defender. To that point every time I played, it was about scoring or trying to score. I didn't really know what a defender did, or was supposed to do. I quickly noticed that a lot of these guys were way ahead of me in terms of their skill on the ball and their speed off the ball. If I stepped forward as they ran at me, I quickly learned that they could dribble left or right and easily beat me. If I backed up, they would take the space and get a shot quickly. Balls in the air were an even bigger problem. I had never really headed a ball, and these balls were brain-bustingly heavy.

After a half-hour of me being turned around and torched either for speed or off the dribble, we went back to drills. We finished with deadly sprints led by Giant Clyde. I made it through my first real practice. Scotnick hadn't said a thing about any individual player. It seemed that the starting positions were pretty much set. There were a lot of juniors and seniors on the team, and the starting positions seemed spoken for, at least at the attacking positions. We also had a superstar, Maurice, an Italian guy who was one of those players you are lucky to see every ten years in high school. Maurice was the focus at practice, and in reality, our coach. Scotnick, it was quickly apparent, was our soccer administrator.

Summer broke, school started, and we were issued uniforms. I got number 15—it quickly became my favorite number. Our school colors—purple and gold—and our Vikings mascot were copied from the Minnesota Vikings. Purple and gold is about as unflattering a combo for a soccer uniform that you could concoct. Our shorts looked like something that one of the girls in Tina Turner's posse would have worn. Our jerseys were thick gold cotton brocade with absolutely no properties of ventilation whatsoever. The only neat thing was the bold "W" across the chest. It was purple, of course, but rendered in a substantial and manly typeface. My jersey fit OK, except for the sleeves, which rode up above my biceps and looked a bit like a women's summer top. The shorts were a problem, though. I had a big butt and big legs. Whoever made these shorts had skinny little high school kids in mind. I was a stocky five feet eight and half inches and 170 pounds. The skinny guys could pull off the short shorts, but mine were so tight in the butt and thigh that I'm sure I had visible jock lines.

With our first game closing in, we had been scrimmaging on the full field. Our home field was a catastrophe. It was basically the baseball field, so you were on either the bumpy outfield grass or the dirt infield. The heavy balls were hard enough to control on the grass; on the dirt they were like bowling balls careening down an alley. As a result, Scotnick wanted his offense to get a lot of high crosses in, which meant the defenders had to practice a lot of heading. The drill that he favored for this was to have a goalie punt the ball as high as he could and have us come forward to head the ball. With a modern ball, this is reasonable, but the weight of these balls was brutal, even more so since we were not taught any kind of technique. Simply running forward and taking the full brunt of the ball falling from the sky concussed me time after time. Had my mother seen this drill, she would have called 911 on the spot.

Based on what little Scotnick had told me—our conversations were two sentences or shorter—I would be a benchwarmer at the start of the season. Our starting lineup, in a 4-3-3 formation would be

Dan M—Keeper

Giorgio	Alain	Doug	Dan N

Clyde #1	Maurice	Clyde #2

Clyde #3	Jerry	Clyde #4

Four Jamaicans, four Italians, one Frenchman, a Brit, and an American keeper. Not one American field player, so I didn't feel too bad. We were all on the bench. Besides, I was a sophomore and a full year younger than other sophomores, so in effect I was a freshman.

Before our first FCIAC game, Scotnick had scheduled a preseason game, against Norwalk Community College. As if I wasn't spooked enough to be playing with older high school kids, we now had to play against an actual college. If our guys were as old as eighteen (I think Giant Clyde was nineteen—a couple of kids said he was over twenty), then some of those guys could be twenty or maybe even twenty-five. The game was on a Saturday, and when I told my dad, I was a little surprised but glad that he wanted to go. It was a home game, and perfect weather. Giorgio, my competitor at right back, was a no-show. God knows where the kid lived—he did not speak English, or at any rate any English that I understood. So Scotnick had no choice but to use me.

"OK, Lilie, you're starting," he said.

I hadn't actually thought that I'd be playing. I thought my dad would watch, give me some download on the team, and that would be that. No Giorgio meant that I would be starting my first ever game against a college team; this after the sum total of my soccer practice experience using a ball, not counting the conditioning days, was five days. I had played five days of real soccer in my life.

NCC lived up to my expectations: they were big, ethnic, hairy, and old looking. I was at right back. Doug was our right-center back. He was big, but on the clumsy side, and one of the fast Clydes was at right halfback in front of me. Maurice was our center halfback. That was my orbit. To my right was the sideline, then a fence. Since it was Saturday, there were a surprising number of people at the game: parents and girlfriends. NCC had most of the possession, but we were doing OK. Mostly that was because the ball hadn't found me yet. If it did, it was surely because we broke down in another part of the field and not because anyone was confident enough to pass it to me. I don't think that half the team even knew my name at that point. Scotnick had made it clear that I had one job and one job only: to get the ball the hell out of our end and kick it up field as far as possible. This was defensive soccer doctrine in the early seventies. And he certainly wasn't taking chances with the only American kid (except for our goalie Dan) in the lineup.

As the game went on, I was at least running a bit. After ten minutes, I was tested: one of their smaller guys, a winger, got the ball past the half line and caught Clyde up field. Smelling fresh sophomore blood, he dribbled at me and then pushed it to try to run around me. But I guessed right. I stopped the ball, and with Scotnick's instructions fresh in my mind, kicked it as hard as I could out of bounds. Without the mandate to overlap and create play up field, fullback is a position of rote defensive responsibility: tackle, clear, and head the ball away. If someone is open, make a pass. Do not, under any circumstances, roll a pass into the middle of the field. Keep goal-side of the attacker. Work with the other three of the back four and push up field for the offside trap. Clear the area after the keeper takes possession. All this I would learn quickly. What I wouldn't learn from Scotnick would be any soccer skills. Those would be vested strictly with the Italians and Jamaicans.

Just as I was settling in to my defensive duties in the second half, we won a free kick. Maurice, our field general and best player by a wide margin, was the only foreign guy who actually tried to communicate with everyone. Like a good soldier, I hung back in my half of the field; to a neophyte soccer defender, the midfield line is your Great Wall, to be passed at the peril of being benched for the rest of the season. But Maurice, with his phenomenal vision of the field, saw that the NCC defenders had shifted to the right side of their goal, expecting a high ball to be played across their goalmouth. I was hanging just inside the NCC half—nothing was near me, so I figured I could at least try out the grass on the other side—and he quickly turned to me and nodded for me to go forward.

I looked at Scotnick and he seemed to be kind of checked out, so I gathered my reserves (it was pretty late in the game and I think we were down 2-1) and made a run down the sidelines. Maurice played a deft ball into space towards the NCC goal box.

I got to the ball, but so did one of the NCC midfielders, scrambling to cover. The ball squirted out and I had another play on it as it moved towards the goal. I could see one of the big defenders moving to close me down and clear the ball, but I slid and tried to direct it goalward.

In the scramble, the NCC goalie had come out, and as the three of us converged on the ball, my foot got there early enough to direct it in. A goal! In my first organized game, playing fullback, in front of my dad, and against a college team, no less. Scotnick was far enough away that he probably didn't get a good look at it. His emotions ranged from brute stoicism to mild amusement. While he did appear to be somewhat happy we tied the game, he made no connection to the goal and me. He probably saw Maurice taking the free kick, a scramble, and a goal. Good enough, and on to the weekend.

I was ecstatic. If nothing else, at least I think my teammates finally knew me, and at least I was athletic enough to get forward and mix it up in front. I had hoped that Scotnick would have seen enough to promote me in my battle to win the position from Giorgio, but Giorgio was Italian and ipso facto a better player than me in Scotnick's eyes.

Sure enough, when the season opened, Giorgio was starting at right back. OK, I reasoned, he was probably about nineteen, so he was older, but I thought that my NCC effort (not the least part of which was that I had actually showed up for the game) would have won me the start. Giorgio could dribble, but that was about it. I couldn't understand how he got through any classes without any command of English. If his dribbling broke down, it was a disaster on the pitch; Maurice would shout out some stuff in Italian, and the three other defenders would have to cover. Giorgio was also smaller than me, and Scotnick didn't like the fact that he shied away from physical play in our end. He was actually more of a modern wingback, ready to overlap and go forward all the time.

After a couple of losses, I got my break, a start. I knew I was in the starting lineup to provide some physical defense, so I set out to play that way. I was pretty big for a soccer player, and I realized that I usually came out ahead on 50/50 balls. That became my trademark. As long as your hands and arms weren't involved, you could hit people pretty hard, assuming you got to the ball first. Tough tackling was not sexy soccer, but it got you noticed by the opposing attackers.

Not too long into that first start, I started to trash talk to the opposition. To an outsider, high school soccer in bucolic southern Connecticut in the early 1970s might sound quaint, but that impression is wrong. Our games, especially with the conference divided into "rich" (i.e., all-white) teams and "ethnic" (i.e., poor) teams, were touchstones for hostility. I started to identify with the multiethnic flavor of Westhill, not that I became such great pals with any of the foreign guys, but because I grew to quickly loathe the pretty boys who played for Greenwich, Westport, New Canaan, Darien, and Wilton. When I say "loathe," it is not in the conventional sense. A lot of them did convey a rich kid kind of dick-headedness for sure, but mainly I was jealous.

Those schools, especially Staples, were a dream. It is a bit absurd, I know, to have gone to high school in a wealthy suburb and talk enviously about other rich public schools. But such was the nuanced pecking order in those days. Even the wealthiest parts of North Stamford were considered to be downscale from Greenwich. Greenwich was an aspirational town, Stamford a place to live. Although I had gone to camp in posh New Canaan, in an absolutely breathtaking part of the town off Ponus Ridge

Road, it was not until my first soccer away games that I began to understand the machinations that went into the psychosocial pecking order of Fairfield County.

Arriving by yellow school bus, the first thing that was evident when you got to one of the rich schools was the landscaping. Boy, did they like to manicure their grounds. At Staples, the first thing you saw was a vast expanse of soccer fields elided to make one giant verdant putting green. And those were the fields for the JV and freshman programs—yes, Staples, with its prescient youth soccer program for the town, had an actual freshman soccer squad. Once parked, if it wasn't too late and there were students still milling around the fields, one other thing was obvious: there were no people of color at these schools. I suppose that Staples had a good number of Jews, Westport being the least "restricted" of the wealthy Fairfield Country suburbs, but the dominant look was white, blond, and waspy. Staples, in fact, was one of the only teams that played in all white uniforms for its away games.

All this whiteness was a shock to my system. For the first nine years of my school life I was confined to fifteen or so other kids who were pretty much like me. Except for my family, my neighborhood was 100 percent Catholic. For the most part, these were practicing Catholic families, and in their way, as distinct from Protestants as the Jews were. I suddenly had two completely new paradigms: the multiethnic, "United Nations" profile of Westhill (and, as I would later learn, Norwalk and Danbury) and the whitey-whitevilleness of Greenwich, Westport, and their ilk. Like much of the soccer world, I would have to choose a side; my side became the common man.

For the rest of the season, Scotnick stayed with a consistent lineup, except for right back. He pitted me against Giorgio, and it became a platoon system. As the only sophomore to start any games, I suppose this should have been satisfying for me, but like any kid playing any sport, you want to be in there all the time. We finished that season with a losing record, something like five wins, eight losses, and a couple of draws. Back then, the season ended in October. Fall was peaking, I had a season under my belt as a true varsity player, and more than anything I was looking forward to the fall sports banquet when letters would be awarded. We did not have a formal JV team, but we carried the JVs as part of the varsity. I was clearly part of the varsity—out of thirteen or fourteen games, I probably started six or seven—and was almost positive that I would be getting a letter from Scotnick.

The night of the awards, held in the school auditorium, was thrilling. This was what jockdom was all about. The season was over, and you could reflect on your accomplishments and bond with your teammates, some of whom would move on, others who would be back with you next year. I was floating—this was vindication for those dreamy days at Bi-Cultural when I thought about what it would be like to play soccer for real. After football and field hockey, soccer was up.

Scotnick took the podium. He quietly summarized a losing season, and went on to the awards. The letter winners were announced: the Clydes, the Italians, the three seniors, and not a word about me! Then came the numbers awards for the JV: both Giorgio and myself. That SOB could not bring himself to award either of us a letter! The sting of not getting a letter was the first time I realized that life is not meritocratic; I deserved that letter. I played half the season as a starter and ran my ass off. I suffered through endless heading drills with soaked soccer balls weighted like kettle bells. I had gotten bruised and battered and logged a hundred miles of soccer and had gotten screwed by a "coach" who neither knew nor cared a whit about the sport.

That fall, there was a collective groan in southern Connecticut. After the Arab nations declared an oil embargo, gasoline was strictly rationed. That single gesture probably created more tension around Stamford than all of the political assassinations in the '60s and Watergate combined. My parents would wake up and plan their day around the filling station lineup. Cars would be backed up twenty and thirty deep at the pumps. There were flare-ups over who was in what line and who was first. As a kid, it was mind numbing. My sister and I would have to sit in the back of the Chevy Biscayne, my mother anxiously sucking on her Newport Lights, fretting over whether someone was going to cut her off.

After several weeks of enduring the all-consuming hell of the oil problem, Stamford was hit with the famous ice storm in late November of 1973. Even from a kid's perspective, there was an apocalyptic quality about this one. The conditions for an ice storm have to be almost perfect—near freezing, but not quite, as the essential component is rain that transitions to ice. Buckingham Drive was a little over ten years old, so the few mature trees that dotted the street stood out as they bent and groaned under the weight of the ice. The power and telephone lines were also draped with ice. We were used to snow—in some of the previous few winters, we had built six-foot-high snow forts in the driveway—but the ice was unusual. With our driveway an ice rink, I took my crummy ice skates out and actually managed to skate on the flat part of the driveway near the garage.

But the sports machine plowed forward. I put away soccer for the winter for another amusement. With the construction of Stamford's Terry Connors ice rink in 1973, hockey registered on the city's sports landscape for the first time. The FCIAC had been playing ice hockey since 1967, and it was natural that a state that straddled Rangers and Bruins territory would cozy up to hockey. Catching the fever, the Stamford Board of Recreation went around to all the high schools late in the fall of 1973 to sign up teams to play a new sport: street hockey. I had been playing hockey with a Wiffle ball in my driveway—mostly with my dad—for years, and if anyone was ready for organized street hockey, I was.

Also, as much as I wanted to start playing ice hockey, the reality was that there wasn't a pond close enough to my house that froze consistently, and with Terry Connors rink a good seven or eight miles or so from my house, there was no way in my wildest dreams that either of my parents would be willing to get me there for skating. With no such thing as indoor soccer, I focused on street hockey through the winter. If nothing else, it was an unbelievable conditioning sport. With a core group of great athletes—including Westhill's first ice hockey star and soccer goalie Dan—we conquered our big intraschool rivals, the Flyers, and went on to win the city title.

I also started getting into the high school groove, thanks to some easier courses and not being in a continuous state of shock from the size of the place and the diversity of the student body.

Thanks to geometry, an easy English teacher, and chemistry, which was pretty easy once you got the basic formulas down, I got my grades up to a point where it wasn't the main topic around our house. With my sister still at Bi-Cultural and my mother slipping in and out of long bouts of depression, the less attention I drew, the better. My family was cloaked in a post–ice storm funk, but we kept it together enough for me to participate in my extracurricular activities, including playing the viola in a regional orchestra.

Westhill, whose music and sports were firmly in the grasp of football—and by extension the politics of funding various school programs—somehow professed not to have enough money to maintain a string music program. This, in the face of spending $11,000 (in 1973 dollars) for band uniforms! I remember this number because there were a hundred kids in the band and the uniforms were $110 apiece. For the brass, wind, and percussion players there was the marching band, concert band, and jazz ensemble, but if you played a string instrument, you had to go elsewhere.

My viola teacher had established a regional orchestra that rehearsed around the county and played biannual concerts. There were a few Westhill kids, but a lot of kids went to Greenwich High. In ninth grade, my first year in the orchestra, I sat so far back in the second violin section that I think technically I was considered offstage. I was barely thirteen, depressed and shocked at being in public school, and barely paid attention to where the other kids were from. The truth is that the only reason I played in orchestra that year was to spend at least one night a week out of my house. Sophomore year was a different story. I was older, smarter, and on the varsity soccer team. In the jock pecking order of Westhill I may have been just another dweeb who wouldn't or couldn't play football, but among the assorted geeks, nerds, and dorks who made up the orchestra, I was a studly athlete.

My confidence was buttressed by two cheeky Greenwich girls—Roanne and Betty. They were both juniors and fun in the way that only two cute older girls who didn't go to your school can be fun. They were quite a pair, a Jew and an Italian, the two groups who made up Greenwich's tiny ethnic minorities. In four years, I remember seeing one dark-skinned kid in my entire time playing against Greenwich High, and he was their goalie. As viola players, we were never treated to the melodic parts of the score. With rare exceptions, the altoregister viola is consigned to the "oom-pah" passages that make up the ballast of orchestral music, giving it depth, leaving the dazzle to the violins and wind instruments. It was best that way because none of the three of us was really that good at the viola. For that we had the sere and judgmental Peter sitting first chair. Peter came in perfectly handy. Always on pitch and a brilliant sight reader, Peter could be relied on to help pick up where we left off. And Roanne, Betty, and I were lost a lot because we spent the better part of our time flirting and kibitzing.

Not that they shared everything with me. They spent a good amount of rehearsal time deconstructing the Greenwich High social scene. Of course I went to Westhill and was clueless about who they were talking about, but I was a decent learner and even a better eavesdropper. Parties, kiss and tells, kiss and no tells, break-ups, crushes, brush-offs were reported on in minute detail. For a fourteen-year-old kid, not long out of the educational ghetto, this was like someone lit the pilot burner for my hormones. Orchestra was suddenly my social life. I didn't mind that the girls weren't against taking the piss out of me. As far as I was concerned, they could have put firecrackers under my fingernails as long as they flirted with me. I had soccer to thank for this. Presoccer, I was schlub, and the sight of upper-class girls would have shredded me before I got out of the gate. When they learned I was on the team, it was the fillip I needed to pique their interest. I was just that much different from Peter and the serious music geeks earnestly blowing and bowing away.

One Monday rehearsal night, Betty asked me out. Not out, exactly, but over. Her parents were going out Saturday, and maybe I'd like to come over. There was one problem: I was fifteen and still needed a ride. No problem, she would pick up and deliver. I didn't let my lack of driver's license stand in the way. She lived in the Cos Cob section, the only working-class part of Greenwich. Slowly, Fairfield County was being demystified.

*   *   *

In the spring, with the World Cup just ahead, my attention turned to soccer more than ever. As a player now, with the numerals to prove it, I started to dig deeper into the media to see what was going on around the world. The Cosmos were decent, with Randy Horton and a few other entertaining players, but clearly, there was a much bigger world out there. To round out my extracurricular activities—according to my geriatric guidance counselor, this is how one got into college—I had a job at the school media center, assisting one of the librarians, Ms. Holyfield, in sorting through the rather large assortment of periodicals and newspapers that Westhill received.

One of these was the *London Times*, a newspaper that seemed to me a lot like the *New York Times*, but with the fantastic twist of reporting on soccer. The London sportswriters were also inclined to a mock-intellectual style of writing, catnip to my young mind. I began to learn a whole new vocabulary, a soccer vocabulary: "overlapping," "centre-halfs," "volley," "pitch," "touch line," "one-touch." There was a whole world of description and soccer erudition that had completely escaped me trudging through that first Westhill season.

It was doubly exciting because there was a World Cup approaching in 1974, to be held in Germany. Here and there I started to read about a team called Ajax, from Amsterdam, and the Dutch National team, which featured most of Ajax's stars. These two teams were purported to be the best in the world at the club and national levels, respectively. The Dutch talisman was a player named Johan Cruyff, a chain-smoking iconoclast who was the foundation of a wholly new approach to soccer: total futbol.

This was the first glimpse I got into soccer as a religion. David Winner, the author of *Brilliant Orange, the Neurotic Genius of Dutch Football*, reveals the basis for the Dutch approach to soccer to be rooted in the notion of 'Maakbaarheid,' the ability to control every aspect of the social and physical environment. Holland, a featureless and flat environment, has fomented a culture of recapturing and reshaping space. This analytical approach to space has been fully realized in Dutch soccer. Winner goes on to quote the Dutch artist Jeroen Henneman, who compares Cruyff and Ajax to Mondrian and Vermeer:

> [Their painting] feels very silent and fresh and quiet and roomy. When you space things it becomes very quiet . . . If you translate that to football, it means it is easier to play because there is more room to receive the ball . . . You went to matches at Ajax and came away with the feeling that you had seen something very special and that only you could see it. But then you talked to other people and you realized that everyone had felt the same thing. There was something spiritual going on.

Although Winner wrote his book in 2000, the Ajax phenomenon had gripped the soccer world, reaching as far as the soccer wasteland of Stamford, Connecticut, in 1973. By the time I saw magazine and newspaper photos of Cruyff and Neeskens, I had become a fan of Ajax and Holland. Eclipsing even the Brazilians with dazzling attacking play, the Dutch were favored in the World Cup, along with the home side, Germany. This was a good versus evil scenario, along the lines of Westhill versus Staples—the worldly Dutch versus the lordly Germans. In photos, the Dutch, with their long hair and flashy orange jerseys, were like touring musicians. The Germans had one or two interesting characters—defender Paul Breitner was an avowed Maoist—but Franz Beckenbauer, the German captain, was clean cut and, well, Teutonic in bearing and manner. Cruyff, by contrast, was a chain smoker and a rebel, refusing to wear Adidas-sponsored gear in the World Cup; instead of a jersey with three stripes, his bore two.

The Dutch captured my imagination to the point where I had started to let go of the local teams of my youth. Why bother with the Mets when there was a sport the entire world cared about? The Mets and Jets were "World Champions" in 1969 and 1970, but where was the "World" part? With teams from Zaire, Haiti, and everywhere on the planet, the World Cup was the only team sports championship that lived up to its billing, and to my thinking, my Westhill team was like a microcosm of the World Cup.

With a bit of sleuthing, I discovered there was a magazine called *World Football*, an English publication. It was expensive, but somehow either I scraped the money together or my dad sprung for it. With *WF*, I could finally follow the world scene, which was thrilling in the run up to Germany '74. What I knew about the Dutch was strictly from reading about them. I had never seen Ajax or the Dutch National team play.

The World Cup began in June with the customary coverage in the *New York Times* and *Stamford Advocate*, that is to say, virtually none at all. There was no television or radio coverage either. My dad was pretty exasperated by this, and taking matters into his own hands, managed to get his hands on a beast of a shortwave radio. Like all the electronics he had, it was broken. His mission at the time was to fix things, and he became the go-to guy for everyone's broken radios and televisions. I don't think we actually owned any of our appliances; my dad simply held on to the ones he repaired until he fixed the succeeding batch and put the newly repaired ones into the rotation.

As the finals approached, I checked the daily progress of the repairs. That giant pile of transistors and capacitors and spaghetti wire did not look like it was ready to deliver the BBC broadcast of the final between Germany and Holland, or that it would ever be ready. But the Sunday of the finals came, and my dad had the thing in a state of semiassembly on the little deck in back of the house. Tuning, we heard the crackle and static excitement of the pregame coming through in lots of languages, none of them English. The BBC was not to be found.

Fortunately, my dad grew up speaking German and could still understand a decent amount. We found a German station that wheezed in and out. All I could hear were staccato bursts of German—frenzied German. Minutes from the start, there was shouting: Holland had been awarded a penalty and Neeskens converted it; my heroes were ahead. The lead was short-lived, of course. Germany came back to win the game "against the run of play," another phrase that I had picked up from the *London Times*.

It was funny, but Holland's loss stung me worse than when my usual teams—the Mets, Jets, and Rangers—lost out. Soccer pushed my buttons. I had become so obsessed with the Dutch and their total football that I felt as if they were playing for my honor. It helped too that Holland, as a nation, was defiant in the face of the Arab attempt to wreak havoc on the Western world through the oil embargo. While many Western nations, especially France, were quick to capitulate and bend over for the Arabs, the Dutch had simply said, in effect, "Fine, we'll go ahead and ride our bicycles." Somehow I concluded this was a show of solidarity with Semitic people all over the planet, but of course it was simply born of Dutch intransigence and national pride. Whatever the motivation, I thought it was badass, and it made me even more of a Dutch soccer fan.

Sometime not long after the World Cup in '74, PBS started showing a one-hour condensed version of what was then known as the English First Division, now the Premiership. Soccer on TV in my neck of the world to that point consisted of the Cosmos and Canal Quarente Uno, the Spanish station. The English game resembled the snail's pace of the Cosmos and the Mexican league as much as cliff diving looked like jumping into a backyard pool. Raucous, chanting crowds, a pace that looked like ice hockey, and ferocity on the field ruled the English game. I still could not see my precious Holland, but there were plenty of stars in the English game, including the spectacular George Best.

The commentary was also fresh to my ears. There was something about the English public school accents that made me feel part of a private club. The English announcers, unlike their American counterparts, would occasionally stop talking for long stretches of action. It was refreshing to have things revealed by the game rather than told to you. My family may not have been willing to shell out for the swim or country clubs, but we could watch PBS with the best of them. It was dime-store erudition, to be sure. I was starting to connect the dots about soccer. It was clearly a foreign sport in the U.S., but it was by far the most popular on the planet. My relatives played when they came here, and so did my dad, and he retained an affinity for it. I liked "American" sports, especially baseball, but soccer not only was a blast to play, it also fed my budding adolescent desire to be "interesting."

At school I did not see a whole lot of my soccer teammates. The economic, class, and intellectual divide at Westhill was pretty powerful. It sounds remarkable, but out of about twenty-five soccer players, I think there was only one other guy—Dan N.— taking a college placement schedule, and he was a year ahead of me. Our goalie, Dan M., was a good enough hockey player that he was offered a "postbaccalaureate" scholarship to play at one of the private prep schools. He went on to St. Lawrence to become the first Division I collegiate player from Stamford. Occasionally I'd run into Maurice or one of the Clydes in the hall and we'd say hi, but that was about it. There was not a single other high school kid who shared my interest in soccer as a fan. If I tried to talk to one of my other friends about it, they'd have some derisive reflexive remark: "girls' sport," "for weirdos," "what's soccer?"

I did get wind of some great news: Scotnick was not going to coach in the fall. I didn't know who was replacing him, but the rumor was they were bringing in a new coach. I was actually excited enough about this news that I went to find Scotnick at the pool after school one day. He confirmed the news and seemed as happy as I was; soccer was drudgery for him, nothing more. In the yearbook photo of the soccer team, he looks like someone had shot his dog.

Spring practice was standard for the football team. It had a big coaching staff and the full attention of the athletic department. Like at a lot of schools, football at Westhill was the athletic department. Without any coach towards the end of the school year, a few of us decided that we should probably kick a ball around and at least try to imitate the discipline shown by the football team. It was an anemic showing. Maurice worked and had a girlfriend, and the remaining Clydes were too unreliable to show up for anything. It came down to me, Dave W., one of the other white American guys, and a couple of the JV dudes.

It wasn't long though before we were told about our new coach. His name was Jim Vadikos, and he was coming to Westhill with a pedigree as a track coach (and state record holder in the 800) from Southern Connecticut College. Good enough, I thought, but did he know anything about soccer? The problem in 1974 for almost every high school program was that there were virtually no seasoned or knowledgeable coaches out there. Staples succeeded in large part because of the tactical genius of Albie Loeffler. Westhill had failed in large part because of the retrograde and insouciant approach of Ben Scotnick.

When we showed up for summer practice and met Vadikos for the first time, he cut a very impressive figure. He was about 6'3", 215 pounds of rock-solid, lantern-jaw athlete. He had thick hair parted down the middle and a booming voice and favored running us into the ground—by example. Unlike Scotnick, who passively stood around with his clipboard, mumbling on about commitment and conditioning, Vadikos was an in-your-face, rah-rah guy who was going to mold us into . . . well, we didn't know exactly, but he was certainly enthusiastic about it. There were about thirty kids out for the first summer practice. We had about eight starters back and a bunch of new American guys (and a couple of foreigners). In its fourth year of soccer, the word had started to spread a bit at Westhill. Only two of the Clydes remained, and, to my relief, there was no sign of Giorgio. Either he flunked out, went back to Italy, or started collecting social security, but any way I sliced it, there would be less competition at fullback.

Vadikos was quick to prove he was no slouch in the conditioning department. The difference between him and Scotnick, though, was that Vadikos ran with us, actually ahead of us. Way ahead of us. The guy had a horse's stride and was immune to sweat or thirst. His threats centered on challenging us to be in the same physical condition that he was in.

Among the new kids were two or three really exceptional athletes. Two brothers—white Americans—came on the scene from a private school in Singapore. I didn't have the foggiest idea where Singapore was, but it sounded exotic and hence soccer-worthy. The older brother, Chris, a senior, was a goalkeeper. He was smallish, about my height, but more slender, and spoke very quietly. Before we were into our second day of practice, Chris had spoken to Vadikos a few times, and whatever he said made Vadikos anoint him our starting keeper. The other big catch was a powerful Haitian named Alex. Like the Jamaicans, Alex had a heavy accent, his laced with Creole dialect. He also had a puppy dog personality, goofy and distracted. But Alex was the only guy who could almost keep up with Vadikos; the problem for Alex, and soon for the rest of us, was that he rarely wanted to do so.

Seizing upon Alex's speed, Vadikos made him the benchmark for our workouts. Unless Alex could win a sprint, we would all keep sprinting. After a two-hour workout, the last thing any of us wanted to do was to bootstrap a guy who needed to dig down and win a race. Alex was a free spirit, as undisciplined as they came. One day he ran, the next day he jogged. He was in America, but still on Haitian time. I am still haunted by pushing through yet another agonizing gallop to the half-line courtesy of Alex's lollygagging.

Vadikos told us point blank that toughness was the most important quality for him—it would have been great to have him on the team. He settled on Dave and me for his central defenders. We were the Americans, and the two most physical players. Dave was a terrific athlete, a pitcher on the baseball team, and very fast. He was commanding in the air, but like a lot of central defenders, he was uncomfortable with the ball at his feet. Our wingbacks were two seniors, another Alex and Dan N., speedy and reliable players, both on the small side. Maurice marshaled us from the center of the pitch, with one of the returning Clydes, Greg, our school 400-yard champ, on the right of midfield. The left side of midfield was our weak spot. Vadikos thought it was enough to have Maurice in midfield and rotated through a bunch of hapless guys on the left side. Up top, the mercurial Alex was on the right, with Jerry in the center and a Clyde, Noel, on the left. We would have been far better off with a 4-4-2 versus a 4-3-3, especially against Staples, but such was the tactical naiveté of Vadikos that he started and ended the season that way.

After staging a semibrilliant academic comeback during sophomore year, I again dipped my toe into honors-level courses. Eastern Standard Time made it necessary for us to start our games at 3:00, which meant we had to hustle out of school on game days. The athletic department authorized early dismissal for us on those days, and our teachers were notified. My last period English teacher, Mrs. Stellbart, had other ideas. The first game, I stood up quietly to go.

"Where are you going?" she asked in front of the whole class.

"I have a game." I said.

"Oh, really, and you think you can walk out of my class just like that?"

I knew that Stellbart had received the memo from the athletic department. I had also spoken to her before classes even started to let her know that I'd have to go early on game days. She was a theatrical sort, enamored with the sound of her own voice, and clearly favored the girls in the class who fawned over her long-winded interpretations of Hawthorne and Thoreau.

"I'm sorry, but I'm pretty sure you got the memo. It's not my policy but the athletic department's. My bus leaves and I have to be on it."

Stellbart glared at me, as if to say, "You can walk out of here, but your grade is going to reflect it, pal." I was not the kind of kid who wanted to get into an "eff-you" situation with my teachers—lord knows I had enough of that with my mother—but she did her best to belittle me. For the rest of the semester—we had eight away games—she busted my balls every time I had to leave. I wound up with a "B" in her class. I'm sure that if it weren't for soccer I would have gotten an "A."

We started the season with a bang, two victories and two ties, ten goals for and three against. It seemed we had the talent to beat anyone, but with Alex and the Clydes, it was a question of who would show up to play on any given day. We also had something new: two girls, my friend Sue and a beautiful, willowy sophomore named Holly, who were "team managers." The year before, we hauled everything ourselves—water, balls, flags, cones. Soccer seemed to be getting a bit more noticed, especially by some of the girls at school. With the benefit of hindsight, I'm sure that Vadikos's glamour didn't hurt in drawing new attention.

After going undefeated in our first five games, we laid an egg—a 1-0 defeat at Stamford High. Stamford was the only team in the FCIAC that had a worse field than we did. It was on top of a rock and strangely short and wide. It seemed like it was only eighty yards long. Goalie punts would bounce into the opposition's box, and the games there had more of a basketball-type feel. It also played into the hands of their top players, Spanish-speaking twins, who, like a lot of the foreign soccer players in Stamford, were rumored to be much older than high school age. Alex was in a crappy mood that day, Vadikos pulled him early, and the twins were pulling the game's strings. The conference featured four superstrong teams—Staples, Greenwich, Wilton, and McMahon.

The previous year, we had gone to Staples and got thumped. I hadn't been able to shake the Staples mystique since first arriving on its verdant, expansive campus. Our scruffy Heinz 57 contingent got off the bus and prepared for our usual kick-around and stretching that constituted our warm-up. Loeffler, on the other hand, had Staples organized like a professional team. The varsity, in their Yale-blue warm-ups—those beautiful warm-ups alone were intimidating; we were lucky to have jerseys—went through a series of specialized drills, two versus ones, one-twos, in a high tempo, well-choreographed manner. All this on their practice field, which was groomed like a billiard table and miles better than our game field. The game field was like Wembley, so good that I remember it was startling how true the ball rolled and bounced. At Westhill's field, every bounce was a bad bounce, and we developed a style that favored long clearances from the defenders and goalkeeper.

This year, Staples was coming to Westhill, and Vadikos had spent the previous week getting us psyched up for them. That 1974 Staples squad was loaded—about half that team went on to be NCAA Division I scholarship players. Sprinkled through the lineup were three monsters—Steve Dickstein, Andy Simon, and Charlie Perlwitz—all about six feet or more and skilled. The midfield was run by the arrogant and combative Murphy brothers, Ken and Kevin. They were real Westport towheads, fair and angelic looking, but direct and skilled players who played angry. The line was led by the meteoric Phil Moen, a sylph of a guy who was so fast and elusive that our entire back four was at his mercy—and we were all pretty fast ourselves. Kevin went on to play at Sacred Heart in Bridgeport, Ken at UConn, Dickstein at Brown, and Moen at URI. A lot of other Staples players went on to play in college as well. They had better players than most of the FCIAC, but a lot of the program's success in placing players derived from the pipeline and relationships that Loeffler created.

Loeffler was a brilliant coach. He had great players, but as a unit, Staples played a style that was as close to Dutch total football as I have ever seen, certainly from a high school team. They were interlinked, superfast blond dervishes. They played triangles to perfection, drawing us into a flat defensive scheme and continually shooting the gaps with perfectly weighted passes, usually to Moen, who, time and time again, shredded our pathetic zone defense that Vadikos devised—a basketball defense. Maurice, whose preternatural cool and field vision could usually be counted on to control large swaths of the game for us, was just as flummoxed as the rest of us. As good as Staples had been the year before when they beat us 3-0, they were astounding on our chopped-up home turf that was half baseball field. They beat us 2-0, and I would venture to guess they had 75 percent of the ball that match. Against teams that possessed the ball like that, Alex, the Clydes, and Jerry would virtually disappear. They had almost no discipline and no desire to win the ball back. They were good when they possessed the ball but were for the most part uncoachable.

In part, it was this last quality that infuriated me and fueled my obsession with Staples. What they had, in addition to a formidable soccer team, was an esprit de corps. They were a team, with a real coach, who understood tactics and training and technique. The Staples guys could shoot. We could not really shoot, because Scotnick and now Vadikos had never played a game of soccer in their life and had no interest in developing their technical knowledge of soccer. Vadikos, who had played some ice hockey, was convinced that soccer was an adaptation of hockey for grass. He devised a series of drills that revolved around contact, including his favorite, the soccer version of "chicken." Chicken involved forming a big circle. Vadikos would toss the ball high, somewhere near the middle, and yell out the names of two players. The object was to get to the ball first. Obviously it was rare that there would be such a discrepancy in speed that one guy would win the ball cleanly. Usually, the chicken drill involved a high-speed collision, which Vadikos encouraged, like a pit bull trainer baiting his dogs before a fight. With the lowest center of gravity on the team, I was strong at this drill, so strong that one time Maurice and I came together, the result being that Maurice was left in a heap. There was a collective gasp around the circle. Vadikos ran over to Maurice, and from that point on, we did not do the chicken drill. Another favorite of his was a drill that involved "running to the post." This was inflicted on the whole team, but mostly on our wings, including a Clyde, and two sophomores, Dave and Rene. The post drill, another unrelenting toughen-up drill, involved Vadikos kicking the ball into the area, with the player about thirty yards from the goal. At Vadikos's command, the player would have to sprint "to the post." Not towards the goal, but exactly to the post. What Vadikos was seeking was a collision with the post, the ultimate toughening-up experience. If one of the wingers, slightly built to a man, even hesitated a bit, Vadikos would have a fit: "David J., you better get tough—I want you going to the post hard." While Staples was playing triangles and mastering moving the ball into space, we were being enticed into high-speed collisions.

Then there was shooting. At his size—Vadikos was three inches taller and forty pounds heavier than the biggest guys on the team—Vadikos could kick a soccer ball seventy yards. The problem was that he could only kick the ball with his toe. The basic principles of kicking a soccer ball—instep to shoot and for long passing, side foot and outside of the foot for shorter, control passing—completely eluded him. He did not even have the most basic idea of how to control a pass or shot. In practice, he would go to kick someone a ball, and with his toe, he would blast it directly at someone, only for the ball to veer sharply left or right as soon as the rotation overtook it.

As even the littlest player today knows, you impart spin to control the flight of the ball. Of course, there is occasionally a benefit to the toe poke, most often when a striker is inside the box with no other options, but the toe kick is not part of the basic repertoire for a player. With the exception of Jerry and Maurice and maybe Chris, no one on our team really knew how to shoot a ball properly. The mechanics of shooting—toe down, body over the ball, making contact in the right part of the ball—must be taught, and taught well. More than other good teams, our goals were garbage goals: rebounds, ugly headers, side-footed shots. In three seasons of Westhill soccer, I think we scored two or three really pretty goals.

That game against Staples changed my whole perspective. After being torched by Phil Moen for ninety minutes, I realized that we had to raise the bar if we wanted to compete. What was it about Albie Loeffler and Staples soccer that made it so brilliant?

I believe that the galvanic factor for Westport and Staples soccer was the acquisition of the Longshore Club Park, a 169-acre former country club on Long Island Sound that was purchased by the city's selectmen in 1960 for $1.9 million. Today, Longshore and the nearby public Compo Beach serve as a public country club for city residents. As far back as the mid-60s, Longshore had youth soccer run by the Westport Recreation Commission. The acquisition of Longshore was a prescient move by the city and was instrumental in creating a democratic leisure class. Other places in Connecticut were far more patrician, and if you were not a member of a private club, you had to make your way to a hardscrabble municipal golf course or dirty stretch of beach. Westport now had a beautiful private club along with the twenty-nine-acre Compo Beach, one of Connecticut's finest. The average Westport citizen, for a small annual fee, was entitled to recreational facilities as nice or even nicer than some of the ritziest private clubs in Fairfield County.

Unlike the other more homogenous wealthy parts of Fairfield County, Westport also was known as a community of creative people—copywriters, artists, and actors who owned summer homes there. On and around Main Street, small-door, independent shops thrived for years before the influx of national tenants. With Compo Beach, the Longshore Club, and the Saugatuck River winding its way through downtown from Long Island Sound, Westport had a maritime feel unmatched by any other town on the southern half of the Connecticut coastline, with the possible exception of Old Saybrook.

Translated to the soccer field, a whole bunch of factors worked in Staples's favor. All of the kids were white and native English speakers. Since the '60s, they had grown up playing youth soccer together, moving on to junior high, the freshman and JV programs at Staples, and finally, hopefully, a starting position in the Staples varsity eleven. They had an enlightened coach who either intuitively came to understand soccer or was a disciple of the sport at the international level, or both. They had fans—1,000 or more could be had for big divisional rival or state championship matches on the Staples hill. And, coming from mostly affluent households, they had a desire to achieve and succeed on the field. Staples had a system of play, but it was not a system that stifled individual brilliance. Quite the opposite: the flexible attacking and supportive play that Loeffler engineered gave his players confidence that was palpable on the field. Any guy at any time could score, defend, and play a one-two, all with near-perfect fundamentals. When we played Staples their talking was nonstop. Terms I had never heard before: "square," "dummy," "tackle." They bossed the game with brilliant teamwork.

Our team, by contrast, was a study in individualism. Like in a pickup park game, each player had his own concept about how soccer should be played. As kids, the foreign guys had grown up playing in school. To them, a coach like Vadikos was at best a cheerleader, at worst a big oaf who was cramping their own personal soccer style. On the sidelines, Vadikos was a maniac; if nothing else he was passionate about winning. His coaching vocabulary was limited to the basics: "hustle," "work," "get there." I was one of his favorites because of my no-nonsense approach to tackling. Not having ever played organized soccer, I adapted my game to what I thought coaches like Scotnick and Vadikos wanted: clear the ball and knock people on their ass. The FCIAC was a tough league. In 1975, in a 0-2 road loss to Wilton, two separate ambulance trips were needed for injuries incurred in the first half. Concussions, broken noses, knee injuries, tears, and strains were commonplace.

As a physical player, I often got the assignment of going head to head with the other team's best player. Ken Murphy, who later played for the University of Connecticut and with Johan Cruyff in the NASL, was my favorite combatant. Murphy was damn good and got pissed off when you got him even a little bit out of his rhythm. If he sprayed a pass or if you won a ball from him, he made it personal. In the four matches I played against him, we would spend most of the game in each other's face, talking smack and getting away with as much pushing, grabbing, charging, and sliding as we could.

It's not that Westhill didn't have talent. Our team had two NCAA-caliber goalkeepers, Chris and a young Colombian kid named Carlos. Chris was short for a keeper and Carlos even shorter. Vadikos, based on Chris's little preseason chat and workout, had anointed Chris our starting keeper, but Carlos, a sophomore, proved so agile and talented, that Chris was moved to striker. Like a lot of our team, Carlos could hardly speak English. Against a team like Staples, this was a death sentence—a goalkeeper has to marshal his back line. Phil Moen would slash and attack with impunity, and all the defenders could do would be to yell at each other: "You got 'im! No, you got 'im."

We finished that season a respectable 6-5-2, good enough for the state tournament. The first team we drew was Conard High School, in West Hartford. We knew nothing about Conard, but we did know that there were a bunch of great teams upstate, especially E.O. Smith in Storrs. On one of those dreamy crisp fall days when iridescent leaves dust the ground, we went to Conard's beautiful grass field and beat them in one of the most cohesive games we ever played.

Deep into the tournament, we drew our next opponent—Staples! An entire state full of soccer teams and we randomly drew Staples. There were two major problems: Between 1966 and then, Staples had incurred a total of zero home losses; and second, during the entire FCIAC season, including preseason and postseason, Staples had been scored on from the field (excluding penalty kicks) exactly . . . zero times. Even Vadikos, with his matinee idol looks and sis-boom-bah coaching moves, was having a tough time spinning this one for us in a positive way. I was excited beyond belief. Not only had we advanced to the last sixteen teams in the state, but we would be privileged to play in front of one of the legendary home Staples playoff crowds.

It was also the first time that soccer was truly on the map at Westhill. Kids—regular kids—at school knew about the team and that we won a state game. There was, dare I say, a buzz. Our two cute female managers, Sue and Holly, spread the word about the game, and soon it was clear that Westhill would have its own rooting contingent at Staples. There were one or two girls from Westhill that I also hoped would go, but it really didn't matter; we had become a legitimate sport, worthy of a fan base.

Nothing changed with Vadikos. He had us running the same routine of head-banging drills. It was like he hadn't seen Staples eviscerate us several weeks before with dazzling interchanges, close ball control, and inventive passing. As long as Clyde and Dave and Rene were willing to collide with the goalpost, our strategy was set.

On game day, I felt like a pro on our yellow school bus en route to Westport. The team was loose to say the least. Alex, clowning in Haitian dialect, was not remotely near the correct frame of mind to play. Maurice, as usual, was a rock, and Carlos was church mouse quiet. We had talent all over the field. Probably the softest spot on the field was my partner in central defense, Dave. Against the weaker teams in the conference his speed and strength in the air were plenty to keep the opposition at bay. Against Staples, he had been a disaster, coming unglued the second Moen ran at him with the ball. To be fair, Moen, who would go on to be named an All-American the following year, made everyone come unglued.

About 1,200 people showed up for a high school soccer game in late fall of 1974. I couldn't believe it. For our home games, we would get twenty or thirty spectators scattered up and down the sidelines. Perhaps the biggest crowd I saw at any of our games before that, home or away, was about a hundred, and I'm sure that was also at Staples. It looked like their whole school was on the hill. We had a contingent come up as well, maybe thirty in all, but they hadn't arrived yet. I felt sadly inadequate. We didn't have team warm-ups, so we were out there in a Salvation Army assortment of gear—gray, yellow, red, whatever we wore on top of our uniforms was our business. Not only did Staples look drop dead, kick-ass in their dark blue sweats, their fans had better gear than we did. I could see Staples sweatshirts, windbreakers, long sleeve T-shirts. It was like we were a visiting team from the Free and Democratic Republic of Stamford, sponsored by some charitable mission.

I barely warmed up. I couldn't stop looking at the crowd, the sheer numbers on the hill. When I wasn't absorbed by that, I was looking at our opponents—Moen, the Murphys, Dickstein. Moen had on his trademark gloves and white turtleneck. He looked like a fuzzy little blond elf; I kept glancing over to see if he might have sprained his ankle or gotten hit by lightning. Vadikos looked like he was going to shit his pants. He decided that Carlos would start in goal, and my Spanish had not improved over the course of the season. But that meant we had Chris at striker, where he had really started to come on strong.

I remember my adrenaline being supercharged. The game started with frantic running and tackling. The Clydes and Alex were into it, and they were as fast or faster than anyone on Staples. When they were on, Maurice could play balls into space and let them run the wings. We tried a slightly different thing with Moen: I was going to mark him high, with Dave behind me, a high-low strategy, instead of being flat across the back, which played directly to his strength. It didn't matter. The Murphys plus Moen on their worst day were several levels better than us on our best.

I felt like I had played a whole game at halftime. My endorphins had crashed, and now I was just plain spent from chasing Moen all over the field. We didn't have a great start to the second half, but our spirits were still high. After forty-five minutes, we still had a shot. Maurice was playing the game of his life, a big-time player playing his best at the right time. We started to rally around him, and we could sense that Staples was unnerved that we were sticking around so long. Mind you, this was a team that effectively had not been scored on for an entire season of soccer—sixteen games or so! I don't care what sport or what level is involved, that is remarkable. At about the sixty-minute mark, we were opened up and Carlos was forced to make a diving save, only to have the ball parried to one of their forwards—not Moen—for an easy tap-in. At that moment I didn't sense failure, only destiny. It was Staples all the way, the fair-haired sexy girls in the crowd, the acute and beautiful late fall sun defining long shafts of shadow on the field. I was happy and ready to get on the bus.

We were still scrapping, though. We had the ball in their end. I saw Maurice cut sharply to the edge of the eighteen-yard box and shoot. The shot was a worm burner, low and hard, but was clearly going wide. And then I saw the Clyde on my side jumping up and down, and then Maurice and Chris jumping up and down. I thought that there must have been a hand ball and they were looking for a penalty kick. But they were celebrating! The ball was in the net. We had actually scored against Staples in the run of play!

We were tied deep in the game against the best team in the state. It didn't matter that the ball caromed off about three players and probably a stray dog before it found its way into the net. I didn't quite believe it. I had assumed that the best result we could have hoped for was 0-0, with the game going to overtime and hopefully penalty kicks, where we stood some kind of chance. Everything on me hurt. My hamstrings were burning, and my calves were cramping, a problem of mine.

Our joy was short-lived. Staples attacked and scored an easy goal at about the eighty-minute mark, and then shut us down. We gathered our stuff and watched the fans mill around on the field. We lost, but I was still basking in the glow of the big event. Our traveling contingent came down to say hi, and we put our sad mismatched jackets and sweatpants on, gathered up our equipment, and rumbled home on the yellow bus. A great season. We had defeated fourteenth ranked Conard and almost took out number 3 Staples. How they were only number 3 is a complete mystery, although they did lose in the state semifinals. The final rankings had us at number 12 in the state.

Reflecting on the season, I concluded that we were better than our record. That we were barely over .500 for the regular season was a testament to Vadikos's profound lack of soccer knowledge. We were in decent shape, but so was everyone else. What separated the top teams from the next tier was cohesion and communication, neither of which we had. Watching Albie Loeffler dispense quiet advice was a clear sign that there was a higher level to the sport, one that I hadn't seen at Westhill. The level of pure talent on our team was exceptional, if not quite to Staples' standard. Chris went on to lead Southern Connecticut to a national Division III championship. Maurice went on to star at Eastern Connecticut. Alex Charles could run a ten-second hundred-yard dash, and the Clydes had talent to burn.

By the time our season ended, I had watched enough soccer, listened to enough commentary, and played with enough players of different nationalities to understand that more than any other team sport, soccer depended on a unanimity of understanding. There were clearly defined national styles of play. The Dutch and total football were largely responsible for ushering in this era of systems, even though the Hungarians in the '50s and the Austrians in the '20s had played the Dutch way. Brazil, of course, was the world's leading exponent of individual creativity and brilliance, melding that with team play. For Brazilian players, it was not enough to win; they had to provide the world with Jogo Bonito—the Beautiful Game—as Garrincha did when he would torment defenders by beating them once, circling back, and beating them again for good measure.

The Dutch system, as beautiful as it was to watch, was a derivative of Dutch practicality. Total football is a system that is based on seeing and measuring space, along with a comprehensive understanding of positional play. The beauty of total football was an accidental by-product of the Dutch system. And that is what I realized about Staples: they played beautiful soccer in spite of their ruthless efficiency. Westhill had three "conflicting" systems: West Indian, Italian, and American. The Jamaicans (and Haitians) were fast and talented but weirdly disconnected with results. It was as if showing up was enough. They didn't really celebrate goals, didn't lose their temper, but just kept everything at a nice even "blood-clot" keel. The Italians were easily riled, easily frustrated, and wanted to win badly. They were, however, overly invested in their own personal soccer universe. If you didn't accept as gospel Italian ideas, Italian teams, and the Italian way of life, you were, well, a piece of merde. Not knowing any other system, Dave, John, and I bought into the Vadikos culture of hustle and head banging. I had pretty decent talent that wasn't extracted one whit in high school. Somehow I made honorable mention All-County junior year, and the coach from Eastern Connecticut wanted to talk to me about playing there, according to Vadikos.

With Westhill athletics starting to make its mark in Fairfield County, the brain trust that made up our athletic department started noodling around with an idea: why not put together an intramural competition based on ABC's popular show *The Superstars? The Superstars* was a winter fill-in programming brainchild of the former figure skater Dick Button and pitted athletes from different sports in a competition made up of ten events. The events included a lot of the basics: a hundred-yard dash, a mile run, swimming, and weightlifting. Kyle Rote Jr., an American-born soccer player who came up through the nascent youth soccer ranks in Dallas, won *The Superstars* three times, in 1974, 1976, and 1977. He led the NASL in scoring his rookie year in 1973, and played largely in the shadow of Pele and the

Cosmos. What Rote did accomplish was a measure of credibility for the athleticism required to play soccer. Here was a guy whose father was an All-American football player who became a soccer player instead. Concentrating on soccer after a football injury, Rote Jr.,was perhaps as influential in setting the course of youth soccer as anybody.

The athletic department made it official: all the varsity teams would be pitted against each other in a multisport competition, including two running events, a couple of field events, a tug-of-war, swimming, and for some strange reason, floor hockey. The last event was doubly strange since pretty much the whole gym staff knew that my street hockey team had won the city championship two years running, and that five soccer players—me, Dave, Maurice, Alex, and Paul—were on that team. I was also in the middle of possibly one of the most awkward moments in high school gym history during our floor hockey "module." Like everyone else in gym, I did what I was told, whether it was dopey-ass square dancing, being "deep-sixed" in the pool at eight in the morning, or floor hockey I was a decent to good soccer player, but compared to the general run of kid, I was like Wayne Gretzky and Bobby Orr combined at floor hockey.

Smitty and Laz were watching one day as I was scoring at will. It was a rout, but what the hell, I was having fun, and I didn't want to seem like I wasn't trying. I kept scoring and Smitty and Laz were getting more and more irritated as the score piled up. Finally, Smitty put down his clipboard and picked up a stick. His Tubbiness was going to come to the rescue of the beleaguered team. The problems for Smitty were that (a) he couldn't play hockey to save his life and (b) he was pathetically out of shape. Anger could only get him so far. With Smitty in the opposing lineup, I was doubly motivated, and we really started to pour it on. With every goal, Smitty, a light-skinned black man, became redder and redder. Exhorting the other kids to "get him (me)" and "stop him," he started to try to keep up with me and stop me. It got to the point where I just felt sad for the guy. I was just a kid in gym class, but I had to figure out whether to try or give it up and stroke Smitty's frail little ego. When they announced that floor hockey would be part of the Superstars, I thought there must be a trick up their sleeve.

From the outset of the Superstars, we knew a few concrete facts: we weren't as strong as the football team or the wrestlers, or as fast as the track team, or as good at throwing as the baseball team. But what we did have was a remarkable group of specialists. On our team were two or three guys as fast as anyone in the school, a star swimmer, a pitcher, and me, a hockey player. The big first test came in the tug-of-war, an event adjusted for weight. We were up against the football team, who had a bunch of their bigger guys pulling, giving us a man advantage. We won, and won easily, yanking them forward in a matter of seconds. From that point on, we were doing well, dueling it out with the wrestling team. With the floor hockey game coming up, they knew who we were and came in with a plan.

As soon as the game started, they put a shadow on me, a kid named Cleve who wrestled at about 138 or so. Cleve didn't know the first thing about hockey—it may have been the first time he ever grasped a stick—but he was as fit as they come and didn't bother to even glance at the orange ball. Cleve ran next to me close enough that I could smell his Aqua Velva–tinged BO. It was pretty damn frustrating and pretty damn effective. Not once in three years of street hockey had I been shackled like that. With a bunch of other strongmen, it was all we could do to win a close game. But with that we clinched the Superstars. Kyle Rote Jr. had nothing on us.

Any inkling that senior year would be a banner year for Westhill soccer was squashed quickly. We graduated seven senior starters, Dave and I were elected co-captains, and I was "promoted" to center-half, Maurice's old position. Vadikos, as a gym teacher, had a wild hair up his ass about recruiting every fast guy in school for the soccer team. His prize recruit, Richard, was a sprinter on the track team. He came out the first few days of practice, was totally lost, and quit. Chris's brother, Paul, was moved to center forward, so the spine of our team was Carlos, Dave, me, and Paul. We had a bunch of untested and frankly subpar underclassmen at the wing positions. With two years of central defending under my belt, I had gotten pretty used to the position and what was expected of you. At center midfield, it was an entirely different matter—you had to create. I was overmatched not only due to my failings as a creator—all my previous soccer training had revolved around clearing the ball out of danger—but also because, with the exception of Paul, I had almost no options to play the ball to in attack. We were overrun by the quality teams and managed a paltry one or two wins before I blew out my hamstring racing in practice. Our second-string goalkeeper, Pete, was so slow and lumbering that a few of us spotted him twenty yards in a hundred-yard race. My hamstring snapped, a sharp and weird sensation. It was my first real injury. I was on the bench for the next three games, my training consisting of marathon sessions in the smelly chlorinated whirlpool tub in the locker room.

There was one highlight that season. The Greenwich High School cute girl dividend continued to pay off in orchestra. I had moved up to second-chair viola, a dubious honor up there with being a slide rule collector or exotic cat groomer—and immediately to my right sat a sensational girl named Liz.

Orchestra became a facile excuse for me to stare at Liz, the sinuous top of her cello resting on her chest. The second I got my driver's license, I was obsessed with asking her out. Soon I would have a chance to see her when we had a road game at Greenwich.

As a city, Greenwich is surprisingly large. Today, the population is well over 60,000, and it is about the tenth biggest city in Connecticut. The high school is huge, in terms of both the student body and the physical plant. In the '70s, the student center was acclaimed as the second largest building in the state, although with Sikorsky and United Technologies having manufacturing plants, it was surprising that a high school would have this honor. Greenwich, nice as it was, did not have the same charm for me as Westport, but for some reason, I did better with girls from Greenwich High than from Westhill. As promised, Liz was there. I said hello briefly; after all, I was there on official game business and I had to be cool. That was perhaps the highlight of my entire high school career: I did not frankly give a rat's ass if we lost 10-0. Liz was there to see me.

We lost, but operation Greenwich worked out for me. Somehow, being soccer captain made me that much more charming at rehearsal. It got to the point where I was so infatuated with her that I probably should have been institutionalized. Lucky for me, I was almost at the end of my driver's ed program. Vadikos himself was my teacher, all but guaranteeing a fast track to freedom. The notorious driving "simulators," aka, "stimulators," were fantastic fun. We would sit in these big rigs, and Vadikos would show some dopey film from the '60s, with tricycles and dogs and toddlers popping out suddenly into traffic. While Vadikos told us horror stories, "The average motorcyclist in the state of Connecticut riding for four years is dead," I had one thing on my mind: give me my goddamn license so I can ask Liz out.

Within weeks of my sixteenth birthday I managed to ask her. The only other time we had gotten together outside of orchestra was when a few of us went over to her parents' house in the Riverside neighborhood to play chamber music. Today Riverside is in the banker's belt, with many of the older shingled homes either torn down and replaced by mansions or added on to in excess. The neighborhood adjoins Long Island sound and Binney Park, about a dozen acres of gently rolling paths and views to the water. Liz's parents were right out of central casting. Her mother brought out warm chocolate chip cookies as we rehearsed in their cozy library. So, this was what Greenwich was about, pretty girls and warm cookies. When I finally had gotten where I wanted to be, on Liz's cozy chintz couch, I started to squirm, aware, even as a teenager, that things would never be quite this comfy again.

THREE

SUMMER GRASS

SUMMER SOCCER HAD been around in Connecticut, but it was new to Stamford in 1976. Chris, through his southern Connecticut connections, was in with a whole new crowd, mostly Caribbean. The Stamford Soccer Club debuted as a U-19 team that summer. The "U" nomenclature did not formally exist, but the teams were basically made up of graduating seniors and underclassmen from college. Our first adventure was to enter the Scottish Games, an annual Scottish sports and cultural festival held in New Canaan, not far from Camp Playland. My family had gone to the Games a couple of times, and my favorite event by far was the tossing of the caber, a telephone pole–sized log. The object was to flip it over and compete for distance. It was a combination strength and balancing act, and it defied physics. New to the festival was a soccer tournament played on the thick, haylike grass of a crude field marked out for seven-a-side play. Along with Chris and Paul, we had added some talented guys from St. Vincent, islanders who seemed to have a lot more will to win than the Jamaicans and Haitians at Westhill. It was kind of odd, fielding a half black Caribbean team at the Scottish games, and, representing Stamford, we were of course the only non-all-white team in a field made up of New Canaan, Darien, and Westport squads. The core of the Westport team was made up of players from Bridge Grill, its summer-league team sponsored by a downtown restaurant.

In the tournament's final game, we were up against Bridge Grill. In a 50/50 collision in midair, I clashed heads with the best player on their team, a guy as good as Phil Moen, but a lot bigger. The guy, unfortunately, broke his nose in the collision, but it brought me into one small degree of separation from soccer royalty. I found out later that his name was Paul Hunter. After a stellar career at Staples and UConn, Hunter was signed by the New York Cosmos, playing for the 1977 NASL champion team that featured Pele and Franz Beckenbauer. Part of the Staples and Westport mystique was how even back in the '70s, the players stayed close to the town after they graduated. Why Hunter would risk his pro career by getting bashed by a hack like me is questionable in hindsight. I'd like to think that I had as much an impact on his game as Pele or Der Kaiser.

Summer soccer proved to be a far better format for learning than high school, the single biggest benefit being that we were liberated from the gym dolts who were conscripted into coaching. Chris and Maurice were playing in college, and our horizon was expanded to towns that were ever further upstate. In contrast to the fall, summer soccer was a sultry affair. Before synthetic uniforms were developed, there were two basic fabrics used to make soccer jerseys: heavy polyester and cotton. Our jerseys were the latter, and in the hot and humid evenings, they would soak through in a matter of minutes, as would my shorts. In the confines of a squishy and smelly kit, it was only a matter of time before you got bad blisters and rashes.

The freedom and beauty of the games more than made up for these little inconveniences. For the most part, we played in a hush, descending on a totally empty high school pitch at about 6 P.M., with the light just starting to fade. High schools, especially more remote suburban high schools, become quietly beautiful without all their students around. One school a fair ways upstate, in Woodbury, was so countrified that it seemed remote, like we were on vacation. An early darkness set in, and bats swooped and dove for insects as the game started. Minutes into the game, a dark, pelting rain started to fall, soaking us to the bone. I could barely see three feet ahead of me, and the puddles made the progress of the ball impossible, but we went ahead. I opened my arms wide and took in the sweet perfume of a Connecticut summer evening.

What good came from not being "coached" also left us exposed. Against Greenwich, an especially nasty game turned into an all-out brawl. Paul wound up on the ground, and then something shocking happened. One of their players, a second Team All-County selection, ran from about ten yards away and kicked Paul in the head while he was down. We went nuts. It was the soccer equivalent of a Rangers-Flyers game during the Broad Street Bullies era. The ref, working alone and helpless amid a sea of fists and feet, called the game and eventually things simmered down. High school soccer had its share of bad blood and more than its share of bad fouls and injuries, but we never had an out-and-out brawl. I was shaken that someone—soccer player or not—could be cold-blooded enough to kick someone in the head. It was sickening to watch and still a vivid memory.

It wasn't like we didn't have our role models by that time. None other than Pele had signed with the New York Cosmos in 1975, getting $2.8 million for five years, an astounding sum for a soccer player in the U.S. He was dubbed the Pied Piper of soccer, and, although his skills had begun to wane, he was still good enough to be a dominant force in the NASL. Soon the Cosmos became the resting place for once-great Europeans looking to ramp down their careers and either escape the dangers of their home countries or extend their glory.

In Florida, in the mid-'80s, I was visiting my girlfriend's cousins in Ft. Lauderdale. The cousins were perfect Floridians— at one point the husband winked at me and asked if I wanted to see something. "Sure, what is it?" He brought out a shiny Halliburton briefcase. He slid it on the coffee table and smiled. "These are my babies," he said. With a thwack, he popped open the case to reveal an assortment of guns to make Crockett and Tubbs proud—a Magnum .44 with a silencer and a riot gun with a sawed-off barrel were his prized possessions. It was a bit of a conversation stopper. What was I supposed to say: "You got some amazing guns there. I'll bet you feel pretty safe here in suburbia."

I thanked him profusely for the privilege of seeing his weaponry and the conversation turned to soccer.

"I heard you are a soccer fan," said the wife.

I said I was a huge fan, I played, etc., etc.

"My neighbor is a soccer player. He's a really nice guy. I think he used to play professionally."

Now, if I had a couple of bucks over the years for every "professional soccer player" I ever met, well, you know the rest of that story. But I was bored, and a little curious, so she suggested we go next door to say hello. A trim, smallish man with close-cropped hair answered the door.

"Hello, please come in."

He introduced himself as Teofilo. It took a few seconds to register, but I realized that I was sitting in the living room of Teofilo Cubillas, the greatest player in the history of Peru and a major star of the 1974 and 1978 World Cups. I was casually sitting with one of the greatest players ever, by accident.

"Cubby," as the neighbors called him, was tickled to death that I knew who he was. In south Florida, he was anonymous, or as anonymous as a world soccer star can be, playing briefly for the Ft. Lauderdale Strikers.

"For me, it was a matter of safety for my family," he told me. "We have many kidnappers in Peru."

It was during the Shining Path reign of terror, and for a high-profile guy like Cubillas, there was a daily risk to his and his family's life. He grew more animated as I asked him about the World Cup and his playing career.

"Come here, I show you something."

He brought me in the bedroom and popped in a videotape. It was dimly lit footage of him playing futsal—indoor soccer—in Peru. I couldn't really make out any of the action, but out of deference to greatness, I fawned over every moment.

"Come outside," he said, "I show you some things."

Cubillas was a bit less than ten years removed from his prime, but still only thirty-five or thirty-six at that point. He took a ball outside and we went to his gently sloped front lawn. If I had ever learned a thing about soccer, I had forgotten it all in that moment. Out of 200 million or so soccer players on the planet, this man, in his prime, was one of the best five or so. In my prime, I was perhaps about number 10 million. He was about to kick me the ball, and I stood there, my feet rooted to the ground with what felt like cement booties. I manage a little side foot return pass. Neatly, Cubillas flipped up the ball, juggled it a few times, and let it settle gently at his feet. His movements were almost silent. The essence of greatness in any ball sport is to calm the ball and do things at your own pace. I recall playing a round of golf once with a guy trying out for the PGA tour, and what I recall most was the absolute lack of sound when he struck the ball.

It was thus with Cubillas. He then went to show me a step-over, actually two step-overs in quick succession. American coaches did not teach or approve of the step-over back then. Scotnick and Vadikos probably could not have discerned a step-over from a slap shot. I think that in American scholastic soccer circles (Staples excepting), anything that didn't involve direct, English-style football was considered unmanly. I had played soccer for over a decade at that point, and I didn't recall seeing anyone, even the best players I had played against like Moen and Hunter, use the step-over. Catching my breath back at the cousins' place, I thanked the wife for introducing me and told her it was a memorable trip and how lucky I was to meet Cubillas. I prayed that her husband would keep his postal tendencies under wraps; did poor Teofilo realize that he fled would-be kidnappers in Peru only to move next to a paranoid maniac with visions of building his own militia?

Cubillas's NASL was part of the "Pele Dividend," the influx of geezers and wheezers from abroad plus a few guys still in their prime. In 1973, the average attendance of the NASL was 5,782, climbing to an astonishing 47,856 at its peak in 1978. That year, the New York Yankees' average home attendance was 28,838. In many ways, this statistic encapsulates one of the central stories of soccer in the United States. Despite being the most popular team sport in New York, soccer labored in such ignominy that in "regular" sports circles, that is to say, non-foreign-born circles, you still had to virtually apologize for being interested in it at all. Back in the days of Bi-Cultural, it made sense: there was no soccer being played anywhere and none on television. The only broadcast of the World Cup final match between Brazil and Italy was on closed-circuit TV at Madison Square Garden and a few other select venues.

But why did soccer still have pariah status in 1978, even as record crowds went to the Meadowlands to watch the Cosmos? I don't believe there is any one answer to this question. But let's start by looking at the positives. Why did attendance for soccer—really, for the Cosmos—skyrocket? It was, of course, due mostly to Pele. But Pele alone would have not sustained the large crowds that were featured for three or four years at the Cosmos' peak. He was followed into the league by other greats: Beckenbauer, Carlos Alberto, Cruyff, Cubillas, and Neeskens, among others. These players were the stars of their World Cup teams in the 1970s. Except for Giorgio Chinaglia, they were not quite at their absolute peak when they arrived in America, but not far off it. In high school, my nonsoccer friends, and that was basically all of my friends, would ask me, ad nauseum, "Why isn't soccer more popular?" I could barely contain myself when I heard this. "It is popular, you idiot. Have you seen a team called the Cosmos?"

Jingoism was at fault here. The insularity of Westhill's Jamaicans and Italians in effect prolonged soccer's pariah status. It was not until the "soccer mom" ascended that enough white American-born kids started to play so that the stigma was dropped. But even today, the myths persist: soccer is a girls' sport, soccer is a foreigners' sport, soccer is for sissies, soccer is only about "running" and "getting in condition." And the sport itself is to blame. Far more than in American sports, theatrical flopping and diving is now a "strategic" part of soccer. While FIFA expresses dismay over this, and instructs officials to penalize what it calls "simulation," the punitive measures have barely curtailed what most American sports fans deride as preposterous histrionics.

During the summer before I went to college, when I had plenty of time to hang out with my friends, I started to get frustrated with the antipathy that so many of them displayed towards soccer. I had gained a lot of self-esteem through the sport, and I had a kind of parallel universe set up with soccer and my "regular" life. Soccer had its own ecosystem. Within that system, my only friend was Paul, that is to say, someone with whom I would hang out if there were no game or practice to play. Paul's brother, Chris, and Dave, who were also on my street hockey team, were good guys but not quite in the friend category. During senior year, I was taking AP courses exclusively, and it was this crowd that especially loved to vilify soccer. It didn't help that it was not an especially athletic group, but an odd fact became clear: in Stamford, as you moved up the educational ladder, soccer was held in disdain. This was completely opposite to what was going on in Westport, Greenwich, New Canaan, and Wilton. In those towns, an actual youth soccer culture was forming, and yes, it heralded the incipient development of the soccer mom. Soccer was a polarizing sport. You were either with it or against it. No other team sport engendered such divisions. If you were a basketball fan and someone else wasn't, then there were no hard feelings. If, in the wrong crowd, I'd get started on the virtues of soccer, I'd immediately get an earful: "It's so boring," "There's no scoring," "There's no action," "Every game ends 0-0." It was like I brought up bird watching

It didn't help that most of the sporting media fraternity was totally ignorant about soccer at best, or openly hostile at worst. The Pele halo led to the *New York Times* boosting the profile of its lone soccer writer, Alex Yannis, along with picking up Paul Gardner's *Observer* articles from London. Even Dave Anderson, one of the *Times*' mainstream sportswriters, would dip his toe in the soccer pool now and then, particularly if there was a story about Pele to be had. But the consensus was that soccer was an interloper. Antisoccer sentiment in the conservative wing of America's three-sport theocracy was as alive and kicking then as it is today. Dick Young, the *Daily News* sportswriter, derided soccer as one of the "up and down" sports, in contrast to the structure of football and baseball. Does the jingoism affect the other side as much as it does here? It seems that German and Italian sports media professionals do not get their panties in a twist about the existence of football or baseball, yet it is great sport in the U.S. for commentators like Tony Kornheiser and Jim Rome to endlessly bash soccer. In 1973, in response to the public's perception that there was too little scoring in soccer, the NASL created a thirty-five-yard line to encourage offensive players to take up positions closer to the goal, providing them with offside immunity up until the new line. While it barely created a scoring ripple, the line further damaged the sport's development here, distancing the NASL even further away from FIFA.

All I knew was that seeing the Cosmos at a packed Giants Stadium with Pele and Beckenbauer playing was thrilling beyond belief. Newly liberated with a driver's license, my parents were more than happy to have me and my friends brave the wilds of I-95 and the George Washington Bridge to go to the games. Paul and Chris and I didn't care if the bottleneck started five miles from the stadium. The big games were drawing 70,000 plus at this point, and it seemed everyone wanted to get there at exactly the same time. At this point in his career, in his mid-30s, Pele had thickened considerably from his prime, in which he was probably 150 or 155 pounds. Playing at about 165, he was slow compared to the other players but still remarkably gifted. Brazilian greats, as they age, tend to adopt a new soccer persona. Whereas a German or Italian star will lose a step, become frustrated, lose playing time, and retire, a Brazilian will refine his game in an ever-shrinking sphere of influence. Where Pele, in 1970, may have covered 75 percent of the field with great effectiveness, the 1977 version would operate over perhaps 30 percent of the field. Today, the once formidably influential Ronaldhino plies his tricks and flicks within an imaginary ten-yard box that he has visually constructed adjacent to the left touch line about forty yards from the goal. He will, of course, venture to the goal if the opportunity presents itself, but if the ball goes past him towards his defensive zone, he will stop his pursuit as if he has hit a brick wall.

While Pele was occasionally great, but more often a bit player, the central defenders on that 1977 Cosmos squad, Beckenbauer and Carlos Alberto, were still nearly in their prime. Never ruffled, powerful, and with the ability to carve up opposing defenses with inventive passes, watching those two was the ultimate master class for a player like me, who had been schooled in the "kick and pray" technique favored by Vadikos and Scotnick.

By this time, Chris was a fixture in goal for the University of Southern Connecticut, a team he would lead to two NCAA Division II semifinal appearances in 1977 and 1978. Chris had reverted to goalkeeper after moving to striker for his senior year to allow Carlos to play goal. I was amazed at how well

Chris was doing—he hadn't even been an honorable mention All-County player and was now starring in college. On the other hand, as an underaged junior, I was honorable mention, and along with Paul, I had carried the team during senior year, albeit a weak team. I was clearly a better player as a senior than as a junior, and with the exception of being recruited by a junior college, Eastern Connecticut, I didn't get any affirmation or support from Vadikos about moving on to the next level. As it turns out, I suspect that there were probably a lot of Division III schools with decent academics where I would have been a good fit for the team. Chris was learning about soccer on a higher plane. He was coached by real coaches and playing with serious players.

For me, after wandering in soccer diaspora at Westhill for three years, I had nothing to show for it. Even being captain and tasting the lower rung of All-County stardom wasn't enough to propel me into Princeton or MIT, where my dad had gone. As an unbalanced adolescent who had to apply to colleges while he was still sixteen, I constructed an entire fable around my titular existence at Princeton. From the literature (Princeton was not on the itinerary of the one college tour my mother reluctantly agreed to—Boston), Princeton appeared to be the perfect place to continue the coddling to which I had become accustomed. Pretty, waspy girls, broad-leaf trees like southern Connecticut, unimpeachable academics, all air-brushed by gentility and grace, seemed to be the perfect tonic for my previous seventeen years of living with a chain-smoking, pill-popping, histrionic, and inappropriate mother. It was like the script of *The Graduate* was unfolding in slow motion.

One of my first and most painful life lessons came with my Princeton rejection. Our school's best athlete, a brilliant math student, also wanted to go to Princeton. Of the six or so of us who applied, he got in—Princeton wanted him for baseball. My soccer was nowhere near Princeton's radar, and frankly I was a notch or two below Division I caliber. With a bit more of a head start, better coaching, and more commitment, I may have gotten there—that is to say, if I was born in Westport, things might have been different.

Chris had solved the equation and was our de facto summer captain, even with Maurice on the team. We had integrated a bunch of new players along with the core from our 1974 team that lost to Staples in the state tournament. One game, a new player was there, a black guy named Weston with a physique like a middleweight boxer. Up to that point, I had played with and against some really good players—Division I players and, here and there, a pro-caliber guy like Paul Hunter. But Weston was a new phenomenon for me: the "Soccer Bitch."

Weston started at striker, and I was on the right side of midfield. Unlike some other guys who looked great but weren't, Weston was a very skilled player who used his power to his advantage. He could shield the ball exceptionally well and dribble with skill and was very fast. There were two big problems with Weston though: he did not pass the ball—to anyone, ever—and he did not utter a word on the field. He was an Adonis of silence, a player who played utterly for and with himself. It was Weston's masturbatory incarnation of soccer. He was not a part of a team, unless there was a team named "Weston," and I was completely flummoxed.

Time and time again, Weston had the ball—he was so fast, strong, and skilled, that he was always on the ball—and time and time again, as I worked to get into space, to create a target, to open the game, Weston completely ignored me. It was humiliating to the point where I thought about quitting at halftime. I asked Chris what was going on.

"He's like that. He sees the game at a higher level."

"But he sure is the silent type. Does he ever talk?"

"Not really," Chris said.

Ouch. Weston was a Soccer Bitch. Life sometimes doesn't work out, because, in fact, Weston was rewarded with a son who became a pro and has been capped for the U.S. Men's National Team. To add to the insult, several years ago, my wife's adult team brought in a special coach for a training day—Coach Weston. I half thought about going down to say hello, but even after thirty years, I was still pissed enough that I had no interest in seeing the guy. Suffering through a half-dozen or so summer league games was more than enough.

The Soccer Bitch is a ubiquitous creature in the realm of park soccer. They are rarely as talented as Weston. In fact, one of the great ironies of the Soccer Bitch is that he is rarely the best player on the field. What is central to the ethos of the Soccer Bitch is that he feels aggrieved and seeks both self-fulfillment and retribution on the field. This is the paradox at the heart of soccer: it is the ultimate team sport that is utterly reliant on individual brilliance. In a sport in which the best players in the world manage about a goal every two games, success turns on one or two flashes of inspiration, or, conversely, on one or two blunders during the course of an entire ninety-minute match. The Soccer Bitch believes he is the arbiter of all things soccer. He is the self-anointed high priest for whom every play is one of his congregants, awaiting affirmation.

The Soccer Bitch thrives in the crevasses and dark shadows of soccer—the parks, the beer leagues, the over-forty pickup matches, the college intramural scene; any venue where a coach is extraneous or unaffordable, he enjoys free reign. Perhaps the most famous incarnation of the Soccer Bitch was Giorgio Chinaglia, the prolific, egomaniacal striker for the Cosmos during their golden era. Chinaglia famously told Pele to stay out of the middle of the field and to keep outside, as the middle was Chinaglia's territory. Chinaglia had self-belief in abundance; that he took it upon himself to try and humiliate the sport's greatest player and global icon was something that was going on pretty much on every soccer pitch on the planet.

Weston was a bit unusual in that he achieved consummate soccer bitchiness without speaking much at all—in fact he was almost mute on the field. Most of the time, the offender delivers an onslaught of "instructional" help, born of his vast soccer experience and inside knowledge of the sport. He is expert at barking orders: "Come to the ball!" "Get goal side!" "Touch!" "Mark-up!" and "Get Out!" are favorites; many of them intended to provide defensive coverage so that he can proceed with inventing and creating, his birthright.

I once saw the Westchester Flames, an A-League team, play with an ex-U.S. National Team player captaining the squad. He was relentless. Yelling, whining, cajoling, and moaning like a grandmother tanking in a poolside game of canasta, I wondered how his teammates could put up with that bullshit. Past his prime and two steps slow, he tried to compensate by being a "leader." He had become a tedious Soccer Bitch.

One of the things that occurred to me around the summer of '76 was that it was the foreign character of soccer that created the petri dish, where petulant behavior could flourish. American sports were taught as offshoots to the military: teamwork, hustle, and the subordination of one's personal goals to the good of the team were essential if you wanted your coach to put you in the game. With soccer, there were so many different ethnic flavors involved that everyone imported their own concept of the sport. How to play soccer is always an open question, even at the very top level. Today, the great clubs of the world adopt a system: there is the Barcelona and Arsenal system, constructed around close control, short passing, and ball control; and there are defensive systems and counterattacking schemes, like the Italian Cattenaccio. Players in Europe are trained at the youth level to fit into the senior team's system. One perennial problem for the U.S. Men's National Team is that there is no real system in the U.S. If you are an aspiring national team player in Germany or Spain or Argentina, you know what is expected of you by the time you reach your teens. In the U.S., even with the Olympic Development Program, there is not enough of an established national style of play to allow a player to tailor his or her game. In most of the top footballing nations, young players are taught to be equally adept at defending and going forward. Nuanced skills—body positioning, working out of tight positions on the field, little offensive tricks and flicks—are passed down from generation to generation.

Maybe Chris was on to something when he told me that Weston saw the game "at a higher level." I had never given a thought to thinking about soccer in any abstract sense. It was enough to play, get tired, and start the whole sequence over again. Sure, I admired Holland and thought that they played beautiful soccer, but the notion of translating that to anything in my realm was not something that seemed possible to me. But remarkably, with Staples and Albie Loeffler, and now with Chris and maybe even Weston, it was right in front of me. In David Winner's *Brilliant Orange*, a history of Dutch soccer, artist Jeroen Henneman describes a "moment in which every player senses perfection." Here he is alluding principally to the arcing pass into space pioneered by Cruyff and Gerry Muhren of Ajax in the '70s, perfected by Denis Bergkamp in the '80s and '90s. The pass into "space" was one that Staples played to perfection. The Murphys and their supporting cast would play the ball around the back of our defensive four to Phil Moen, making diagonal runs behind our flat-four formation. Westhill and our other hapless FCIAC colleagues had been at the mercy of a Staples squad playing a junior version of Ajax. I don't know whether Loeffler was deliberate about this or that he just knew intuitively that it was a style that would break down other teams. Henneman goes on to tell David Winner that he believes "The idea (of this type of pass) is quite Dutch." From my experience, it is equally Westportian.

What was it that Weston was seeing that I didn't? In my view, he held the ball way too long. He did not fulfill the hoary American sports maxim of "making everyone around you better." Maurice did that and it fed on itself: you wanted to work hard for someone like that, someone who would reward your runs with a perfectly flighted ball to your feet or a level square pass. What I think Weston saw, basically, was that I sucked. My entire soccer life until that point was an indulgent, self-fulfilling fantasy. In my own mediocre way, I had actually climbed the ladder, sort of like being promoted to Assistant Regional General Manager and being given the corner cubicle. Not only did I suck, but also pretty much everyone I played with sucked—even Maurice. It had little to do with individual talent. Maurice, Alex, some of the Clydes, and even I had talent. What Weston's behavior revealed to me was that I did not understand soccer. I didn't get the nuances of space and time and measured runs and body positioning and how to strike the ball and how to defend. After three years of varsity soccer, I was a neophyte, and to prove it, Weston did not pass me the ball. In the months before I went off to college, I reflected on this. Weston's selfish play had a modicum of merit, painful as it was for me to experience it firsthand. Staples made it clear that I, along with my Westhill teammates, was lacking, even inept. There was something to excellence, to gaining an understanding at a higher, more demanding level. This concept had eluded my only two coaches to that point, and it had eluded me. If you look at the Staples soccer alumni site, today, in 2012, you get a sense of the success of the graduates of its program. In his book *The Autumn of Our Lives*, Fred Cantor reveals the ingredients that made the Staples soccer program so successful. Its alumni include authors, pianists, physicians, financiers, and myriad other professionals. More telling is the camaraderie and collective sense of being part of a special program. On my way to college that fall, I knew I had lots to learn, about soccer and everything else.

FOUR

No Parking

THE BACKDROP OF what was happening with the Cosmos was extraordinary. For a kid who grew up in a soccer wasteland, pushed to the fringes of sportsdom, it was the ultimate geek's revenge. The '70s were an abysmal decade for the city. In 1972, my grandmother, having sold her house in the Jamaica Estates section of Queens, moved with her sister to a twenty-eighth floor apartment in the Mayfair Towers, a characteristic white brick, post-war rental building on West 72nd Street. The building itself was nondescript except for the fact that it had astounding Central Park views from the upper floors and that it is next door to a far more famous building, the Dakota, where John Lennon lived before he was insanely gunned down.

My dad dreaded nothing more than driving into Manhattan. There was only one thing he hated more than driving, and that was parking. He had an elaborate routine that consisted of pulling to the front of the building to let my mother and sister out—and sometimes me—after which he would circle the block fifteen or twenty times looking for street parking. Even back then, Manhattan street parking signs required the decoding skills of a Navajo to figure out whether, in fact, you were in a tow–loading–bus stop–no parking anytime—fuggedabout you, schmuck—zone. It wasn't until the '80s that Mayor Koch came up with his cheeky "Don't Even Think About Parking Here" signs, but the effect was the same. After fuming and hair pulling, my dad usually resigned himself to pulling into a garage and paying the six bucks. I do remember one or two times when he dropped us off and didn't appear for an hour or more—I'm guessing that he camped out in the car with a book, waiting for a spot to open up.

The Upper West Side these days is not so much a neighborhood as it is a fantasy world constructed by baby marketers. In the mid-'70s it was flat-out dangerous. Even at age twelve, I was not allowed to go out to the street alone. Nearing bankruptcy, Manhattan, hat in hand, approached the federal government for a bailout, only to be famously told to "drop dead" by President Gerald Ford. Ultimately, the Municipal Assistance Corporation devised by Lazard banker Felix Rohatyn created the financial framework for a long, slow comeback. The troubles of New York City in the '70s evoke the country's problems today, with the stakeholders today being primarily foreign governments.

New York City was full of angry people. Overcome by post-Vietnam and Woodstock sentiment, and the aftershock of the energy crisis, corporations fled the city's onerous tax structure for the accommodating suburbs, including Stamford. Parts of the city that are now full of life and commerce, like Times and

Union Squares, were overrun by drug dealers, hustlers, and thugs in the '70s.

Fortunately for soccer, one enterprise that was thriving was music, specifically Steve Ross's Warner Communications, which acquired the legendary Atlantic Record Company run by the Ertegun brothers. To appease the brothers, Steve Ross founded the Cosmos and threw the flagging NASL a lifeline. Shortly after creating the team, Pele was pursued in one of the country's biggest sports business ventures, a bicontinental saga with the U.S. State Department weighing in via its de facto soccer ambassador, Henry Kissinger.

I was fascinated by Kissinger, because he looked and talked exactly like my German-Jewish relatives. Here was a guy who looked like he could seamlessly appear at one of my family's Sunday deli and pastry orgies, except that he had the ear of presidents. He was also a self-professed soccer nut. Kissinger prevailed on the Brazilian government and Pele himself to sanction the Black Pearl to come to America for the express purpose of being its soccer emissary. How Steve Ross and Warner put together a nearly $5 million dollar deal for Pele during a time in which Hank Aaron was making $200,000 a year and the Cosmos hometown was bankrupt is, if you think about it, a marketing miracle. It was not immediately apparent that it was a soccer miracle.

I would argue that the New York Cosmos were the ultimate Faustian contrivance, and in contrast to most observers' opinions, it actually set soccer back a generation in America. Players like Paul Hunter and Alain Macca, the NASL's first collegiate draft choice, were the exception not the rule; the league was a sideshow for the Europeans and South Americans seeking to close out their careers here. The fact that some of the

Europeans, for example, Giorgio Chinaglia, were here at the peak of their careers does not negate the fact that by becoming the resting place for foreign-born soccer talent, the NASL put into motion a construct for professional soccer in America: aspiring to mediocrity.

Starting when I first started to kick that red ball around at Bi-Cultural, I began my lifelong defense of soccer—as a sport and philosophy.

"Why," my friends would and do still ask, "Is soccer not that 'popular' in America?"

My answer, after forty years of wandering in the American soccer diaspora, is definitive: Give Americans the best soccer in the world, and it will be as popular here as anywhere else on the planet. I contend that if you imported the Premiership to America—the players, the stadiums, the weather—the average attendance would be second to professional football and that for the top four or five clubs you could put 80,000 fannies in the stadium every Sunday. Americans have the best team sports in the world. Our hockey, basketball, and of course, baseball and football (who else plays these but us?) are unambiguously the best leagues of their kind in the world. Why should Americans suffer with a professional soccer league that would rank somewhere between tenth and fifteenth in the world? The fact is that Major League Soccer draws crowds that are consistent with its talent level. For the World Cup and when the great teams of the world appear here, the crowds swell to capacity.

Sadly, the marketing vessel that was the Cosmos crashed and burned in the aftermath of Warner's debacle with the failure of Atari. The Cosmos' victory in 1977 did little to stoke World Cup fever for Argentina in 1978. By that time, I was living in Boston, which had ethnic pockets and an NASL team but was firmly rooted in the firmament of the Celtics, Red Sox, Bruins, and Patriots. The junta and repressive Argentine regime of Peron had systematically been incarcerating and murdering political dissidents. On the soccer front, Cruyff elected to sit out the World Cup for personal reasons.

The year 1977 was the first year that I didn't spend a summer in Connecticut. My girlfriend at college went back to Albany for the summer, and I had two part-time hospital jobs, including one in which I rolled a device called a plethysmograph around to postoperative patients. The plethy attached to the patients via cuffs and was used to determine the rate of blood outflow, and hence clotting risk. I was all of nineteen, with no training whatsoever, but by dint of a badge, a machine, and a white hospital jacket, the patients welcomed me like I was Dr. DoRight. I remember one woman who started taking off her clothes before I had a chance to tell her I was just a lowly technician. My other gig was being a lab assistant to a firecracker named Dusty, who was running a genetics research project. She was obsessed with the Red Sox pitcher Dennis Eckersley and had a great monologue that featured a washing machine, Eckersley, and good times.

As a Connecticut Yankee in the Red Sox court, I was held hostage to the insufferable rantings of Red Sox fans, who in their own provincial way were as bad as Yankee fans. I had to admit that the trappings of Fenway—the walkable neighborhood, the looming hulk of the Green Monster, and the intimacy of the Park—were fantastic. It all made me wish that they played soccer there. It was pure heresy to feel this way, even as a student. I was attending Boston University, a big, cosmopolitan campus with a very large contingent of foreign students. BU—code name "Big and Ugly"—was the Westhill of Boston-area colleges. Much as I tried to shake off the internationalism and impersonal nature of

Westhill through my pathetic aspiration to attend Princeton, I was bitch-slapped right back to reality, getting stuck at BU.

In large part, this was due to the ineffectual nature of my sweet natured but incompetent guidance counselor, an older woman who was completely clueless about the college admissions process. In another manifestation of the "good enough" approach of Westhill, the better students were somewhat left to fend for themselves, with the truants, miscreants, and vocational-tech kids absorbing the vast majority of the administration's attention. My parents were of course assured that their kid would glide into MIT, zip through premed, and ascend the ranks of the world's great neurosurgeons by age twenty-seven. That was the plan all along. Instead, I found myself, humiliatingly, at my mother's alma mater, a school best known as a safety school, without any plan whatsoever about what to study. In truth, BU had some fantastic departments and a great faculty. Its philosophy, music, and communications departments were the equal or better than anywhere in the country. What BU suffered from— as did the city of Stamford and Westhill High School—was a lack of identity. Huge and fragmented, with a campus that is literally ass backward—the beautiful part of the campus along the Charles River is an afterthought, and the concrete jungle of Commonwealth Avenue serves as the school's "Quad"—BU is an agglomeration of a dozen or so different colleges.

Without having a clue about BU varsity soccer, I went to talk to the coach about the possibility of a tryout. It was a brief lesson in the mercenary politics of collegiate varsity athletics: walk-ons are viewed as an affront to a coach's recruiting talents. In general, a college coach will do everything in his or her power to discourage walk-ons, unless they possess extraordinary talent. At the margin, a coach has little or nothing to gain by giving a walk-on a roster spot. BU played on Astroturf, an early version that was both bouncy and rock hard. The coach had gone on about the surface and how different it was from grass and unless I had experience playing on it, it was unlikely that I would make the team, etc., etc. And he was pretty much right. After grass and dirt, playing on that turf was like a weird new sport. The ball just rocketed around. Low balls shot through like lightning, and anything kicked high would bounce like a superball. The turf was also unbelievably hot and smelly. It was September, and hot fumes rose off like a smelting plant. It was freshman year at Westhill redux: hostile coach, crap surface, no friends. I was going to have to be content with indoor intramural soccer.

Among the ethnic groups at BU was a big contingent of expat Iranians, politically aligned with the Shah, generally wealthy, and in the U.S. to get educated. It hadn't hurt that a lot of them got nifty aid packages. They were also great soccer players. I had put together a pretty formidable intramural team, most varsity high school players and really good athletes, including one class-mate from Westhill, Frank, who had not played soccer in high school but was a wrestler at 147 pounds. Frank could crank out twenty-five one-armed push-ups without a lot of trouble. Even with our beefed-up squad, the Iranians, speaking in staccato Farsi, destroyed us with a one-touch game that was a revelation, even by Staples standards. They had adapted a game to indoors, and it was very different from outdoor soccer, which has patches of leisurely, even laconic moments. Indoor soccer, whether futsal (without boards) or with boards, is nonstop frantic action.

As good as the intramurals were, there wasn't a lot of soccer buzz at BU or in Boston. There wasn't a breath of soccer in the papers, radio, or television. We would show up for our games, play, and go home. When the 1978 World Cup was approaching, I was lucky to see one or two preview articles in the *Boston Globe*. For anything in depth, I had to hit the world newsstand in Harvard Square and buy a copy of *France Football*. Once the tournament started, the *Globe* at least provided game results, and I was able to track the tournament. Holland was still my team, even though Cruyff stayed home. My favorite player was Johan Neeskens, a take-no-prisoners midfielder who was Tonto to Cruyff's Lone Ranger. Even without Cruyff, Holland was still the world's leading exponent of Total Football.

As the semifinals approached, I saw an ad that the games would be shown on closed-circuit TV at a theater in downtown Boston. The ticket price was $20, a pretty substantial amount in those days for a student, but I was committed. It was a terrific atmosphere, with Holland scoring the winner against Italy. I spent another $20 for the final, which I had thought would be vindication for Holland after outplaying Germany in 1974. Holland, bright and direct, was the better team over the first ninety minutes. At 1-1, with minutes left, a neat Dutch move down the right looked like a sure Holland goal. The Argentine fans had littered the field with so much confetti that it was getting difficult to spot the ball. But with the keeper Fillol beaten, the ball rolled against the post and the game went to overtime. In the extra sessions, it looked almost as if the Argentine secret police had told the Dutch that they would not get home safely unless Argentina emerged victorious. Mario Kempes ran through the Dutch like they had eaten bad enchiladas. Kempes scored twice, and that was the death knell for Total Football: two away World Cup finals, two defeats.

It was about this time that I started to connect the dots with soccer and realize that it was more than just a kick in the grass. When the Dutch received their runners-up medals, the team refused to salute the Argentine dictatorship that ran the country and the tournament. This was soccer doing its dirty business. At the same time that they were putting on a World Cup that gave German reporters a basis of comparison for the 1936 Olympics in Berlin, the Argentines were running a program of political imprisonment, torture, and murder that they inventively called "The Final Solution." Including such specialties as electrogenital torture and murder by flinging people live out of airplanes into the sea, the Argentines were able to deceive most of the world into thinking that they were simply pursuing sound political principles.

The German captain, Berti Vogts, not as tenacious a political critic as he was a defender, noted glibly that "Argentina is a country where political order reigns. I haven't seen any political prisoners." As semifinalists, the Argentines needed a 3-0 result or better against Peru, led by Cubillas, who would finish the tournament tied for the second-leading scorer. In one of the great lay-downs in sports history, Peru succumbed 6-0 and returned home stoned on the plane. I would not really understand the degree of repression and horror until I read Jocobo Timerman's harrowing account of his imprisonment and torture at the hands of the military police. His book, *Prisoner without a Name, Cell without a Number*, describes his ordeal in Argentine prison camp from 1977 to 1979, where he was systematically tortured as a purported enemy of state. The World Cup in 1978 was basically a giant propaganda arm of the government—literally, inasmuch as it retained the public-relations consultant Burston Marstellar as spin doctor. None other than America's alpha soccer fan, Henry Kissinger, was front and center as an Argentine apologist, lamely alluding to Argentina's "Great Future" during the Cup.

With soccer as metaphor, soccer as proxy, soccer as theater, watching the '78 final was an intense experience, cinematic and tragic (if you were a fan of the Dutch, and as I reasoned, free expression). With the swirling streams of white and black confetti and the pony-maned Kempes galloping through the Dutch defense, the game, if slowed down, was a tableau worthy of Dali or a Fellini dream sequence. It was more than just a Dutch defeat—I felt as if my political liberties had been violated. My soccer sensibilities had also been crushed. Everything bad about the sport was displayed by Argentina in the overtime period. Every bit of physical contact, no matter how slight, was a chance for an Argentine player to be sucked into the ground as if by some kind of reverse volcanic osmosis. The Argentines had begun to perfect a move that I will call the "infinite log roll," wherein a player goes to the ground and rolls as if he had caught fire. As if it was not enough to dive and spin and flail about continuously, the Argentines stopped to argue their points, wagging their fingers and scolding the referee. Had they been playing another South American team, who knows how much the game would have devolved? The contrast with the stoic Dutch was striking. In years to come, with Maradona leading the team, the Argentines continued to set the world standard for soccer histrionics. As great as he was, Maradona was an equally great diver who perfected the art of pushing the ball, initiating contact with a defender, and belly flopping.

Right and wrong were still constructs I was working out. I had jettisoned pretty much all the trappings of formal Judaism; since my Bar Mitzvah, I lost the plot, in part because of soccer and how it "internationalized" me. When I was a kid, there was a simple dichotomy: Jews at school, Catholics in the neighborhood. Soccer brought the world to me in the form of the Clydes, the

Italians, and my friends who boarded in Singapore. Also, after seeing the same four girls from kindergarten through eighth grade, I quickly saw that there was a whole big universe of girls out there. I had spent a heroic amount of psychic energy beating down my parents' proselytizing about only going out with Jewish girls. I understood the argument but rejected it. For me, soccer was empowering and bestowed a worldview that was unattainable through other sports. When you played soccer, when you thought soccer, and when you dreamed in soccer, there was an implicit connection with the greater world. There were no baseball-playing Iranians or hockey-playing Jamaicans (at least not in the '70s and '80s).

When I transferred to Cornell, in 1979, we played an intramural team who called themselves "The Third World." They were a lowly college intramural team but had banded together for empowerment. I admit that I thought it was strange, sort of if I had called a team I put together with a bunch of Jewish kids from New Jersey and Westchester "The Ghetto Yids." Soccer made you insular and worldly at the same time. The sport was global, but its thinking distinctly local. Your allegiance was first to your town, then your region, then your country, then your continent, and then to the sport. The Italian guys at Westhill, when they thought about soccer at all, were all about Juventas.

For me, trudging through soccer diaspora, I had only one choice: pick up the thread, if possible, for the Israeli National Team. Somewhere in the crevasses of my brain that had otherwise purged any allegiance to religious convention, I retained a Jewish cultural imperative. For me, the manifestation of this wasn't literature, or the abundant culture of Israel and Judaism, or fealty to any particular sect or way of life but soccer. Soccer offered a lot of what religion had to offer: devotion to a sect, rituals, ceremonial garb, internecine squabbling and occasional warfare, and higher authorities who issued proclamations from their court. Soccer was the ultimate ecumenical game: inclusive to a fault. It did not discriminate in any way: other sports had distinct body morphologies and tended to break along racial lines, at least at the professional level. Hockey was a white sport, basketball mostly black, football strangely segregated by position. Soccer was an astounding study in contrast.

Unbeknownst to me, there was a velvet evolution going on in the '70s. I was born in 1959, a second-and-a-half-generation kid fitting neatly between the Euro-escapees on my dad's side who were part of the great Jewish soccer exodus. The "Muscular Judaism" preached by Max Nordau had done enough to get Jews in Hungary, Austria, and Germany to start their own sports clubs and to cultivate a degree of athleticism that dovetailed nicely with many of the assimilation fantasies of many European Jews. What momentum the immigrants had with resettling their sports clubs in Queens and Brooklyn began to dissipate once things started to get more comfortable. America offered the luxury of having your old world community and being accepted by wider society. Soccer was the perfect transition, but as a distinctly "un-American" sport, it began to lose its appeal for first-generation Americans. With the profile of soccer raised by the Cosmos, kids born in the '70s were part of the great first wave of youth soccer. The legacy of the Cosmos had little to do with the quality of soccer they played or the impact the team had on professional soccer in America. Two Jewish "fixers," non–soccer players Steve Ross and Henry Kissinger, had revived the spirit of Hakoah and its sister clubs through central Europe by legitimizing the sport in America in the middle part of the decade. David Hirshey chronicled the

Cosmos through their championship decade and has become the spiritual father of what Lizzy Ratner has termed the "Soccer Jew." Safe in their American roots, soccer had become anointed by Jewish parents as a safe alternative to football. Basketball, which had extensive Jewish roots in the 1940s, had largely ceded its status to blacks. It could be argued that for Jewish kids in America, basketball had morphed into soccer.

The soccer dividend of this period gave birth to a generation of Jewish kids who gave the sport a bit of star power. Jon Stewart, Ethan Zohn, Franklin Foer, and other Jews have mixed media success with a soccer subplot. Ratner, in her 2006 article goes on to quote David Hirshey: "It's considered a fashionable sport again. It was fashionable in the late '70s and now, after almost 30 years, it's somehow reignited again in a different generation of fans."

One of the compelling things about soccer is that you don't have to be big to play. Since a soccer ball is played on the ground for the most part, there is no intrinsic advantage to being tall; in fact, having a center of gravity lower to the ground probably helps. Being closer to the ball conveys an advantage in terms of a player's ability to shift his weight and direction. Being tall clearly is better to deal with balls in the air, and central defenders and goalkeepers are for the most part the tallest players on a team. But if you look at the creative position on the field, the positions occupied by attacking midfielders, wingers, and withdrawn strikers, the sweet spot seems to be in the 5'7" to 5'10" range. Among Pele, Maradona, Cubillas, Bremner, Gemill, Keegan, Best, Ardiles, Zola, Valderrama, Zico, Giggs, Xavi, Ribery, Sneijder, Iniesta, Messi, Fabregas, and many more, none would probably take a thirty-two-inch inseam. If you saw any of those guys busing your table at the local Tratorria, you wouldn't give them a second glance. Not so with a selection of NFL, NBA, or NHL stars. This is not to say that there aren't lots of big, talented soccer players. The big and tall men's list is equally as long, but many more of them are strikers and defenders.

FIVE

Upstate

CORNELL WAS ALMOST as big as BU, and its varsity soccer team also played on Astroturf. At Cornell, the big sports are hockey and lacrosse. By the time I got there, as a junior, it was much too late to harbor any thoughts about playing varsity soccer. I played intramurals and refereed a bit, and there were lots of good players who fell through the cracks en route from their high school teams to college.

I had stopped going back to Connecticut after my sophomore year at BU. When my first summer in Ithaca came along, I looked for a pickup game and saw some promising action on campus at Schoellkopf Field. It turned out that the scrimmage was a practice for an amateur team, Ithaca United, made up predominantly of Cornell varsity players. They were not a friendly bunch. In fact, I recall that the whole enterprise seemed pretty grim, a bunch of guys who acted like they had been sentenced to play soccer by an evil regime. It didn't seem to help that the Schoellkopf Astroturf was just a shade more forgiving than the rock hard surface of BU's Nickerson Field. The speed of the ball on the surface was wicked fast, and the pace of the game equally so. It was obvious that there was not a whole lot of stock placed in mastering the subtleties of the sport. The chief attribute that most of the Cornelians seemed to have was equine stamina.

I was so perplexed by Astroturf—especially Astroturf in its early incarnation—that I started to think that it was at the heart of the difficulties that soccer encountered in getting established in America. It's easy to conclude by looking around the world and seeing poor kids improvising with dirt lots and wadded newspaper balls that a soccer player can emerge from just about anywhere in any environment. One of the most startling photographs I have ever seen is the one where the starving and desperate men on Ernest Shackleton's ill-fated Antarctic expedition have colonized an ice floe with a game of footie. Like golf on the moon or in the desert, it is amusing to connect your sport with some unattainable context. Hot plastic imitation grass laid thinly on a bed of concrete was as forgiving as Shackleton's ice floe. As it had almost ruined professional football with endless fractures and concussions, the brutal heat, artificial bounces, and soul-sucking qualities of Astroturf did little to help soccer in the U.S. In England, the Queens Park Rangers installed a turf field in 1981 and several other English clubs followed suit. By 1988, the English Football Association had grown so disgusted with the surface that it was banned. Fans complained that the ball looked like a Superball, pinging around all over the place. Players complained of joint pain, carpet burns, and injuries that otherwise would not have occurred on grass.

In Connecticut, even the three bad public school fields—Westhill, Stamford, and Rippowam High—were natural, even if by "natural," it meant dirt. Playing on turf, any ball kicked higher than ten feet or so had the potential to bounce over your head. Worse yet was the complete inability to use spin to play the ball into space. In *Brilliant Orange,* the sculptor Jeroen Henneman illustrates the spatial genius of the former Dutch great Denis Bergkamp through the curved pass played behind an opposing defender. The essence of this pass was that it required a cultured approach, with enough weight and spin to get behind the defender, but not so much as to let the ball run through to the goalkeeper. With Astroturf, there was no chance to even think about playing a pass like this. What spin could be imparted to the ball would actually create the opposite effect, where the ball would gain momentum from the spinning action. Grass, by contrast, "bites" a ball and slows it, providing the entire impetus for the tuxedo-wearers like Bergkamp who orchestrate a game. As the English FA discovered, turf was undermining the sport.

Just as pernicious as Astroturf were the overall trappings of professional soccer. In its nascent pro days, the NASL had to adapt to existing stadiums, mostly built for American football. It is common knowledge among stadium architects that an entirely different set of planning constructs goes into soccer versus football. In fact, a soccer stadium has about as much in common with a football stadium as does a linebacker with a midfielder. Everything from the rake of the seats to the acoustics to the metrics for planning distance between the playing surface and the stands is different between the two sports. And of course the playing field itself is very different. For soccer, the field is typically 120 yards long by eighty yards wide, in contrast to football's one hundred yards long and fifty-five yards wide. The huge difference in width is vital in soccer, but in adapting to American field dimensions, the sport lost its width, severely curtailing the role of overlapping wingbacks. If you look at the modern game today, most of the great teams employ fast outside backs who are encouraged to get forward as much as possible. It is often at the edges of the field where space is found. Chinaglia was heretical in criticizing Pele, but in a way he was right: there's more room to create away from the center of the pitch.

With the exception of the Cosmos, watching an NASL game was a desultory affair. With a few fans strewn around a cavernous football stadium and all of the football yardage markings visible, a professional soccer game in the 1970s and '80s looked a lot more like a pickup game than anything resembling high-level European soccer. Throw in a bouncy artificial surface and sometimes the game could be mistaken for a circus act.

What I tried to impart to my friends was that soccer was a dreary affair here because it was not played in the proper context. It would have been laughable if Pete Rozelle let the NFL play in a cricket stadium or if Clarence Campbell let the NHL play on a speed-skating oval, but that's almost what it was like in the early days of pro soccer. It translated right down to the rank amateur level. The Ithaca United crowd wasn't too happy about a "walk-on" but finally let me run with them. It may have been the least amount of fun I've ever had playing soccer. The Cornell varsity players were all in shape and good athletes, but the game was strictly kick and chase. One of the big backs would settle the ball and try to bang a fifty-yard pass over the top of the opposing back four. I took up an outside midfield spot, which for that style of play was like being a spectator. It was Route 1 football all the way.

At that time, the phrase "sexy football" had not been invented. Today, sexy football is all but a precondition for success at the highest levels. For teams like Barcelona and Arsenal and Brazil, winning with style and élan is essential. The ball must be loved, caressed, and nurtured. Passes must flow with grace and beauty and imagination. Flicks, tricks, and deception must be used to unnerve and embarrass the opposition. Ronhaldino, whale-like for Milan compared to the young sylph running through the English defense en route to Brazil's World Cup triumph in 2002, is focused almost exclusively on perfecting an ever-shrinking zone of sexy football, in which he can employ his soccer circus act. So much do owners and coaches want to elevate soccer to an art form, that it has become essential to the process. In a dazzling recent comment melding sexy football and the Soccer Bitch, the elfin former Israeli star Eyal Bercovic lobbies to become the new coach of the Israeli National Team: "I have everything: clever playing, inspiration, freshness, chutzpah, attacking play, sexy football, interaction with the players— nobody understands them more than me. The only thing I don't have is experience as a coach."

In other words, credentials, schmedentials. Sex sells baby, and get used to it, it's the new wave of football. The hip-hop mogul Jay-Z, contemplating an investment in Arsenal, confirms that he knows little of the business end of soccer. Why would Jay-Z rather buy into a sport he knows nothing about versus, say, a stake in the Kansas City Royals or the Memphis Grizzlies? Could it be that he fancies sitting in the Arsenal box with dishy Euro-lasses flanking him while Arsenal dazzles with its sexy football?

David Winner, in his deconstruction of English football, *Those Feet*, gets to the heart of sexy football and its absence in

England. Throughout its history, Winner argues, English football has been expected to display Lionheart qualities: strength, power, energy, fortitude, loyalty, and courage, while eschewing unmanly attributes: delicacy, cleverness, sleight-of-foot, and imagination. Perhaps the institutionalization of sexy football began with the great Dutch star Ruud Gullit publicly asserting his preference for Portugal over Croatia in the 1996 European Championships due to the fact that the former played sexy football. Gullit went on to explain that sexy football is when "players play with skill and style, when they express themselves playfully, reveal their fantasy, and when it's a joy and pleasure to watch."

The Ithaca United workouts left me sweat-soaked and lifeless. There was no joy, no pleasure, no art, just a whole heckuva lot of running back and forth on the hot Astroturf. I felt like I had been punished. There was also a form of hazing going on. The teammates didn't take kindly to an interloper—sharing the ball, or being halfway friendly for that matter, was not on their agenda. My overtures were met with derisive chuckles, half-grunts, and cocked eyebrows. Understandably, they didn't know my game so well, so they were loath to share the ball in obvious situations. I had to work twice as hard to get the same pass that one of the guys from the team would get. With all that, I was still glad I scrimmaged with them that summer. If nothing else, I saw that with the exception of two or three really talented players, there was not that much to college varsity soccer outside of being extremely fit.

Somehow, there was a great divide in American soccer. The Cosmos were obviously an avatar of sexy football, a pastiche of international styles—Brazilian, German, and Italian mainly—that came together as grand entertainment. But there seemed to be almost no recognition at the scholastic and collegiate levels that dribbling and clever passing and holding the ball were admirable and would lead to success. In fact, the opposite seemed to be the case with most American coaches. With the notable exception of Albie Loeffler, it certainly was the case with the coaches I had encountered. Vadikos and Scotnick were strictly proponents of the long ball. To them, soccer had to adapt to their simple notion of what it took to be successful at the sports they knew: track and field and swimming. The common denominator between them was conditioning, apt for running and swimming, and essential for soccer. The difference was that conditioning was perhaps 80 or 90 percent of swimming and running, with the balance being technique, while for soccer being in shape was necessary, but just a departure point for mastering the nuances of the sport.

That the damn English were to blame was at the root of the problem. As part of the Cosmos halo effect, PBS started to broadcast English Division I (Premiership precursor) matches in a condensed, one-hour format. Soccer the English way—running, long balls, heading, and more running—became soccer the American way. Whether it was the common language or the fact that England provided American kids with the most cultural exchange opportunities, or the influence of English and Irish coaches, the prevailing ethos in American soccer was adopted from the UK, winning out over the European Continent and South America.

To this day, this prejudice is in evidence. When I lived in New Rochelle, in Westchester County, I walked down to New Rochelle High School to kick around on the new field turf they installed. It was the day before Thanksgiving in 2005, and there were a couple of college kids out with a ball. They were good, one of them really good. It turned out he was a starter for Georgetown, and a top player in his conference. I told him that I watched a fair bit of college soccer and was a bit disappointed with the lack of creativity or ideas in the attacking third of the field. He told me that the players would love to attack and be creative but that his coach had him on a very short leash. In college, free substitution is allowed, and it is an easy decision to yank a player if a coach gets ticked off.

Cornell, smaller than Boston University, still had quite a bit of international flair, and good intramural soccer. One of my main goals for transferring was to increase my chances of getting into a prestigious graduate school. I applied to five schools for transfer: Union College, the University of Rochester, Brown, Pennsylvania, and Cornell. I got in to all of them except Brown, which apologized profusely and noted in its rejection letter that it only admitted a handful of transfer students each year. It boiled down to the two Ivies. I scraped together enough cash to visit Philadelphia. I thought that if I felt the Philly vibe, then I'd go with Penn, otherwise, I'd have to make the trek to Ithaca.

I visited the Penn campus for the first time in July of 1980. At the time, the neighborhood around the Penn campus was decidedly not gentrified. I had made reservations at one of the few hotels on University Avenue, a Ramada Inn. The temperature had hit the midnineties, and a brutal urban heat wave had hit just as I arrived. My room was up high but had a rancid, dead skin and cigarette smell, the scourge of badly managed independent hotels. The air conditioner kicked on with powerful fan action but had long since lost any powers of cooling. I dropped my bag off and set out to see the campus. The Locust Walk was nice enough, taking in Wharton and some of the older buildings, but it was still every bit as urban in feeling as BU. It was also summer, and most of the students were gone. The heat was brutal, a three T-shirt kind of day, and I grabbed a quick bite and explored the area around the campus. It was decrepit, but in that specialized, student slumlord kind of way. It wasn't a place you'd want to live or shop or do much of anything in except speed through to get to your classes. The fact that so many urban campuses suffered from surrounding blight for so many years is an interesting phenomenon: was it that the demand for real estate in such close proximity to a university was so high that there was no need for landlords to maintain or improve their properties? Or perhaps it was a case of regression towards the mean: students, slovenly by nature, deserved crappy real estate. As if they had discovered that students have lots of disposable cash (lots of it from student loans that blow up on them years later), landlords have miraculously transformed college towns all over the country into minimalls offering the same types of luxury goods and services that you'd find in upscale locations anywhere else. An investor group near the Yale campus recently opened a boutique hotel, The Library, that wouldn't be out of place in the Meatpacking District in Manhattan.

That night in the Ramada I felt like I was camping in an Indonesian jungle, albeit one that had been fogged by Merit Ultra Lights, semen, and a strange room deodorizer. The heat somehow grew in intensity, with the "air conditioner" functioning strictly as a means to blow the fetid, humid air into every crevasse of my room. I wet a towel and laid it over my face; even the towel smelled like burnt smoke. I lay awake until about three or four in the morning and decided that I would bust my move to Ithaca.

Cornell did play up its Ivy Leagueness to my amusement. My favorite dining hall, not surprisingly called "The Ivy" room, was a collegiate gothic confection with bas-relief carvings of the eight ivy crests, in all their colorful glory. There, I could eat my Salisbury steak and cheesy potatoes while basking in the glory that is the Ivy League. The fraternity and sorority structure was also a complete novelty. As an admitted transfer student, I was sentenced to life in West Campus, which was a rodent warren of dreary, postwar dormitories called "U-Halls." In a fortunate turn of events, I wound up in above-standard facilities, with a private room in the Psi Upsilon fraternity house. After a series of increasingly dire offenses, Psi U was finally banned from the Cornell campus and evicted from their home. This was not long after the release of *Animal House* and before there were any specific rules prohibiting hazing of pledges. It was rumored that Psi U had committed a litany of actual and titular crimes, including locking pledges in the squash court with a keg of beer, killing a deer and mounting it on the front of the house, attacking students with homemade water bomb catapults, and a whole array of sexual assaults. Shortly after I moved in, all of the downstairs windows were shattered in an early morning attack, presumably by disgruntled Psi U boys.

Their loss was certainly my gain. Built in the teens, Psi U was a Tudor mansion from the Gatsby age. The main level included a grand entryway flanked by an enormous living room with fireplaces, window seats, and a paneled library leading to a grand formal dining room and giant commercial kitchen. On the other side were the bedrooms, most of them singles, along with the bathrooms. The second level contained more bedrooms, but the real benefit was the lower level, which contained the infamous squash court and a basement rec room. There were no amenities or facilities in the rec room, but there was something fascinating. In the twenties—I am guessing not too long after the house was built—an artist painted cartoon murals on the wall. The scenes were done in bright colors that had faded badly, but the images were still crisp. The content was disturbing: blob-like monsters chasing "lesser" beings into shadowy spaces. The monsters were nefarious and menacing, in the manner of World War II–era cartoons depicting Fascists as fang-bearing vulpine creatures. The murals had no theme other than search and destroy. The illustrator was clearly gifted; the quality of the pictures was the equal of any comic book, and considering that the images were nearly sixty years old when I first saw them, they seemed contemporary. From a thematic standpoint, I suppose the murals resonated with the mission of the displaced Psi Users: you can never be too nasty. I heard years later that Psi U had been reinstated to the Cornell campus and that the murals were going to be restored.

Cornell was highly factionalized. There were seven colleges that made up the Ithaca campus, four of them endowed and private and three of them part of the New York State system that was part of the congressional land grant legislation that was intrinsic to the founding of the school by Ezra Cornell and Andrew White. Cornelians ID themselves by first asking, "What school did you go to?" There is a hierarchy of prestige, with Arts and Sciences and Engineering at the top and the School of Human Ecology at the bottom. Scholars and slackers abound in all of the schools, but central to this elitism is an attempt by the private Cornelians to align themselves more with the rest of the Ivy League and less with their proletarian, state school kissing cousins.

In 1980, the seminal work in the deconstruction of the social hierarchy of colleges was published. Lisa Birnbach's *The Preppy Handbook* burst my Ivy bubble badly when both Cornell and soccer were deemed unpreppy. In a simple flourish of her typewriter, Birnbach tapped into my primal anxiety about not being preppy enough; my old nemesis Princeton was of course anointed as one of the gatekeepers of preppydom, along with lacrosse and just about anything relating to East Coast prep schools. I knew that Birnbach had glossed over the preppy aspect of soccer; to be sure, by this time, there were thousands of private and public school kids up and down the East Coast playing the sport. In fact, soccer was the default sport for kids with little or no athletic talent whose parents wanted them involved in something after school. That the scholastic soccer coaching mentality regarded running and conditioning as the sine qua non of soccer was perfect: if you could hustle, you could make the soccer team.

Birnbach's book was funny, acerbic, and disquietingly familiar no matter what end of the prep spectrum you were on. As a kid from a profoundly unpreppy family who had a first row seat at the preppy circus in Greenwich, New Canaan, and Darien, it was a bitter pill to swallow. Preppiness was not something you could manufacture. It was instilled, cultivated, and genetically engineered. Looking at it from an insider's point of view, the exposé must have been equally painful. There is only so much irony that can be attached to vomiting.

Birnbach would have been amazed had she known that my prep duck was broken at Boston University, an avatar for unpreppiness. Among the Jews from New Jersey and the Catholic kids from Rhode Island who made up the majority of the miscreants, dope fiends, and party animals who lived on my floor in the aptly named Warren Towers, was one Janet Haupt, a blueblood from Philadelphia's Main Line. How Janet wound up at BU was mystifying. Her retrousse nose, full and fearsome breasts, crystalline voice, and perfectly coordinated pastel sweater sets betrayed her protestant lineage at every moment. She was a Daughters of the American Revolution poster girl, good-looking but large-hipped and broad-shouldered. Janet was like some strange preppy emissary that dropped out of central casting to bestow a shred of finishing school enlightenment on the huddled masses.

In my case, her special gift was to teach me a sport that almost defined the essence of indoor preppiness: squash. BU was a school that did not get hung up on tradition. True to its roots as a commuter school, it did not have a single squash court back then for its 25,000 students. In order to consume squash, we had to venture across the river and wrangle some kind of intercollegiate deal with Harvard. In order for Janet to teach me the ropes, I invested in a solid ash Slazenger racquet—wood of course—that looked like a tennis racquet in miniature. Its clear lacquer and black, red, and yellow striping held me rapt in the weeks before we were able to reserve a court. Janet and I didn't have any kind of personal connection; she had an appropriately preppy boyfriend named "Dunc" who captained the lacrosse team at some small New England college. We all thought that he was fictitious until one weekend he actually showed up, tall, tan, and relaxed, in dramatic contrast to the pallid, pockmarked BU stoners who lived on my floor.

Squash and lacrosse—these were sports that Birnbach, who had gone to Brown, classified as legit preppy sports. Soccer was too sweaty, too proletarian, and too accessible to be prep-cool. All along, I had wanted to be a Dunc type, but I was too late for lacrosse, which was played at only a couple of schools in Fairfield County. I had to satisfy myself with the thought that had there been lacrosse at Westhill, I would have been a decent, maybe even a good player. With Dunc gone during the week, I suppose that Janet was a bit bored and happy for the attention. Janet could play, too. She could hit rail shots like nobody's business, thumping the ball down the wall with authority. We used the hard "American" ball and scored games with a fifteen-point "must" system, with points scored on every rally, irrespective of who was the server. As you get better at it, squash takes on a hypnotic quality. The muffled thud of the ball, rhythmic thwacking, and damp, chilly courts make for a strange and oddly compelling pastime.

It wasn't until I got to Cornell that I really got the full flavor of squash. Looking to explore the new scene after my transfer, I grabbed my trusty (and sturdy) Slazenger one day and headed to the squash courts at Cornell. The mere fact the Cornell had squash courts seemed to almost vindicate my transfer from BU. I went up just to practice on my own but found another kid there, practicing rail shots. I introduced myself and he did the same— Dave Grumman, was his name, which, I noted, was the same last name as the name of the facility we were in.

"Grumman? Are you by any chance related to the person who endowed these courts?"

"Yes," he said. "That was my grandfather."

Wow. Grumman was the scion of the founder of Grumman Aerospace, one of the pioneers of the American aviation industry. I was rallying on a court with blueblood. My grandfathers were self-made guys who owned solid businesses. My mother's father was a street-fighter type from the Lower East Side who started peddling fish as a young kid to help feed his family. It was unlikely that he ever knew what squash was, even the vegetable, but he would have been damn proud that his descendant had sufficient leisure time to bang a small rubber ball off a wall with a trust-fund kid.

Ultimately, my association with Janet did more harm than good. While sentenced to two-and-a-half years of hard urban labor at a huge, impersonal, and drug-addled campus, Janet teased me into thinking that I had the DNA to be a prepster. In high school I had just enough to do with Greenwich High girls to reel me in: was it conceivable that a kid with zero prep DNA could be emancipated into a life of squash and martinis by the poolside? At least I got the bug to transfer to the Ivy League. So what if I picked the biggest, grayest, coldest campus among the Ancient Eight? At least I could rub shoulders with guys like Dave Grumman. But as Janet herself was a chimera, so was my fantasy about becoming an ersatz WASP.

Six

Pampas in Chicago and Kaffefutbol

AFTER GETTING MY degree from Cornell in January, I got a job at its business school, running numbers and compiling data for a woman working on an alumni outreach database. It was great prep for business school, lots of fudging, hypothecating, and pretending we had a grand mission. My boss reported in to an officious middle-aged guy who always seemed harried while doing absolutely nothing. It was a cold winter, and the main excitement around my house was that the pipes froze a lot and we needed the services of a specialist called an "arc" welder. I lived in a tiny box of a house at 315½ Eddy Street, and the property was situated so it got barely any sun. The arc welder had equipment that could generate an electrical connection through the frozen tundra and get the water moving. After enduring two brutal Cornell winters, I got to the point where I figured the weather could hardly be worse anywhere, including Chicago. I was wrong.

If there ever was a greater promise of soccer than moving into a graduate dorm called International House, I would like to know. This was my first stop at the University of Chicago, in the early summer of 1981. The school was an academic oasis in the middle of the city's vast South Side. At the time, there were two or three street gangs who made most of the area to the immediate north and south of the campus pretty inhospitable to student folk. Whether or not it was the stuff of urban legend, the stories about violence perpetuated upon unsuspecting Chicago students was enough to keep me from roaming past 53rd Street. The decline in the quality of the neighborhood away from the campus was dramatic. If you went downtown on the "El," you had to either hoof it home from 61st Street in the Chicago permafrost, or worse, wait for the bus that connected to the campus on a schedule that must have been set by the Indian Railway Commission. The times that I walked home from that El stop were some of the briskest walks I ever took. Ithaca had a crap climate, but Chicago's was worse. For the two years I was there, it was in a mud and ice cycle. The winter of 1981 was so cold that I did not take a shower or bath—or for that matter get much near any running water—for a week. It was in the deep double-digit negatives with the wind chill, and the snow was two or three feet deep. Downtown was virtually abandoned for days. The commuter rail somehow kept running, and for amusement my roommate Jim and I braved the cold to go downtown. Except for a handful of cross-country skiers, we had it all to ourselves. I would rhapsodize about the solemn beauty and stillness of the Wrigley Building and the Palmer House except that I had my entire face covered except two tiny slits for my eyes and remember nothing except that I was freaking cold beyond my imagination.

Jim was a Texan, as voracious a reader and scholar as anyone I have ever known. Soccer was a complete enigma to him. Fortunately, the business school—the GSB—was chock-full of foreigners. The rumor on campus was that the graduate intramural team to beat was made up of the Chicago varsity players, who were allowed to play "up" with the grad students but not with the other undergrads. I made friends with a German guy, Bob, who told me that he ran track and played some JV soccer for Harvard. I had wanted to name the team Blue Star, the successor name to the Prospect Unity Club. Bob, a Berliner, was OK with that, but he wanted to append the name of a club team from his youth—Vorvaerts ("forward" in German), so we became a German/Zionist hybrid team entered in the graduate students' league. Right before our first practice, the business school had a race day. As much as I liked to run around chasing a ball or a puck, I didn't go for races. There was something too pack-like and purpose-driven in a foot race for me. I wasn't into endurance for the sake of endurance. There had to be something to get my blood up—getting hit or hitting—to make me run to exhaustion. The two school races were a hundred-yard dash and a 5k. Bob won them both with ease—the 5k by almost three minutes. If he was half the soccer player as he was a runner, we would be a pretty decent team.

I cobbled together a few other guys, including a rugby player I knew from Cornell named John. He signed on as a goalkeeper, which was perfect, since it is by far the most difficult position to fill when you are playing casual soccer; everyone wants to score. Just by putting the word out, several other guys signed up, including two Division III players and a little Belgian named

Phillipe. We basically had a starting lineup of experienced, mostly collegiate-level players, and I was pretty excited. The first couple of games were easy wins. Bob started up top at striker, and he was damn good, a combination of speed and great finishing. There was no one early on who could come close to staying with him. I played in the center behind Bob, and one of the ex-college players, Jamie from Ohio Wesleyan, anchored the defense. With John solid in goal, I had a sense that we would run the table and capture the graduate school title with only the varsity team standing in our way.

My great miscalculation was forgetting about Argentina. Specifically, a bunch of Argentine guys from the business school. Not having ever met an Argentine—my defense partner Alex from Westhill was Chilean, about as close as I got—I didn't really know they existed in such great numbers at Chicago. When we lined up against them, they didn't look imposing at all. In fact they were pretty runty looking. But there was one guy in the middle who looked solid and very confident. I would later learn that his name was Gerardo Leon. On that day, his name could well have been Diego Maradona. Gerardo dominated us from start to finish, orchestrating breathtaking passing moves and finishing plays with ease. He changed gears like a Ferrari and had close control that was freakishly good. Apparently, he played high-level youth soccer in Argentina until an injury got him off track from a pro career. I had seen a lot of good foreigners play soccer: Italians, Iranians, Jamaicans, Irish, and Americans from Westport. The Argentine style was a revelation. It was apparent from watching Gerardo that there was always another gear, another level of understanding, and a better way to play. The central brilliance of soccer is exactly what its detractors detest: it is a freethinker's sport in which improvisation and spontaneity are essential. The more you think, the better you are. Hockey has some of that in its DNA, and so do lacrosse and basketball. Baseball pitchers and boxers need to think on their feet, but in no sport does so much free-form thinking go on as in soccer. It is also unique it that possession of the ball is continuously contested. Only hockey shares this quality (lacrosse, basketball, and football are technically sports in which possession changes, but they are fundamentally sports in which teams take turns), and the speed of hockey creates frequent turnovers. In soccer, possession is both art and science. The Italians famously counterattack through their Cattanacio football, playing resolute defense and breaking quickly to the attack. For the Brazilians and the Spaniards, possession of the ball is so important it is practically a de facto national requirement; the sporting press in those nations is outraged at anything less than stylish victories.

Before we had to play the varsity, we had a game against the medical school team. That game forever changed my perception of the Hippocratic profession. I suppose that none of them had yet taken the oath because they were, almost to a player, the nastiest bunch of guys I ever played against. They singled out the smallest guy on our team—the Belgian Phillipe, who was about 5'2" and maybe 125 pounds—and fouled him every which way. The match was way too much for the poor student referee to handle. The game degenerated into fouling, cursing, and threats. If that was the future of medical care in America, we all had something to be scared about. We hung on to win and finished out against the varsity. They were as good as advertised, organized and talented. Even an academic powerhouse like Chicago attracted pretty decent athletes—the second year I was there, the basketball team had a great run, and the school was pretty competitive in a bunch of sports. The main field at Chicago was the Amos Alonzo Stagg Field, named after the football coach who presided over Chicago's run as a national football power. Banning the sport after the death of one of its players in the 1940s, Chicago reverted to Division III status, but the school still boasts about its glory days in football.

We lost a close game to the varsity. I found out that a few of them played for a team called Pampas in the South American League that played on some fields off Lake Shore Drive, so I checked it out one weekend. It was my first glimpse of "festival" soccer. An encampment along the lake consisted of South and Central American families who seemed to bring the entire contents of their residences to the park. Hibachis, coolers, volleyball sets, beach balls, umbrellas, blankets, mountains of prepared food, and decorations were unpacked as four generations of families lolled about while the games went on. As relaxed and familial as the picnicking was, the games were intense. It was barn-burning, take-no-prisoners soccer. The South American game, as I saw from playing the Argentines, was a distinct subclass of soccer, built around triangles and quick passing. They were expert dribblers, but dribbling was used as a means not an end. Dribbling South American style created space for teammates who were constantly on the move and unafraid to play a ball square or even a negative (backwards) pass to open up space.

Having spent most of my life in the suburbs, it wasn't until I got to Chicago that I was able to see the urban soccer scene close up. With our quirky intramural team, the Blue Star Voerverts, I started to think more about the history of German-Jewish soccer. As café culture in Art Nouveau Vienna ascended along with the popularity of football, the sport might have been called "Kaffefutbol." Soccer and political affiliations grew from the cafes, and teams not only represented regions, but ideas as well.

Benny Feilhaber's story is one that started in prewar Austria. His grandfather left the country for Brazil, with the family winding up in the U.S. Feilhaber walks on to UCLA, makes the U.S. National Team, gets noticed by Hamburg, and goes to Germany. Full cycle in three generations. With Blue Star Voerverts, I couldn't help notice that Bob and I had fashioned a miniature German reunification of sorts.

The German word "Vorstadt" denotes the working-class suburbs of Vienna. The subtext of the Vorstadt as it related to the Jews—and by extension Jewish soccer clubs—was that the Vorstadt represented the "people," in contrast to the Jews, who were to be considered trifling aliens. From the *Illustriertes Sportblatt*, a prewar sports publication:

> Rapid [Vorstadt] is a team of the people and never neglects its roots. The Green-Whites are a "Vorstadt" club in the best sense of the word. Amateure [Jewish club] is "a team of soccer mercenaries dazed by the fog of the coffeehouse."

Wow, what a concept. Coffeehouse culture in 1920s Vienna was associated with theater, journalism, and the literary arts. Soccer lovers were known to be bibliophiles and progenitors of provocative thought. As Lizzy Ratner notes in her article "Plotz Like Beckham," the soccer Jew has a decided literary bent, with editors and authors holding court to discuss the geopolitical implications of the sport. In my case, it dovetailed nicely with my new favorite activity—going to prolonged brunches at the Medici Coffeehouse on 57th Street in Hyde Park and eating way too many chocolate croissants washed down by its strong, bitter coffee.

I was nearing the end of my lease near the other side of campus where I rented a small bedroom next to the kitchen in a classic Chicago tenement building. That I was still alive after living there for most of a year was a testament to the human capacity for enduring extreme punishment. The three other "roommates," really four, including the leviathan of a fiancée of one of them, were out of hell's central casting. Karl was a night student in the business school and a manager of a supermarket by day. He was rail thin with a thatch of oily black hair pulled over to one side exposing an asymmetrical bald pattern that demanded one's full attention. He had a very angry case of acne that was exacerbated by having his hands all over his face, rubbing and probing. As skinny as Karl was, his fiancée was a bloated witch of a thing, as pale and flaccid as they come. They were not there much except for the evenings, which began with a huge meat fry-up, Karl having sourced some of the primest and tenderest cuts of fillet for his undernourished lover. My room, hard by the kitchen, soaked up the grease fumes as if my bed was on the fryer itself. Karl would recite the dreary details of his day over the sizzling of the steak, which he eventually plopped on a plate, to be gobbled up greedily by the giantess. It was lurid *cinema verité*. The sanest of my three roommates, Mark, at least grasped the nightly irony of skinny Karl leading his lady to the feed trough, and it was so painful to witness that after they retired to Karl's bedroom, we would have to have a debriefing in a kitchen, like two strangers who have just seen a fatal accident.

Then there was Craig. Craig rented a room in the flat, but lived with his girlfriend in another apartment. Apparently this was an arrangement he wanted to keep secret from his parents. Every three days or so, he would rush in, throw his bags down and frantically ask me or Mark whether his mother called.

Craig gave us strict instructions to not disclose his whereabouts under any circumstances. Playing the beard for Craig got old, and one time his mother started pressing about whether he was at his girlfriend's—at least she knew he had a girlfriend. I said that I guessed there was as good a chance as any, but that I wasn't sure. Not long after that Craig came back and flew into a psychotic rage—I had betrayed him, how fucked up this was, don't I ever dare talk to his mother, etc. In short, the guy was a classic University of Chicago undergraduate mess, emotionally disturbed and on the lam. Mark, for his part, was quiet, a mathematics student and profound introvert who did not speak unless spoken to. He was more like a pet than a roommate, but in concert with the others, he added to the general aura of depression and repulsiveness of the apartment.

With the World Cup in Spain approaching in June of 1982, I packed up my few boxes of clothes and books and kissed Karl and the smelly walk-up goodbye. I had nowhere to go but back to International House, which rented rooms by the week. Aside from the cavernous hallways and loud echoes whenever a door opened or closed, it was a decent place to live, and most importantly, I could watch the World Cup on the big TV in the downstairs lounge. In my fantasy soccer life, I would have been always surrounded with knowledgeable and enthusiastic fellow fans, a moveable feast of soccer, like a friendly pub in the English countryside. The tournament opened, and I got to the lounge about a half hour early to make sure I got a seat to watch Spain open against Honduras. Surely, the "International" House would be buzzing about the World Cup. I walked in and saw three or four guy lazing on the sofa and chairs, watching a game show.

"Hi—you guys ready for the game?"

A couple of the guys shrugged. "What?"

"The World Cup. You guys are watching, right?"

"Don't know," said one. "Whatever. Put it on if you want."

Those guys really didn't know that the World Cup was on. I walked over to the TV and changed to the Spanish broadcast station, still the only channel that showed the games. Despite PBS's occasional forays into broadcasting English and Italian soccer, there was not a whiff of American network broadcast interest. That dream apparently died when Steve Ross was unable to get FIFA interested in having the U.S. host the 1986 World Cup. The Cosmos were bleeding to a slow death by the time the 1982 Cup came around, and if you wanted to see the games, you'd better have had a good UHF antenna. At I-House, I had to construct my own out of several wire coat hangers. The group in the lounge stared at me like I was some kind of freak as I twisted and grunted and dangled the homemade antenna out of the window. Still, the picture was grainy. Finally, after about a dozen Tecate commercials, the feed came in live. It was in Spanish, and the picture was close to unwatchable, but dammit, it was the World Cup.

It was a fantastic tournament. Two matches, Italy versus Brazil and Germany versus France, are considered to be among the best Cup games ever. Without a job and classes, I parked myself in front of the TV every day and watched every minute of every match that Univision televised. It did not matter to me that the other folks regarded me like an oddity at the zoo.

"Who is that strange dude watching Poland play soccer with a bunch of loud Spanish broadcasters?"

By the time that Joel Battiston, a French forward, was rendered unconscious in a collision with the German keeper Harold Schumacher, I was in my own soccer trance, dreamy and euphoric. The French "Four Musketeers" midfield embodied

Total Football in all its interchanging glory. Led by Michel Platini and Jean Tigana, to my mind the most underrated player that I have ever seen, the French barnstormed with Gallic swagger. Tiny Alain Giresse darted around the pitch like a water bug. Platini scored, and Tigana played box-to-box midfield in a way that should be used as a training video today. Sadly, I watched alone, even when there were other people staring at the TV. Soccer was still an oddity.

I did find a pretty decent pickup game at Stagg Field. With a training regime that consisted mainly of polishing off several croissants at the Medici, I was not in prime condition, and one day I felt my knee go slack. It was a meniscus and patella combo pack that put me out for a good three months. My partner in Medici crime was my friend Jim, an anthropology grad student from Tyler, Texas. Jim was a paradox; he managed to have a languorous East Texas drawl and to speak quickly. For a guy from an archly conservative part of the country, he espoused a socialist bent and freely quoted from the various impenetrable (for me) anthropology structuralist texts he was reading—Derrida and the like. He found a room in a prewar apartment near the landmark Frank Lloyd Wright Robie House on 58th Street. Another room opened up and I grabbed it.

That was a quantum leap forward from the ghetto trappings in the meat fryer asylum with Karl et al. Jim and I each had a bedroom in one wing of a gracious four-bedroom apartment occupied by Mrs. Pierce, an Austrian Dr. Ruth doppelganger, who had lived in the apartment for some forty years and occupied the two bedrooms in one wing. The kitchen was shared, and Jim and I were allowed to use the living room, with the caveat that we were to act like adults and keep things clean. Mrs. Pierce was a child psychologist and Freudian who fancied nude midnight raids to the refrigerator. Catching her flaccid little rotund figure with ballooning breasts sagging near the floor like inner tubes in the harsh kitchen light at midnight was a bracing foreshadow of old age. Her father had been a composer of some renown in Austria, and she claimed to have sat in Mahler's lap as a child. I am sure she is dead now, but I would have liked to have had the chance to ask her about café society in prewar Vienna. In particular, I would have asked her about Matthias Sindelar, the Austrian soccer star known as the Grandmaster.

In a cloak-and-dagger life, Sindelar was perhaps the greatest soccer star of the years between the two world wars, an iconoclast who shunned the Nazis after the annexation of Austria in 1938. Sindelar whose high forehead and wiry frame suggested an artist, refused to play for the national team that the Nazis formed out of the remnants of the old Austrian national team and the German side. In the last game played by the Austrian National team, a matched dubbed the "brotherhood" match by the Nazis, Sindelar ran to the Nazi bigwig box to gloat after Austria had taken a 2-0 lead. Later, after the usurpation of Jewish property was declared legal, he bought a street corner café in his boyhood district of Favoriten from a Jew, possibly for fair market value at a time when Jewish property was routinely "sold" for a fraction of its value. Continuing to consort with Jews, many of whom had been his fans when he played for FK Austria Wien, he remained under Nazi suspicion and died in his apartment at age thirty-six from carbon monoxide poisoning. Many conflicting theories surround the death of Sindelar. His death had all the trappings of the bleak and nefarious dissipation of life under the Nazis. Was he murdered by his girlfriend, who died in his bed, or by the Nazis, or perhaps by gangsters to whom he owed gambling debts? Had Sindelar actually paid good money for the café or seized an opportunity to get in on a favorable deal? Was he in fact a Jew who had kept his identity a secret? Strangely, little has been resolved about Sindelar's death, nor has he achieved any significant recognition from the Austrian people or government, despite the fact that he was one of the nation's greatest sportsmen.

Sindelar was known to be a darling of café society and its principal constituents—dilettantes, flaneurs, and the bourgeoisie. Why is it that soccer, a sport of motion and continuity, holds café culture rapt? It would be considered silly, almost heretical to link a café with football, hockey, or basketball. Baseball, which could well use a shot or two of caffeine, is not much debated over a ristretto and biscotti. I believe that the answer is that soccer and politics are inextricable. The simplicity of soccer—the singular aspect of the sport that makes it so loved (and loathed by some)—makes it universally accessible. The sport lends itself to being politically hijacked. The Jews looked to soccer for assimilation and acceptance, the Nazis for reinforcing their nationalistic agenda that began with a systematic cleansing of Jews from all aspects of sport. Today, the paradox of soccer continues. American blacks are latecomers to soccer and barely know of it in the inner cities. But black Africans, poorer still, are nuts about it and appear in greater numbers throughout the top leagues in Europe. A tough-guy sport in Europe, soccer in the U.S. is considered to be way down the toughness pecking order—a distant fifth or sixth perhaps, after football, hockey, lacrosse, and basketball. Baseball, without any contact save for the occasional home plate collision, is somehow considered a "tougher" sport in America.

Reading about Sindelar, I am better equipped to understand why I played angry at Westhill. Think about what Sindelar did. If he was in fact Christian, then it seems almost surreal that he would have killed himself in political defiance of the Nazis. If he was Jewish and hiding it, then why wouldn't he just have high-tailed it out of Dodge and gone to South America or the U.S? The fact is that he was loyal, standing by the Jewish leadership of FK Wien and continuing to fraternize with his Jewish and libertarian colleagues after he revealed his "treasonous" tendencies. In the rare air of bucolic Fairfield County, circa the late 1960s, circumstances were surely less violent, but there was plenty of religious tension, at least as an undertone. The same undercurrent of bad blood and anti-Semitism that supported the Vorstadt in its invective against Jews was present when the older brother of one of the kids I played football and softball with in the cul-de-sac came up to me one day out of the blue and told me that the Jews killed Jesus. He might just as well have invoked the favorite anti-Semitic insults of the Hakoah-era, "Dreckjude" (dirty Jew) and "Judensau" (Jew Pig). I led a dual life: Jews at school, Catholics in the 'hood. It imparted a weird splitting of values. I couldn't quite reconcile the proselytizing from school with the neighborhood animus against Jews. Soccer, mostly to its detriment, lends itself to crusading and jingoist behavior. There has never been such a thing as a "baseball war" or a "basketball war," but Honduras and El Salvador infamously conducted a "Soccer War" in the seventies. The existence of Hakoah FC largely can be explained as a soccer war—Jews had been slowly excluded from Austrian sport and gradually formed their own clubs. As Hakoah asserted itself as a force in the highest levels of Austrian soccer, systematic violence became a parallel ritual to the games. Without knowing any of this history when I was a teenager, I had strangely assimilated it. I suppose a lot of it had to do with my grade school and the prevailing theme of persecution against the Jews.

Well, yes, that was a good introduction, but where did one go from there? I remember being completely flummoxed when one day in sixth grade, several yarmulkes full of sand were hurled through the open casement windows to our classroom—anti-Semitism in broad daylight in Stamford. The teachers just kind of shrugged it off—they didn't even have a context for it. It was kind of strange, and I took it as the same passivity and disinterest in the physical world that was manifested in our lack of gym or organized sport. What I didn't understand then was that this rejection was active; sport had been tried as an equalizer but had comprehensively failed. Hakoah was disbanded, its players scattered all over, and physical culture was usurped by war and survival.

After we had been smoked by the Argentines in that intramural game, I started to get to know some of their players, including their star, Gerardo. We arranged to play them again on the Midway for fun. After the game, Gerardo asked me a question that I had been asked at least a dozen times before: "Where are you from?" This was the basic soccer question. Where you were from told someone everything: how you played, how you thought, what were your strengths and weaknesses. The problem was that the "U.S." or "America" was not an acceptable answer. At the very least it was an answer that required a footnote: being an American branded you as a soccer arriviste, a naïf, a dilettante. It was as if someone asked you what religion you were and you answered "vegetarian."

The question itself was a compliment. The subtext was "Hey, you're good, where you from?" When I lamely mumbled that I was American, Gerardo said he was surprised—he thought I was Argentine! That was all I had to hear. I did have one of my better days the second time we played. Their short passing, one-two style was infectious, and we played them much tighter the second time around. With all the crappy coaching I got through the years and the fact that I was a complete soccer independent, there wasn't a whole lot of feedback—good or bad—to take away and work with. Gerardo's comment temporarily gave me soccer vapors: acceptance into the global fraternity at last.

Still, it did not resolve how to answer that war horse of a question. Of course I was an American and damn proud of it, but as far as soccer was concerned, I needed a new cover. I thought that maybe I should start answering that I was from Israel. That would provide an exotic imprimatur, and certainly sounded foreign enough. Since Israel was hardly on the world soccer tier-one radar at the time, no one would have an opinion about its football, so I couldn't be branded one way or the other right off the bat. In hindsight, a foreign identity would have served me well at Westhill. Instead of immediately being consigned to the back line, Scotnick would have put me up top, where I would at least have learned to shoot by trial and error. As it was, I spent three years of high school soccer in a complete learning vacuum.

Winding up my second year of business school, there was increasing pressure to do what comes most unnaturally to any graduating student: find a job. Unlike a lot of my classmates who seemed to have crawled out of the womb with a closetful of pinstriped suits and yellow power ties, I owned just the one suit that my dad bought for me for my Cornell graduation two years earlier. It was a nice Brooks Brothers suit but made of heavy winter tweed. As interview season started to peak, I felt like a sherpa stranded on a Cote D'Azur beach—sweaty and overdressed. I didn't learn the secret to business school until the very end—it was not about what you knew, but how you marketed yourself. Success was predicated on hitting the preinterview trail hard and early. Attending business school for two years was a mere formality. If you didn't have your "A" game from day one—and at that time the only "A" game was aspiring to be an investment banker or management consultant—you were dead. Back then, there was something called an "invite list," made up of pre-selected students who managed to concoct the correct potion of grades, looks, charm, and moxie. As one who was emphatically not part of this inner sanctum, I did the next best thing, which was studying these lists. What they revealed should have been pretty obvious: the same students were being recruited by all of the prestigious firms. It was musical chairs within musical chairs. Twenty-five or so of the top of the class was being sucked up to by the same fifteen or so firms. The other four hundred of us were left to the industrial scrap heap: energy companies, manufacturers, advertising shops, and, horror of horrors, commercial banking. Commercial banking was the default strategy for the bottom of the class.

There is a stale joke about medical school: "What do you call a medical student ranked at the bottom of his class?" Answer: Doctor. Not so in business school. In the post–Jimmy Carter recession, before Ronald Reagan's avuncular but hollow presence miraculously got the economy back on track, the job market was in its worst tailspin prior to the Great Recession of 2008. The stock market had yet to make its big bull run of the '80s, and the commercial banks, notably the "money center" banks, were eager to admit MBAs to their training programs. I knew I had a shot at getting a job in banking, but I had to solve the problem of how to answer the question of why I wanted to become a commercial banker. The agonizing truth was that I didn't have the slightest desire to go into banking. True, I had a degree in finance but had barely grasped the esoterica of the prevailing theories at Chicago: the Random Walk Theory and Dividend Irrelevance Proposition.

The latter, in particular, was almost completely opaque to me. I understood what it was meant to be in English—more or less that an enterprise's share price was not affected either way by its decision to pay dividends or not—but when it came time to translate this to math and accounting, I was flummoxed. It did not help matters that I had a financial accounting professor on the verge of divorce who mercilessly graded her exams on a curve, notwithstanding the fact that seven CPAs were in Intro Accounting. My opinion, along with others who were not CPAs, was that CPAs should not have been allowed to take the Introductory Accounting class and that perhaps they were there to get an A, making them more enticing for the magic carpet ride that was the interview invitational list.

But maybe this is all sour grapes, a by-product of not belonging to country clubs, of being from Stamford and not Greenwich or Westport, of having a dad who was more of an intellectual than a wheeler-dealer, of having a mother who spent the bulk of her adult life sitting or lying on the same spot of her sofa, prattling into the phone about being slighted by everyone around her.

Along with my friend Aviva, another accounting refugee, I pretended like I was above the pesky world of high finance and its evil twin, making money. We glorified the more "artistic" aspect of business, or, as other business schools called it, marketing. Although it technically had classes in marketing, Chicago did not believe in the concept. I was duped into taking a course that had an "A" written all over it, something like Basic

Marketing, or Introduction to Marketing Theory. After getting beaten up by accounting, eviscerated by corporate finance, and thrashed by econometrics, I needed the tonic of talking about the merits of Diet Coke versus Diet Pepsi in a touchy-feely way. What I failed to realize was that Chicago, in all its data-gathering glory, was not about to let its guard down with marketing. From day one, it was a knockdown, drag-out session of bitch-slap equations, formulae, and statistics. Marketing, in fact, was the exact opposite of what it should have been, an easy gut class. Because it was tainted as a nonquantitative field, marketing was the Napoleon of the business school, seeking to overcompensate with a blizzard of higher math.

Another friend, Andy, played along with me, pretending to be put off by the course while breezing through with yet another A. If merriment and mirth were the criteria for a good grade, I would have been fine, but our goofball, bad-suit wearing, mustachioed professor wanted to see some math, and somehow my bad jokes and outbursts did not resonate with him. Aviva had already taken a couple of marketing courses and was put off enough by the whole enterprise. "Hey," she asked me one day, "Did you ever think about advertising?"

No, I had not. If marketing had no status at Chicago, advertising was its blind and crippled love child. Aviva convinced me to go to an open house at the Leo Burnett Agency. Free lunches were the cornerstone of the business school experience. I never ate better than during my two years of business school. Figuring that I could live with the stigma of feigning interest in advertising as a career for an hour or two in return for a prawn and roast beef spread, I agreed.

We were led into the main conference room and seated— lunch was waiting of course, and a couple of slick executives introduced the company. They dimmed the lights and showed us a dazzling short film, a promo of, well, a promotional machine. There was no soft sell that day. Burnett was desperate for Chicago grads, even ones who flirted perilously with flunking accounting. My instincts told me that I should heed Groucho Marx's advice: any club that wanted me was certainly not worth joining.

That foray into the advertising underworld reinforced my disenchantment with the relentless onslaught of analytics to describe every facet of business, as served up by the Chicago Graduate School of Business. Jim and his disaffected cabal of overworked anthropology graduate students were way more interesting to hang around than the business-school crowd. I was in a state of retarded academic development, and I still wasn't prepared for the soul-crushing world of business. Rumor had it that fledgling investment bankers and consultants worked sixteen-hour days—a prospect I found terrifying enough that I believed I was fortunate to not be in the orbit of the interview invite lists.

In a last act of desperation brought on by the prospect of graduating without a job and seriously in student loan debt, I wormed my way on to a couple of commercial bank interview schedules, one for Mellon Bank and another for the pompously named Manufacturers Hanover Trust, a big New York Bank with roots in the garment and factoring business. As they say in soccer, going to New York was, for me, against the run of play. After Stamford, Boston, Ithaca, and now Chicago, I was looking forward to a westward move—preferably California, where I tried to get into Berkeley for business school but was put on the wait list.

It was not to be. "Manny Hanny" had a Chicago quota to fill and saw me as fresh meat for its training program.

"Why are you interested in commercial banking?" the recruiter asked me, as I knew he would. It was the most obvious question, and, just as the business school students ranked commercial banking about 120 notches below investment banking, so did the recruiters need to assuage their inferiority complex by hearing the interviewees genuflect about their organization. In the two or three months that made up the interview season, I had come up with nothing of substance to reply to this most basic of all questions. What was banking, after all? It was putting out money for a greater rate of interest than you paid on it. How on god's green earth did one construct a convincing story about how this made for a compelling career choice?

"Well, to be frank, I have always had an abiding interest in earning a 275 basis point spread on corporate tier-two loans. As far back as sixth grade, I can recall being mesmerized by loan covenants and secretly playing 'loan committee' with my sister behind my parents' backs."

The one thing I was looking forward to while waiting to find out if Manny Hanny would make me an offer was the trip to Europe that Andy and I planned that summer. We had lined up the usual European backpack tour, with a flight to Brussels and the all-important Eurail pass. Come June, Andy and I were setting out for Europe. Not long after we finalized plans for the trip, Manny Hanny served up an offer of $32k/year to enter its six-month credit-training program. My Jacksonian ambition of expanding westward was taking a detour to New York.

PART TWO

New York & California

SEVEN

Boroughs to Brahmins

DESPITE HAVING LIVED twenty-eight miles away from Times Square for the first seventeen years of my life, and having both parents and both sets of grandparents born in New York, I knew next to nothing about the city. During our furtive visits to my grandmother's apartment in the Mayfair Towers on the Upper West Side, my parents treated the excursion like we were making an amphibious landing in Somalia. My mother would raise the level of hysteria as we neared the building.

"Auntie (my mother's aunt) wants to get the hell out and go to Florida, but Mother won't go. Look at this place, it's a hellhole."

My dad, anxiety ridden about the parking situation, would look at her blankly: "Should I circle around again or just let you out?"

"Let me out. Jessica can come with me."

Sometimes I'd jump out too, depending on how hungry I was, but usually I'd go with my dad. Scrambling around Columbus and Broadway from about 71st Street to 75th Street was my only brush with touring around Manhattan. It was only much later in life that I learned that one of the finest natural history museums on the planet was a five-minute walk away. My family preferred to make a beeline for the twenty-eighth floor of the Mayfair Towers and settle in with the appetizing platter, groaning with salty fish and cheeses.

In the span of one generation, it is remarkable to think of the difference between how I spent my Sundays and how kids today spend theirs. It is almost unthinkable today for kids not to be running themselves to exhaustion doing some kind of sport on at least one day of the weekend. My Sundays typically involved going to one or the other of my grandparents' house, parking myself in front of the TV to watch Rocky and Bullwinkle, and stuffing myself silly with bagels, cheese, smoked fish, cakes, yogurt, and whatever else would fit in my fat little face.

In my grandmother's post-Depression/holocaust/shtetl mentality, any activity you did was de facto robbing you of precious calories, which had to be restored twofold, in the event that you were again called into action. My grandmother lived with her sister—a Boston marriage—after my grandfather died. My aunt was merciless about food; making the rounds with huge platters of roast chicken, stuffing, and assorted Jewish specialties, some of which, like stuffed derma and tongue, was stuff I wouldn't go near today. She would ask if you wanted more. Of course there was only one answer to this question; answering "no" meant that you were suffering from oxygen deprivation and needed an immediate second helping of chopped liver to restore normal thought patterns. Not waiting for you to respond at all, she would begin ladling out copious balls of fat-laden protein and rich starches onto your plate. It was little wonder that I flirted with husky sizes through grade school. If it wasn't for the cul-de-sac games of football and softball, I would have been a rolling dough ball as a kid.

The kitchen byplay between my grandmother and her sister was always a show.

Grandmother: "Ott, did you check on the chicken?"

Aunt (hard of hearing): "Of course I checked on the chicken."

Grandmother: "How is it?"

Aunt: "What?"

Grandmother: "The chicken, how is it"

Aunt: "The chicken? How is it?"

Grandmother: "Ok, I'll check it."

The schedule at my grandmothers' was roughly like this: snack, immediately upon entering the apartment, followed by lunch, served promptly fifteen minutes after the snack, followed by a midafternoon minimeal, in the event that you were feeling peckish. In between meals and snacks, I was free to refuel from the refrigerator.

At my paternal grandmother's in Queens, the culinary imperative was even worse. As much as my mother's mother fancied herself a cook—and she was a decent Old World cook—my dad's mother was an expert baker. This meant that at those German-Jewish family gatherings, she would bake four or five different cakes. Her two specialties were Grimmelkuchen, a buttery coffee cake, and mocha butter cream cake. She could also turn out perfect strudels and assorted cream cakes, and the overall quality was as good or better than a fine Viennese bakeshop. As a child, unsupervised at these events, there was no other way than to sample all of the desserts—cakes, cookies, pies, terrines, and candies. I would eat dessert until my teeth throbbed—the decay actually taking place in real time—and my gut audibly groaned. I would become woozie and at least on one occasion almost delirious from the post-bacchanal blood sugar crash. If the Beats had used Grimmelkuchen as a recreational drug, my grandmother's house at 58-52 Northern Boulevard would have been their crash pad.

With my new job at Manny Hanny, my grandmother in Queens suggested that I could live with her to save money. She lived alone in a three-bedroom, semiattached row house and spent three months of the winter in Florida. It wasn't my ideal scenario, but rents in New York were high even back then, and I took her up on the offer. Queens was not my first choice of places to live. Psychologically it was two steps backwards from Stamford. It was as if I had singlehandedly reversed the onto-logical path of progress.

My parents had actually gotten things right for a change. In the span of two generations, they had gone from boat to Ellis Island to the Lower East Side (and the Bronx) to Queens and finally to Stamford, a leafy validation of the struggles that preceded them. They did stop short of the golden ring; after being settled in Stamford for a while, my mother, seeing friends and neighbors trade their starter homes for larger homes in Stamford and other richer towns on the Fairfield County coast, began to pine for Greenwich. As comfortable as Stamford was, Greenwich held the allure of having the best of everything: hous-es, shopping, schools, clubs, beaches, cars, and attitude.

I had brought this cycle abruptly to a halt. Queens was defeat. Manhattan was the place to enjoy life as a young single guy. I would have liked to have seen a study showing the difference in the likelihood of hooking up as a single twenty-something guy living with his grandmother in Queens versus living in a studio apartment on the Upper East Side of Manhattan. And recreation was another problem. Manhattan had gyms and cool parks. While there was soccer in Queens, it was mainly played on dusty patches of parkland scattered throughout the remains of Flushing Meadow Park, where the 1964 World's Fair was held. Woodside was about as urban as it got. I think every inch of the hamlet is either asphalt or concrete.

It was strange moving into the house on 58th Street. As much as Queens was considered the "garden" borough of Manhattan—and Queens does here and there evoke a sense of being treed and green—it is mostly an act of urban deception. After high school I lived in two urban places, Chicago and Boston, and a semirural one, Ithaca. I was not a stranger to cities, but Queens caught me off guard. In recent years, Queens has been recognized for its diversity and vast array of ethnic restaurants and shopping, but it has never been able to ascend to the ranks of hipness. Brooklyn, by contrast, has become white hot, with its prewar architecture and abundant loft space. With the exception of Douglaston, Little Neck, Malba, Forest Hills, and parts of Bayside and Flushing, the housing stock in Queens is pretty utilitarian.

My grandmother's house on 58th Street was close to Northern Boulevard, a commercial spine that was not designed for walking. While 58th Street was tree lined and nicely shaded in the summer, Northern Boulevard was a vast hot tarmac with faceless auto dealers, diners, and gas stations. Woodside was like a place that had been shaken inside out with its innards on the outside. Even in its downtown area, Woodside was in the shadows, the elevated tracks of the subway obscuring the sun even during the middle of the day. Devoid of parks, Woodside makes do with schoolyards.

Not being able to afford a gym, I would take a ball and kick it against a concrete handball wall and try to improvise some kind of workout routine. Occasionally I would take to the streets to run. The numbered streets and avenues of Queens, frequently intersecting at oddly oblique angles, make for very confusing navigation. Unlike Manhattan, you can't count on making a series of turns to lead you back where you started. I'd try to keep the jogging to a fairly desolate stretch of 37th Avenue.

Being deserted was my main problem. I had a strange, bicameral existence. By day I was in midtown Manhattan, tucked into the 38th floor of a depressing skyscraper on Third Avenue. From the early morning swelter and crush of the subway to the cafeteria lunches and elbow-to-elbow walks to and from the subway, I was suffocated by bodies in Manhattan. Queens was a wasteland except for cars and taxis, which pinged through the intersections with third-world impunity. If you saw a live person walking on a Queens street, except from a parking lot into a diner or a store, you had to be concerned. It was like an urban area, except without youth, vigor, and any hint of sexiness.

For that, I had one threadbare connection to the swinging single life. Paul, my friend from Westhill, was a banker, a real working banker and not a training-program wonk, who had smartly deferred his MBA and gone straight to work. Paul had a membership to the newly open Vertical Club, the Studio 54 of health clubs, five or six stories of spandex-clad singles on the make. Like the Lincoln Square Synagogue on the Upper West Side, cheekily known as "Wink and Stare," there was precious little working out going on at the Vertical Club and a boatload of flirting. Like me, Paul had let the soccer slide. His brother Chris, our goalkeeper at Westhill, had decided to make a go of a coaching career after playing at Southern Connecticut and briefly for a pro indoor team. Chris had scored a coaching job with a U-12 girls' team.

One day I got a call from Paul. "Chris wants to know if you want to play in a match he's organizing in Connecticut."

"Sure, who's on the team?"

"Weston and a bunch of the other guys from his indoor team."

The thought of being reunited with Weston, after seven or eight years had passed, was still unappealing. But I had met some of the other guys—all from the Caribbean, and they were decent.

"Where's the game, by the way?"

"Ever hear of a guy named Peter Brant?"

"Not really."

"He's a very rich guy who lives up in North Greenwich. Chris coaches his daughter. His buddy is Brian MacNally who owns a bunch of restaurants in the city."

"That's it?" I asked. "We're going to go to Greenwich just for a pickup game?"

"No—there's a little bet on the game. Ten grand."

At this point I got a little quiet. I hadn't heard of Peter Brant and I was way out of soccer shape. Doing two sets of tepid bench presses while crotch watching at the Vertical Club didn't quite translate into being Navy Seal fighting fit.

"What's the catch? Who's McNally getting together?"

"A bunch of busboys according to Chris. Lots of Brazilians."

I did a little research on Brant. Turns out he was, indeed, very rich, having made his money in the paper pulp business. He became a patron of the arts, and Andy Warhol in particular, having bankrolled *Interview* magazine. To indulge his interest in polo, Brant did what any self-respecting gagillionaire Connecticut mogul would do: he constructed a regulation polo field and 10,000-seat grandstand along with a minicompound to house a team of ten-goal Argentine polo professionals on his estate, White Birch Farm, in the Conyers Farms section of north Greenwich.

When you live in Connecticut, it becomes second nature to become addicted to "house porn." Everywhere you look, you are smothered with residential fantasy. My freshman college roommate Roger and I—he was from Bethel, about twenty-five miles up bucolic Route 58 from Stamford—would tour around in each other's hometowns (well, in my case we'd go to Greenwich) and gawk at the houses. Looking back, it is very queer that we did this. I guess we were metrosexuals who were ahead of our time. As far as being a house-gawker was concerned, I was experienced, having traveled the full length of suburban confections like Ponus Ridge road in New Canaan and Round Hill Road in Greenwich. It was a simpler time, way before the financial bloat on Wall Street created tear-down fever (along with the 30,000-square-foot mega house), but there were still some pretty spectacular homes to be seen in southern Connecticut.

I went jogging with hand weights a few times down 37th Street and convinced myself that I was in shape for the game. The last soccer I had played with any kind of competitive impetus was in graduate school, and that was seven versus seven, a far cry from the structure you needed to play a full game. With smaller sided games, there are nominal positions, but basically everyone goes forward and everyone tracks back. My last real position had been center midfield, at the heart of the team, and with the caliber of players Chris had assembled, I knew I would not be running the show from midfield. In fact, the more I probed, the more it sounded like our team would basically be a bunch of semipro players from Branford, with Paul and me making up the numbers.

The Saturday of the game, I got in my big bomber of a car—a '73 gray-green Impala that got about five gallons to the mile and headed north to Greenwich. I had ventured pretty far north in Greenwich, but these directions had me going for miles north of the exit on the Merritt. I had the feeling I was in Litchfield County by the time I saw the turnoff to Conyers Farms. Divided into ten-acre estate parcels, including Ivan Lendl's property at one time, Conyers was developed by Peter Brant and was intended to be a refuge for people who could not stand the hurly-burly of regular Greenwich.

Brant's place was a 200-acre spread with a whole lot of equestrian stuff going on. There were houses, outbuildings, stables, the polo field, acres of gardens, and spur roads heading off into the distance. I had arrived, but did not have the faintest idea where to park. The expression "how the other half lives" became clear to me that day. This was not what my mother used to call people who "had money." This was startling wealth. It was strangely vulgar and mannered at the same time, like Tom Wolfe in his white suits. I drove around for a bit, gawking, wishing that Roger were there to share the moment. For a house voyeur, it was the ornithological equivalent of spotting an ivory-billed woodpecker. No one would believe me if I told them what I had seen.

Finally, I saw a few assorted rice-beaters and jalopies parked by a vast expanse of grass—telltale signs of Caribbean soccer players. I parked and got out to breathe some of the most fragrant air I can recall. It was overcast, and the air, if I can recall it properly, was laden with floral and horse notes—it was as if Martha and Ralph had come together to create a scent called "Greenwich." I could envision the ad: a swarthy Argentine ten-goal polo player comes riding in from the distance. He takes off his helmet and shakes his thick, shoulder-length mane of jet black hair, a couple of strategic beads of sweat showing on his angular tan cheekbones. Coming out to meet him is supermodel Stephanie Seymour in a diaphanous summer shift. She is bearing a basket of freshly picked raspberries and a flask of homemade energy drink. He drinks greedily as the ad fades to the Connecticut horizon with the honey-toned voice over concluding the pitch: "Greenwich . . . the Scent for Men."

I walked towards what I thought was the direction of the field. Beyond a gravel path and a stable, I saw a grandstand—not really a grandstand as I drew closer, but what looked like half a stadium adjacent to the biggest piece of manicured grass I have ever seen. It was a regulation polo field. In person, a well-groomed polo field looks like an infinitely extruded billiard table, without the slightest undulation or defect. It seems like something that would be scientifically impossible to produce, like a banana without a peel. How could they get a piece of land so flat and level? I have no idea what it costs to install a polo field, and I suspect that very few people do. If you have to ask, well, I suppose it's not for you. During his very public split with his second wife, Stephanie Seymour, it was estimated that Brant was worth between $400 and $500 million.

In the distance I saw some black guys. I walked over and found Chris.

"Wow, this is a decent spot." I said.

"Nice, right? He's not hurting."

I asked him where to change. Chris pointed to a large building, a stunning shingle and stone carriage structure.

"There's a locker room in there. Check it out."

I ambled over and went into the building's lower level. The locker room was tricked out with fancy millwork, granite flooring, and fixtures better than a nice country club. It had about forty lockers, and off in the corner were showers, along with a steam room and whirlpool baths. It was like a small, super-upscale health club, and this was just the lower level of one of the many outbuildings on the property. I wanted to go upstairs but didn't want to be caught snooping, so I headed back out to warm up. Next to the polo field, there was a soccer field marked off. The vastness of the polo field so dwarfed the soccer field that it seemed like the latter was designed for Lilliputians. The playing field part of Brant's estate was so big that he could lay out a regulation soccer field next to his regulation polo field without it even making a dent on the visual landscape of the property. I was fully intimidated. I asked Chris about the 10k bet.

"The one condition," he said, "is that he (Brant) has to play."

"But does he play soccer?"

"No, but he's a great polo player."

I didn't care if we had ten Westons, if you have a soft spot on the field against a really good team, eventually they will exploit it. Not that I had any great prospects for my performance.

"Where are you going to play me?" I asked.

"Probably at right back," he said. "I have to see who shows up."

Showing up, always an issue with the Caribbean guys. Hell, even if they showed up, they didn't always show up. The other side started to trickle in, Brazilians as promised. It was very cinematic: two different ethnic groups meeting to play the world's game on a giant bucolic estate in the wealthiest town in the country. The aggregate annual earnings of every player in that game (save for Brant himself, of course) would not have kept the horses fed for a week at White Birch Lane. Eventually, all our guys got there and got dressed. Weston and a couple of guys I knew from summer league were there, along with a bunch of guys I had never met. It's always a challenge playing with new guys. You don't know what someone's preferences and tendencies are. Are they fast? Quick? Deceptive? Physical? Do they share the ball or take an extra dribble or two? Or, like Weston, are they consummate egoists, out for their own personal glory?

One guy who had definitely been out for personal glory was Edmund Converse, the Bankers Trust president who assembled the land for Conyers Farms in 1904. "Conyers" was the Old English spelling of Converse, and throughout the early part of the twentieth century, the property was a working farm that supplied much of the food supply for the city of Greenwich and was one of its largest employers. Skilled laborers and artisans were brought in to create outbuildings and architectural follies, including a gigantic pipe organ for the original estate and a forty-foot-high clock tower.

Like Matthias Sindelar, Converse, who died in 1921, died with some suspicion that he was murdered. Peter Brant, no stranger to the tabloids, bought the 240-acre property in 1980, at the age of thirty-four. An arts patron, Brant continued the tradition of architectural curation at Conyers Farms. Of the some thirty players assembled at the field that day, I think I may have been the only one more focused on the construction techniques used in the assembly of the stone and shingle locker room than the game itself.

During warm-ups I felt like I was in Las Vegas, staring at a tromp l'oeil polo stadium at some cheese ball hotel like the Paris or the Luxor. Polo for the masses. Steve Wynn may yet do it—construct a regulation polo field around which would be four 1,500-foot-high towers each containing 8,000 hotel rooms. It could be called the Sky Chateau or Chateau Polo and would be yet another cultural touchstone for the $12.99 all-you-can-eat crowd.

More than any other time in my life, class distinctions were illuminated for me standing on Peter Brant's soccer field. There we were, fifteen Caribbean guys, mostly high school grads or in community college, plus Chris, Paul, Brant, and me. Having gone to schools with lots of rich kids, I thought I would have been prepared for seeing wealth in action. But the gulf between Peter Brant and me was a veritable polo field. He joked with his buddy McNally but only made a superficial effort to chat with anyone else. He was cordial, but detached in a way that suggested "you can visit my estate, but you are not my guest." It wasn't anything explicit in what he said or did, but by his body language I could tell that he wasn't going to brook casual banter with any of us.

The sky was getting dark quickly, and Chris sent out a starting lineup that had Paul, Brant, a few others, and me on the sidelines as subs. We started well and took a 2-0 lead. About thirty minutes into the first half, I went on at right back, with Paul in midfield. We kept the pressure up and kept the lead at halftime. In the second half the sky opened and it started to pour. Brant was a world-class polo player, and in decent shape, but clearly not a soccer player. Chris pushed me up top, and with us leading 4-1, I found myself at the edge of the box with a good look at goal. I shot and scored: 5-1. We added another to make it 6-1, and with everyone completely drenched, we hightailed it to the field house to change.

I was prepared to head right back to the city with Paul, but Chris came around and said they would have some food and drinks upstairs. The second floor was totally different than the gym and lockers below. It was set up lodge-style, but with polo substituting for the hunting. It was a shrine to the sport and to Brant's White Birch Farm team, one of the top teams in the country and a feature on the domestic circuit. When I got upstairs there were a few players from both teams, and also about six or eight of Brant's friends—social register types who had come to watch the entertainment. It was weird. They were decked out in their whale pants and Greenwich club gear, and it was definitely like being paraded in front of the Royal Court. I was frozen— thank god Paul was there, because between the Caribbean guys and the loafer set, I was frozen in social time. At their best, the Caribbean guys were awkward conversationalists. I could only imagine what the opening line would be with a guy who had a $100 million trust fund and lived in Bonaire Farm: "Blood-clod, sum soccer game today, mon."

I got some food and sat down staring at the wall. Paul came up, and we were talking for a minute or two, when Brant's wife appeared and started walking around handing things out to our team. When she got close to us, I looked up and smiled. Without saying anything, she smiled and handed me a check. It was for $100—I had gotten my first and last ever payment for playing soccer. Paul chuckled. "Chris had to pay those guys to show up. Nice little bonus, huh?"

Basking in the glory of being a soccer professional lasted about five minutes. After I reflected on it, it was more humiliating than anything. I wasn't that much younger than Brant, and I probably had a swankier education, but here he was treating me like the hired help, flinging a hundred bucks at me so he could be diverted on a Saturday. Also, he made ten grand on the game, so even after paying the team and springing for the buffet, he made a few bucks. That was chump change to Brant but seemed like a fortune to me. And I wondered about the other guys. They seemed stunned in the headlights. Most of those Caribbean guys scrambled around doing blue-collar jobs and playing soccer for a little cash on the weekends. For them, it was like a trip to a parallel soccer universe where megawealthy folks get their rocks off. And get his jollies Brant did, gloating over McNally when he finally showed up in his après-soccer attire. Looking every bit the dashing polo mogul and foreshadowing another mogul, Roman Abramowitz, Brant, without saying a word to me, gave me a very down and dirty lesson on the economic imperative of sport: open your checkbook and the best will come.

If it was not my destiny to conquer Greenwich, then at least I could move to Brooklyn. After deciding that commercial banking was too much of a soul-sucking enterprise, I decided to join a boutique real estate firm and learn the business from the ground up. One of my cohorts had an apartment in Park Slope and was looking for a roommate. I bid Woodside and my grandmother farewell and took the room in a bright floor-through apartment on President Street, in the heart of the neighborhood.

Park Slope in the late 1980s was a far cry from what it is today. Seventh Avenue was the only really decent commercial street. But two differences between Queens and Brooklyn immediately jumped out: the architecture and the park. Brooklyn is a borough of distinguished-looking brownstones with quiet tonal character in browns, reds, and grays. Queens is dominated by brick homes and looks more institutional, the newer stock of brick homes lacking the gravitas of the brownstone. The big idea in Brooklyn is Prospect Park. Because it is not as commercialized as Central Park and not as heavily trafficked, Prospect Park has acquired a more naturalistic patina than Central Park, which on busy weekend days can resemble a theme park.

After moving into the apartment, I had no idea whether there was soccer in the park, but I discovered a pickup game on the broad lawn near the eastern entrance where I lived. It was decent, but the attendance was unpredictable, and one day I decided to head further south, into the wooded valley off the edge of the great lawn. I came to a clearing and saw a very high-octane game going on one day—all black guys. The next day, I headed back a little earlier, and when they showed up I started to kick around with them. There were soon about a dozen guys, and I learned they were all Antiguan. Right off the pace of the game was fast. There was also a purity about it. When you have a "United Nations" game going, with multiple ethnicities, it can be a real dog's dinner; every individual has a different idea of how soccer should be played. When there is only one ethnic group, there is a tacit understanding of how to play and, equally important, where to play. You see this phenomenon when national teams come together with very little practice time, and they play with a cohesion that approaches, and at times surpasses, that of the best club teams in the world. When soccer is started at a young age, the combination of muscle memory, imprinting from watching older people play, and a general ethos about what style your country plays comes together and becomes a national style. With the Antiguans, there was pace and an emphasis on one- and two-touch passing. More than any pickup game I had ever played in, there was no time to linger on the ball. It was close to the game I saw near the Montmartre, with North Africans. In the film *Pelada*, the filmmakers playing pickup in France note that the game resembles a cross between soccer and martial arts. In Brazil, with its tradition of the African martial arts and dance hybrid of Capoeira, the emphasis on fluid, creative, and attacking soccer follows naturally.

One thing that struck me was how different the Antiguans were from the Jamaicans I had played with at Westhill. If you were apt to draw a simple conclusion, you would guess that two small Caribbean island nations would produce players that were similar in temperament and playing style, but in my experience this was far from the truth. The Jamaicans I played with were enigmatic and tended towards being phlegmatic. The Antiguans played a more positive, supportive style of soccer, and they worked harder when they didn't have the ball. I enjoyed playing with the Antiguans as much as anyone I have ever played with. It may not have been because they were Antiguan per se—more likely, it was because I was the only non-Antiguan out there. In the ravine with the Antiguans, I felt like I was playing soccer with all the static removed. They had a created an intriguing little niche in an offbeat, deserted spot. Having played with a hodgepodge of nationalities my entire life, I had always believed that soccer involved too much petulance and arrogant behavior. You had to curry favor to get the ball and be stoic when your teammates blatantly fucked up. By the looks of it, it wasn't that way for the Antiguans, and it wasn't that way for the Argentines at Chicago or Staples High School. Soccer poetry was out there if you hung around long enough.

Other than that, Brooklyn was almost as deadly dull as Queens, hard to believe in the 2010s when Brooklyn is one of the Fauxhemian and Celebutard centers of the planet. My room-mate Bruce and I would try to artificially create excitement. Without money, this usually meant striking out for other parts of Brooklyn, either on foot or by subway, and using our keenly honed sense of real estate intuition, we would hypothecate value where we saw potential.

Our problem was that we were about twenty years too early. Under David Dinkins, an affable mathematician who just wanted to be loved, New York degenerated into a giant crack den, suppressing development, growth, and confidence in the city's prospects. The pattern in New York is that things happen in Manhattan and then trickle to the "other" boroughs, although in recent years this trend has been reversed, particularly in Brooklyn, where hipsters and new ideas have flourished against the backdrop of the rejuvenation of the Williamsburg, Red Hook, and Dumbo neighborhoods.

But Bruce and I, without a gym, and one-half of a girlfriend between us (Bruce's girlfriend lived in Boston and only came down occasionally), we were urban nomads. A good Saturday workout for us consisted of walking to Fort Greene and, while admiring the magnificent brownstones, lamenting the fact that the neighborhood was so dangerous. We would then hoof it to downtown and, in true Brooklyn fashion, buy a pink rubber Spaldeen ball to use for a handball in one of the empty-vest-pocket urban "parks" that are found all over the city. It was always hot, and we were desperate for air conditioning. Part of the New York City hazing process was to suffer the indignities of street life through wandering in the brutal heat. The main challenges were finding a place to piss, finding something cool to drink, and finding a place to sit, that didn't (a) involve sitting on empty crack vials or (b) involve getting harrassed or worse by a crack addict.

Even getting to work was an ordeal. In New York there is no such thing as linear, crow-flying distance. Rather, it is the location, and more importantly, the quality of subway stops that matters. Our apartment was equidistant from two trains, the D, in downtown Park Slope at 7th Avenue, and the F, at 9th Street in the other direction on 7th. Our preferred train was the D, which inexplicably became the Q at random times, which was only preferable because the Q wasn't as crowded. Both trains went the sky route, that is, on a bridge over the East River en route to Manhattan. The pattern of our summer commute was like this:

Bruce: "What train do you want to take today?"

Me: "How about the D. Maybe we'll get a Q."

Bruce: "OK."

All suited up, Bruce would shove some food in a bowl for his Himalayan cat, Simon, and off we went. Sweating easily by the time we reached the station, we'd enter through the turnstile where we were met by a swelling crowd of other professionals and lower-status workers eager to get to work.

"Is it hot in here, or is it me?" I'd ask Bruce. We doffed our suit coats and braced for misery.

Sadly, in today's progressive energy environment, where carbon footprints are being reduced and renewable energy sources are being developed, no one has thought to harness one of the world's most potent forms of heat generation: the New York City subway platform. If it was 92 degrees and 86 percent humidity outside, the numbers spiked a good 30 percent inside. How on god's earth did a perpetually dark, masonry-enclosed space get to be so hot? This was one of life's basic mysteries back then.

During the Dinkins regime, everything was left to go to hell. The subway platforms turned you into a slathered side of grilled meat, the cars were smelly cauldrons of hate and fear. Festooned with graffiti outside and inside, a car would lurch to a stop, its air brakes squealing with the intensity and force of a symphony of air horns. Sometimes the doors would open, sometimes not. Sometimes they would open very slowly only to slam shut in your face, leaving you to wonder about how poorly the trainman had been treated as a child. If the doors did open, you would be forced to walk the gauntlet, or should I say, a gauntlet of rear-ends. The defensive posture adopted by a New York City subway rider who does not want to let you on is to show you his or her ass. And in general, this is not an ass designed to be shown in a J. Crew catalogue, but a bagel-fed, wide-bodied, not-taking-any-prisoners kind of ass.

If we were lucky enough to actually get on a train, then the fun started. Before leaving the station, the doors would start a sequence of slowly opening and slowly closing, sometimes five or six times. A garbled message would come on over the loud-speaker: "Passengers . . . clear . . . door . . . can't . . . move."

With the car not moving, the riders would start grumbling and with each open/close sequence, the conductor would get more and more pissed off, reaching a crescendo: "This train will not move until the door is clear!"

With the doors finally closed, the train would slowly, very slowly, start to roll, and then . . . lurch to a sudden stop. Newspapers and briefcases would fly right into your coriders lap, as if people weren't agitated enough about being late and having sweated through their outfits. Barely feet out of the station, the train would stop in the darkness of the tunnel—hot dark and airless, packed shoulder to shoulder, with the audio silent. It was hell, and this was the start of our morning commute. On cue, the true denizens of the underground—the crackhead beggars, would start their assault on the car. With no air circulation, smell traveled quickly, and the addict's fug could be detected from a car away. Often limping to exaggerate their plight, the beggars would slowly, agonizingly, drag themselves through the car, making just enough bodily contact to cause folks to contort themselves away from a grubby hand, or worse, a soiled lump of trouser or free-swinging satchel. This was the golden era of begging, when harassment was practically institutionalized. The beggar operated with absolute impunity, bordering on outright aggression. Coming down from a crack-high-imparted desperation and an aggressive stance that proved intimidating, some panhandlers earned several hundred dollars a week or more.

Finally, leaving Brooklyn, the train would start to ascend over the East River, chugging like freight running out of coal. It would then stop on the bridge. After five or ten minutes of silence (except for more muttering and cursing from the riders), the garbled, universal New York City subway message would come on: "We have . . . congestion ahead . . . we . . . will . . . be . . . moving . . . shortly."

No explanation, no reason, no logic, just complete stagnation. If it wasn't your day, the homeless guy would suspend his begging in your car—sometimes so close to you that you feared wearing his special scent all day.

This was the basic conundrum of commuting to Manhattan in the 1980s—arriving at work thoroughly spent and sweat-soaked, all before you had a chance to even start your workday. Bruce and I worked for a wacky little commercial real estate firm in its boutique real estate brokerage group. It was a mix of "hitters," that is to say, people connected to money and investors, and a bunch of pretty smart young people out of college. The doyenne of the group was a Park Avenue lawyer turned residential real estate broker, who was part society lady, part street fighter, and part impresario. The hitters were led by Abby and Megan, the former a hard-boiled, thirty-five-something Jewish gal with an edge and a bunch of downtown investor clients. Megan was younger—late twenties—and her claim to fame was being married to a rising New York syndicator and developer. He was developing a tower on 3rd Avenue and thus had demigod status among me, Bruce, Sam, and a couple of the other younger guys, including the "head" of our department, a southerner who affected the pose of a Virginia gentleman to great effect with women. He and Megan worked a have and have-not system in the office, the hitters having their own clique, while the junior folks nibbled at the edges, trying to get in with the cool kids.

One of the perks about the firm was that it was at 600 Madison Avenue in the heart of the Plaza district, the most expensive in New York. At lunch, on a budget, the obvious move was to pick up a sandwich and head to Central Park. Bruce and I befriended one of the assistants to the residential brokers, a ninety-something-pound Asian woman named Kim. We would eat our sandwiches, people-watch, and head back to make cold calls and push paper. One day, one of the first hot days of early summer, we headed over to the lake, sat down by the bank, and unwrapped our sandwiches. Without a word, Kim stood up and unwrapped herself, stripping down to a tiny white bikini. She calmly lay down and started tanning. Bruce looked at me, and I looked at Bruce. I knew at that point that I had to move to Manhattan. Later that summer in Fire Island, I was jogging on the beach. When I came to the clothing-optional stretch, I saw a familiar silhouette—Kim out for a frolic.

During the time I was at the kooky firm, I took my broker's exam and met a guy named Brad, who looked like a Ralph

Lauren model. Like me, he went to Cornell, but unlike me, he went to the Cornell that existed in the realm of Dave Grumman; that is to say, the monied, influential Cornell that had churned out legions of industrialists and successful engineers through-out the previous century and a half. Brad was tall, trim, and had graying temples. He wore simple classic clothes and was one of those guys who seemed to be created by a stylist, everything in place. He was also a master builder and a pioneer in the south-ern part of Soho, having bought a freestanding building on Crosby Street in 1985, with a plan to convert full floor units to coops. He took the top floor for himself, which had the poten-tial for a dramatic roof terrace, but since there was no elevator, you had to climb twelve flights of stairs. Brad was in the middle of converting the project, with his buddy Jim doing a lot of the work. I got interested in the building and the neighborhood, and Brad soon recruited me to do manual labor, a trade-off I didn't mind since I got to hang out in Soho and learn a bit about construction. Absent a gym membership, it was also a decent way to stay in shape.

Brad was a talented designer, and for the first time I started to see beyond plain vanilla architecture and construction. Of course, it helped to have a few bucks. Brad's taste leaned towards elegant cherry bookcases, steam showers, and custom-made rose planters for his deck. His aesthetic was rustic-modern, with a hint of Indonesian retreat and a soupçon of industrial chic. It seemed like the perfect apartment.

In the course of helping Brad out and getting my real estate salesperson's license, I decided to get serious about getting a job in real estate development, a discipline that was way too "pragmatic" to have gotten on the radar in any capacity at the University of Chicago Graduate School of Business. The more I looked around, and the more I got exposed to the inside world of real estate dealings at the boutique brokerage firm, the more it became clear that the built environment was the focus of a lot of money, and it brought together a lot of different talents and disciplines. If I was able to get a real job in Manhattan, then it was a short matter of time before I could move to Manhattan.

As cool as it was playing soccer with the Antiguans in Prospect Park, I wanted to check out the scene in Central Park. I wondered whether in fact there was any soccer in Manhattan, which seemed to be populated by the rich and the poor, without a lot of ethnic pockets except at the very northern tip of the island. The poor residents of Manhattan, mostly black and Puerto Rican, were into basketball and baseball and definitely not soccer. There were busboys by the ton, to be sure, but didn't they just work twelve-hour shifts and go home to Ozone Park or wherever?

I found a job with a company that had the pretentious sounding name of The Littlefield Property Corporation. Littlefield was a UK Trust Company, which meant that the majority of its shares had to be held by life insurance companies. In addition, Littlefield's chairman held shares in trust for a British orphanage. Littlefield was quintessentially British, with one exception—the chairman was Jewish. Besides him, the board of directors was made up of a group that clung to the notion of British superiority with vitriolic fury, a red-wine-swilling, gay-bashing, racist bunch of entitled do-nothings whose main objective with its U.S. operations was to concoct reasons to bring their wives over for extravagant holidays.

Watching *Mad Men* today, I see that there was little progress with regard to the way the British viewed society and the workplace. For the cadre of directors and executives that ran Littlefield, maintaining protocol and enforcing the hierarchy was everything. One day, my boss Fitzwilliam called my colleague Tony and me into his office to deliver some good news: we were going to each be getting a company car. I had no idea why. I commuted by subway, bus, or foot to work everyday from my apartment on West 86th Street, and our big project was in Manhattan. Once every two months or so I went up to Connecticut, where we owned a few parcels of raw land and kept a very entertaining local lawyer on retainer in the event that we wanted to rezone the parcels. For that trip, I took Metro-North from Grand Central and walked to Beecham's office from the Milford train station.

We also had the unfortunate distinction of owning a good chunk of downtown Buffalo. Occasionally Fitz would tell me to get up to Buffalo to check on the profligate duo that ran our investment up there—a fat cat attorney who was a friend of the chairman and our property manager Tom. With the exception of the land we owned in Monroe, none of this required a car.

"You guys are getting a car, but I've got to talk to England. I'm getting a Lincoln—Walker (the vice chairman) has a Mercedes, of course, and a Lincoln won't show him up when he's here. I don't know what you guys are gonna get. Why don't you do some research and tell me what you want."

Weird. Even in 1988, parking in Manhattan cost a ridiculous amount, and it was a titanic hassle to get the parking jockey to get your car in and out, especially in the crowded, Upper West Side garages.

"How about parking?" I asked. "It's almost three hundred a month."

"All right, we'll figure out the parking. Do some research."

I spent more time at Littlefield researching cars, going out to lavish meals (both with and without the Brits), and going to mindless meetings than I did actual work. It was the go-go '80s, and money had a life of its own, pinging from the banks and investors to lustily conceived real estate projects without a whiff of a tenant. In our case, Fitzwilliam engineered the perfect recipe for a disastrous project: overpay dramatically for the land, or in our case, an "assemblage" of smaller improved lots that could be combined to create a larger project, select a location that was off-pitch, and underwrite the project with unrealistic rents and lease-up projections.

Enabling this show was a cast of New York real estate apparatchiks led by an indomitable force of nature named John Pearson. Fitzwilliam was obsessed with Pearson. He referred to him as an "Irishman," ostensibly as a slight, but partly in an insular way, implying a sense of unspoken brotherhood. Pearson was everything that Fitzwilliam wasn't: big, loud, gruff, rich, entrepreneurial, and misogynistic. He was a street brawler who was the most successful commercial real estate broker in the country for many years running. During the time that Fitzwilliam worked in the corporate real estate department for GTE, Pearson was the firm's corporate leasing agent. After being eased out of GTE, Fitz landed the Littlefield job with the mission of getting Littlefield established in New York.

Fitz was driven crazy by some of the consultant contracts he inherited, including some of the law firms we used. One of them had gotten the company invested in the pistol-hot markets of Danbury, Buffalo, and downtown Los Angeles in the 1970s. The firm was on retainer for about $13k/month—in the mid-1980s! In the days before shareholders were vigilant about these sorts of things, no one ever thought to look at the bills that closely. What I got was a lot of bitch sessions in Fitz's office.

"Holy cripes, did you see this legal bill?"

He pushed the paper across his desk. I looked at it—the number usually ranged between $13k and $17k per month. I was all of twenty-six years old, not at all wily in the ways of pricey consultants, but it still seemed a lot.

"Yes, that seems like a lot," I said diplomatically.

"That's a crap load of money." Fitz, as white a man who ever lived, with white tufts flanking his shiny head, would turn crimson, his only real sign of being angry. "Wait'll the vice chairman gets a load of this one. This has gotta stop."

This would go on for an hour, what passed for work at Littlefield. In the meantime, Fitz himself had become accustomed to the high life, courtesy of his own expense account. Our in-house counsel and CFO was the anti-Fitz, a mumbling and persnickety guy, who counted every bean that came in and out of the office. He was perfectly named: Myron. Myron was fond of saying everything smelled like "wet shit." And he invoked that phrase most often in conjunction with Fitz's expense accounts. So there was basically a knock-on effect, or a massive case of projection: Fitz would rail against the lavish habits of the English board members and the pricey consultants, and Myron would rail about Fitz's excesses. Some days at "work," I would shuttle between Fitz and Myron's office, each confiding in me about the other's personality deficits.

As time went on, it was clear that what mattered at Littlefield was status. The same obsessive accumulation of status created the distinction between Westport and Stamford, between Peter Brant and Brian McNally, between Brad and me. The gradations of money—between making money, having

money, and having a lot of money—dictated what you thought
of yourself, and presumably what other people thought of you.
The term "hitter," which the uber brokers Abby and Megan used
to describe certain real estate investors, was expressly about
money and how freely an investor used it. A hitter bid high and
closed the deal. Other investors kicked the tires and hemmed
and hawed. If you snoozed, you lost. Littlefield was not about
hitting, but about posturing. Absent any real power, Fitz and
Myron used the power of the expense account to make a state-
ment. If we were out to dinner there would be fretting over the
wine list.

"What do you think about the Gavi?" Fitz would ask.

"I prefer Barolos. Is the table getting fish or meat?" Myron
would chime in, always the pragmatist.

"The Brits would get the Barolo. At eighty bucks a bottle, I
might add."

"The Barolo it is."

The next day of course, Myron would have me in his office,
bitching about how Fitz didn't care—frankly never even looked
at his expenses. Fitz desperately wanted to be a hitter. To this
end he joined a club—the Union League Club. The ULC was
founded under the pretense of preserving the rights of emancipated slaves. To my youthful eyes, entering the attended
entrance of the club, nothing could have been further from the
truth. In fact, there was a lantern jockey air about the place that
suggested that the "freedom" of men of color extended to them
picking up wet towels and refilling glasses of iced tea. Sure Fitz
addressed them by name, and they snapped into action when
he beckoned for another glass of white wine—insisting that it
be cold—or asked for a couple of shrimp salad sandwiches. The
whole enterprise smelled like a rat and I felt goofy about it.

After trouncing Fitz in squash yet again, he made the same creepy suggestion: "Hey, why don't we get a sandwich and eat it here."

"Here" meant the locker room, as in eating your sandwich in your sweaty clothes inside the locker around a dozen or so other sweaty white men in various states of undress. Not exactly a crusader for hygiene, I never quite got comfy with staring at the nether regions of the hirsute members of the Union League while I scarfed my sandwich. The uniformed black man brought the tray and set it down in the locker. I glanced from my plate, to a flaccid white butt, and back to my lunch. Fitz, mustering his angst-ridden Catholic school and Marine Corp resolve, lustily bit into his shrimp salad. I was being hazed. My idea of lunch was at a clean table, with a tablecloth and silverware. I liked to wash my hands. I was never in the military, but this was like eating in battle conditions, shrimp on toast substituting for the MRE.

Myron, a nonathlete, was specifically excluded from Fitz's and my sporting diversions. When Fitz hired me, he was fifty-two years old and I was half that age. When you're fifty-two, you are on the steeply evanescing part of your athletic curve. It occurs to me now that Fitz hired me partly to test himself, to see if there was any vestigial bloom of his youth left by testing me on the courts. We played two sports together: tennis and squash. For tennis, we'd play at the New Canaan swim and tennis club, on crisply manicured clay courts. He would manage some pretense about going to look at our land in Monroe and Milford, and we would do a half-hour drive-by and then head to the club. In truth there was nothing to look at in Milford and Monroe. The former was about a 200-acre parcel of rolling knolls and streams that was zoned for office use, while the latter was a landlocked, undevelopable hunk of woodland property that seemed perfect for pheasant hunting and pretty much nothing else.

On a Friday, Fitz would call me into his office. "Whaddya say on Monday you take the train to New Canaan and we'll put on our hiking boots and look at Milford and Monroe."

"Put on your hiking boots" was code for "Let's fuck off all day on Monday."

It's plausible to periodically tour an investment property to make sure everything is maintained, but land? If you've seen it once, you've seen it. In the intellectual Sturm und Drang that defined the Fitz versus Myron cold war, these boots on the ground property tours were to Myron yet another example of Fitz's profligacy and lack of focus. Myron, while Fitz was flubbing yet another second serve into the net, would have been reforecasting the monthly forecast and redoing everyone's expense report with the totals carried out to four decimals.

If Peter Brant was the real deal—a hitter's hitter—Fitz was the great pretender. As he tried to have some of John Pearson's charisma and machismo rub off on him, he was also desperate to adopt the patina of the Connecticut gentleman. The first time I heard his wife's name—Muffy—I had all I could do to not choke on the remnants of the bagel stuck in my teeth. That Muffy was an equestrian and boarded a horse that made Fitz blush with fiscal fright every time he mentioned it, made the story so rich it hurt. Fitz had two kids, a prodigal, athletic son and a dicey, anorexic daughter. If he wasn't wringing his hands about his daughter coming back at 2 A.M. from some party, he was fretting about his son's lack of playing time on offense for the New Canaan Rams. Money, horses, clubs, expense accounts, and the goddamn Brits. It was opera buffa incarnate.

I thought I hit the jackpot with soccer when I was hired by an English firm. I had visions of flying first class on British Air to London, where I would be wined and dined by our staff and taken to see Arsenal or Tottenham play, or maybe both. I thought it would be nothing but soccer, soccer, soccer to talk about with the staff. But to a man—and there were only men working for Littlefield over there—not one had even a passing interest in soccer. The issue of class and sport had reared its ugly head. For the hyper-class-conscious Brits, the aura of sport was crucial, and soccer was squarely the domain of the blue-collar guy. This was especially true during the 1980s, perhaps the acme—or nadir, if you like—of soccer hooliganism in the UK. To the university O-level snobs who populated the executive ranks with their business cards full of trailing credentials—FRC, RCS, Fellow of this that and the other thing—soccer was the provenance of toothless, rampaging scoundrels. To ram home the point, Littlefield was a major sponsor of Ascot and handpicked some of its execs in the satellite offices to fawn over the horse and crumpet crowd. Fitz, invited the first year that I worked for Littlefield, was practically jelly-legged for the three or four months leading up to his trip with Muffy.

When I sat in his office, there was only one thing to stare at: the "executive" commode, which could be glimpsed when the door to the bathroom was left open. Apparently, having a private crapper was an all-important point of negotiation for Fitz, once he learned that all of the board members in London had one. And that—the concept of the private bathroom—was another sociological fillip: did a private john convey a sense of authority? Was it symbolic of an executive who was pressed to the last second, rendering a walk to the hall bathroom a waste of precious executive decision-making moments? Or was it simply there to obviate having the underlings see the boss with his pants down?

"Muffy's gonna have to get out and get a whole new wardrobe," Fitz said as I stared into his bathroom. "You can't just show up to this thing wearing your jeans and flannel shirt."

Even though I was half his age and worked for him, Fitz was lording Ascot over me.

"I'll have to swing by Paul Stuart and see if they have a sweater or something I can wear over there. Maybe a sport coat too."

Myron, of course, was not invited to Ascot. When Fitz traveled—which was rare—Myron went about trying to reorder our little office of thirteen or so people into a simulacrum of a large accounting firm. In my case, as a budding young real estate developer, Myron would call me into his office under some social pretense—wanting to talk about Fitz or how some meeting went—and would then start to run the entire project budget from scratch. I had a computer that ran Lotus 123 spreadsheets, a pretty rudimentary setup, but Myron was strictly old school, and ran the numbers with a freshly sharpened number 2 pencil and a yellow legal pad. He would scratch away, as I fought off sleep after a big lunch. Please, please, can't somebody lob an urgent call into Myron? I had to pay some semblance of attention, because he would periodically ask for inputs—"how many square feet was the retail in the subconcourse?"

Without Fitz around as an escape hatch, I knew that it would be a long week while he was sunning himself at Ascot.

* * *

One thing I realized with maturity was that my chosen field, real estate development, was not a career but an up or out profession. It wasn't exactly that I wasn't good at it, but that I had failed to crack the code. I was not a member of the Lucky Sperm Club, bequeathed an empire by my dad and uncles to cut my teeth on as a young buck, pretending to actually work while knowing that I had several hundred million in the bank (or pending while the old man was still alive), and pretending to work every day. The alternative was figuring out how to get "opium," other people's money, specifically big institutional money that you could deploy on your behalf in a fund, skimming just enough off the top for yourself to get rich. Based on the few brokers and young developers who contrived to set up their own funds, this was a result of a mystical cocktail that consisted of luck, pluck, balls, ego, and hard work, although, like Coca-Cola, I could not tell you the specific ingredients.

As for the LSC members, I ran into enough of these to staff the cigar lounge of the Billionaire Boys Club in perpetuity. There should be an ironclad rule in the workplace—no one is allowed to wear a suit that costs more than ten times your age. As young guys in real estate, Bruce and sometimes my friend Sam and I would head down to St. Laurie's, an early adopter of the "Men's Warehouse" formula, and pick up one or two (usually one) ill-fitting off-the-rack suits that were purportedly "hand tailored" but fit like two slabs of cardboard. These were glued and fused like model airplanes, and god forbid you should get caught in the rain in a St. Laurie suit, because it warped like American cheese under the broiler. But if you had a meeting with an LSC kid, they would come in wearing a made-to-measure suit made from the good stuff, the drape just so, the buttons functional, the buttery smooth weft of the fabric up in your face like their cologne and slicked back hair. Unlike guys like me, hired guns who were paid a salary to speak using proper grammar and relied upon to create spreadsheets that projected project costs and IRRs down to a gnat's ass, all you had to do to be an LSC kid was to show the fuck up. That was it, you just had to be in the room and represent the Money. The Money was always right no matter how retarded the people were on the other side of the conference room table. Another job that the hired guns had was to nod in vehement agreement with anything the Money said. If they proposed that you run down Madison Avenue with your pants down around your ankles with a chicken mask on, my job was to commend them on their insight into how to get a deal done.

At one point, I was hired by a British company that specialized in running highly profitable clothing marts. They were one of the most nimble and forward-thinking companies in the space, with large holdings on Kings Road in Chelsea. As an investor in Littlefield, they popped over to the New York office a few times and got a bug about owning an office building in Manhattan. They paid me cash on the side to start sourcing an acquisition, and for the better part of a year, I tried to get them a neat little asset, 1776 Broadway, a 135,000-square-foot class B building at the corner of Broadway and 57th.

It was a chance for me to make the leap from schlub to mogul. My deal was to get paid to negotiate, and if I was successful, I'd get a piece of the deal. Not a big piece, but even the tiniest ownership interest would have given me a toehold in the business. The two main negotiators on the other side were Bruce and Mike. Bruce was the young partner and the asset manager, and Mike was the big Macha, the syndicator, as they were known back in the day. A syndicator was someone who raised investor cash to buy property. They were the general, or managing partners, and for their effort, they got a piece of the transaction, usually around 20 percent. It was a pretty sweet racket when the Feds allowed for accelerated depreciation, and the tax shelter benefits for wealthy investors from these transactions were 100 percent per year or better. The best part? A building could be complete shit: falling apart, poorly run, practically vacant, but as long as it generated tax losses, it was a fantastically profitable venture.

The corollary to this was that prices for commercial buildings were bid up by syndicators. My buyers were foreign, and not so smitten with the idea of piling up gigantic tax deductions that they couldn't use anyway. I settled into a groove, meeting every Wednesday afternoon with Bruce. He was a smart guy who acted dumb, or a dumb guy acting smart, I was never sure: more street fighter than book smart in any event. In the days before scanner and Internet war rooms and computerized due diligence, you had to look at paper, and lots of it, to figure out what was going on with the leases and the asset. Bruce trickled this out in dribs and drabs, and he and Mike dangled a big asking price in front of me. I had a Sisyphean task: the more we negotiated, the higher the price got. They knew that I was fronting for a UK group, and it was clear that they smelled a giant payday. What they didn't know was that my guys were as shrewd as anyone, real junk and muck dealers. I was happy. I'd spend two or three hours between meetings in a conference room at the building and phone conversations with Bruce that went on in circles. I'd fax a bill through and my guys would immediately mail out a check. I suppose it didn't hurt that the pound was (for a change) crushing the dollar. It was clear that the hunt was as appealing as the idea of actually owning an asset in New York.

Every third meeting or so, Mike would blow into the room, late by ten or fifteen strategic minutes. He was a big guy with a

Queens accent. His sole mission was to threaten me with pulling the deal on account of my team "not performing."

"Tell your guys they're not performing."

I had no idea what "not performing" meant. We were in contract, with a ninety-day due diligence period, and I was trying to review as much information as a guy with another full-time job could, but they wouldn't really open the "real" books, that is to say, the nonsyndication books, for me. In other words, the whole damn building appeared to be losing money. I couldn't say exactly how much, because a lot of what I got were investor spreadsheets that showed how with such and such a loss applied to income at a certain marginal tax rate, wasn't this an unbelievable investment. Which it was, no doubt, except for my guys wanted to know how much cash flow the building itself generated.

As the negotiations progressed, I was getting more confused. There were huge gaps in occupancy that I couldn't reconcile. Was the building 90 percent occupied? 70 percent? 50 percent? No one knew for sure. More telling was the fact that the more I probed, the more jittery Bruce and Big Mike got. Hubris started to take over. My guys kept reducing their offer and Big Mike increased his. The gap between the buyer's and seller's expectations grew, and my dream of owning a piece of Manhattan real estate died.

Speculative development and tax syndications started to go downhill with the TEFRA enacted by Congress. No longer would projects be viable on the basis of fat tax deductions. With the retrenchment, there were fewer real estate jobs, and new development was much harder to finance and get off the ground.

EIGHT

Number 1 Local

MAKING A LIVING wage for the first time in my life, I launched an assault on the Manhattan housing market, which was emerging from its most recent period of bleakness into a whirlwind of condominium construction. I found a building I liked, a strange little sliver of a thing shoehorned into the southeast corner of Amsterdam Avenue and West 86th Street. The apartment was a perfect example of what a young person should not have bought—narrow with high ceilings, a tiny footprint, and no built-ins. The Packard was developed by Sackman Enterprises, a coop converter turned developer. Sackman was a slick sales operation, but short on overseeing construction quality, especially with the exterior waterproofing of the Packard. My huge windows leaked water from the first rain, to the point where I would have soaking towels all over the apartment when there was heavy rain.

My sills had turned to cottage cheese, and the wind whistled like the kazoo section of the Salvation Army Band. In the mid-1980s there was a condo building boom in Manhattan, and subcontractors were being whisked quickly from job to job. Quality control was thrown out for speed, and the Packard was a big victim. The building was seductive because of the huge, multipart windows facing Amsterdam Avenue and east towards Central Park. In a city filled with lots of dark apartments, the ones in the Packard had tons of light. The problem was that they leaked often and badly. It got to the point where I might as well have pitched a tent on 86th Street.

I closed on the apartment, unit 7A, in June and moved in about a week later. On my first real commuting day to and from Manhattan, I came home on the number 1 local train and started walking east on 86th Street. Two white guys were sprinting full speed diagonally across Amsterdam Avenue, in hot pursuit of a black guy. They caught him smack in the middle of the street, threw him down, and hogtied him: an undercover bust. Welcome to the neighborhood, brought to you by the friendly folks who ran the notorious crack den, Sabu's, at 85th Street, which I had somehow failed to noticed on my neighborhood tour.

Come to think of it, when I looked down at the ground, I started to notice more of the little glass vials with the brightly colored caps, crack vials, on many of the side streets of the Upper West Side. The west side, more liberal and tolerant of the downtrodden than the east side, also was the home of a number of SROs—single room occupancy facilities—that were Manhattan's version of the welfare hotel. One block, West 92nd Street between Broadway and West End Avenue, contained three or four of these facilities. Where the welfare hotels stood, there was an entrenched culture of drugs and idleness. The bigger ones, including a notorious SRO near Macy's, were major crime centers, where pedestrians were advised to steer clear.

If I headed east from my apartment, things looked better, especially as I neared the park. By design, Amsterdam Avenue was the "poorest" of the avenues, intended to be a service spine of sorts for the wealthier streets at the edges of the island and Central Park. So walking on West 86th Street towards the park, the architecture gets grander, the lobbies more ornate, and the buildings better attended. Celebrities, locked out of tonier and snootier east side cooperatives, flocked to Central Park West. Central Park is also Manhattan's playground, although its creators, Olmstead and Vaux, would have been put off by any play more structured than bird watching. But the park has selected spots with sports facilities, including softball, tennis, basketball, and running and bridle trails. What was notably missing were any soccer fields. Manhattan had 2.5 million residents, and in its biggest park there was not a soccer goal or hint of soccer anywhere. But there had to be pickup soccer somewhere in the park. It was vast, it was flat, and there were definitely enough foreigners working in the restaurants and buildings to make up hundreds, if not thousands of teams.

On my first exploratory venture, I found a game. It was tucked into a little clearing at about 83rd Street, beyond a playground and a knoll and close to some softball fields. It was basically a dust field, and big trash cans were dragged over for goals. There were a variety of nationalities there, but the core group was Mexican, a stocky and stumpy looking lot. Soccer on West 83rd Street reflected the admixture of unrelated businesses and mysterious properties on its length, from Riverside Drive to Central Park West. The strangest stretch was between Amsterdam and the park. Small loft buildings, Cuban sandwich shops, chopped-up brownstones, and vacant lots gave that section of the street the feeling of an animated urban montage scene from the Top Cat cartoon, in which Top Cat and his henchcats run ragged over the municipal police force, a take-off on the Bowery Boys series.

There was a tailor shop I went to on 83rd, where the trappings had not been touched in several decades. The proprietor was a dapper Cuban man who seemed to accumulate archival clothing and drapery without regard to ever finishing a job. There were suits lying around in strange shades of green and brown with giant, bat-like lapels and shiny fabric that suggested that their owners were long deceased. The shop was like a lot of others in Manhattan where the path of gentrification had not reached or paused. The cartoonist Ben Katchor did a brilliant strip called Julius Knipl, Real Estate Photographer, that captured the sad beauty of the peculiar commercial elements, that when knit together, created Manhattan. Tailor shops, water tanks, ground-floor bead emporiums, bodegas, noodle shops, painted advertisements, steam holes, second-floor massage parlors, all gradually took on a patina of neglect, but at the same time created a nostalgic counterpoint to the new high rises and white-hot development and retail scene in the city. If you scratched the surface, there was still a parallel universe of old technology business in Manhattan.

While I was briefly in the banking industry, part of my training assignment was to identify a "beat," or an area that might be fertile for new business development. I decided to go west to 9th Avenue, where there were a bunch of video houses. I had no idea what actually went on at these places, many of which were called "postproduction" facilities, but whatever they were it seemed far more creative and laid back than the uptight banking office where I worked at Rockefeller Center. There, in the oppressive summer heat, the banking officers sat on the mezzanine level and worked the phones all day and passed giant binders—loan committee requests—back and forth all day long. Like the Politburo, the hegemonic influence of the loan committee was omnipresent. I was being groomed to be the consummate suit; in fact, the cut of one's suit seemed to be the most important thing about commercial banking. The officious Duke grad who was a year ahead of me and had graduated the training program to become a full-fledged Junior Officer blathered on and on about his suit wardrobe: how many he owned, when he changed over from his winter to his summer wardrobe, what was the best color to wear for client meetings.

As the summer wore on, I found more and more excuses to get out and pound the pavement. I was like a documentary photographer without his Leica, searching out New York City street life and making mental notes. One day, to escape the dreariness of the banking floor, I went out on a client "prospecting" tour. The clouds darkened to a shade of charcoal, and a monsoon-like rain opened up quickly. I was in my best dark gray banker's suit. It was too late to duck for cover, and I got soaked quickly. In the driving rain, the city takes on an imposed peace. There is shared agony: ruined umbrellas, a favorite skirt or suit ruined, fine leather shoes turning to wet cardboard. With nothing to do but embrace the wet, I kept the tour going, traveling a few miles up and down 9th and 10th Avenues, stopping in the lobbies to get a tenant roster. I knew that day that I loved New York, but hated banking.

With Littlefield, there was little pressure to work late or impress coworkers. Fitz had an hour and twenty minutes back to New Canaan, and Myron liked to hit the town, having traded in his dreary suburban New Jersey colonial for a two bedroom on the Upper East Side that he shared with his second wife. That left me free to bolt out at about 5:15, enough time to get the shuttle at 42nd Street to Times Square and the number 1 train uptown to 86th Street. The problem was that at rush hour, both Grand Central and Times Square—the shuttle nexus—were packed. The pedestrian traffic flow for the shuttle was like a bumper car ride: a combustible surge of people frantically trying to make their trains. It wasn't unusual for it to take fifteen minutes just to swim upstream against a tide of humanity to get on a shuttle train, especially just as one was letting out its passengers.

If I were in a hurry, I'd have to make like Harold Lloyd in *The Freshman*, zigzagging his way through the opposing defensive line on his way to a miraculous touchdown. Cursing, battling New York City commuters are a fierce lot. And the MTA did its best to provide an incendiary context for anger. There must be a decree in the New York City subway charter that all platforms are kept at 30 degrees above the outside temperature, but only when it's hotter than 80 outside. That puts the average summer subway platform temperature at about 110–120 degrees. Wearing a suit and moving fast in those conditions was a crazy workout. It's a wonder that gym culture ever got a foothold in New York.

Juking and hustling, I would scramble from the 86th and Broadway stop, hopping to the left side of the staircase to bolt around the folks meandering up the right side. After racing to my apartment, I'd grab my stuff—my gear consisted of cotton shorts, a jock, a T-shirt, and sneakers. Usually the game would be on by the time I got to 83rd. The custom was to just jump in, even if you made the teams uneven. This part of pickup soccer culture is much different than basketball, where you wait until there is another full team to challenge the on-court winner. Some pickup soccer just adds and adds until the game resembles a thirteenth-century Italian Renaissance town-on-town fandango. The question of what position to play starts to become an issue when a game gets bigger than four on four. Until that point, everyone pretty much is going up and down, attacking and defending. Usually there are one or two people who are genetically predisposed to either attacking or defending, and those folks quickly assume their innate positions.

What gets hammered home with park soccer is just how democratic the sport is. The core group of players were Mexicans who seemed descended from beer cans. If you glanced at one of them quickly, the take away was that they were virtually square in shape, heads eliding into shoulders without the benefit of a neck. They were also kind of chubby, many of them with barrel chests and more than a hint of gut, a body shape that looked good for shielding the ball and maintaining control, but not the body of an athlete. But these guys had an economical, short shuffling running style and seemed to be powered by solar batteries. Not only were they quick—not fast per se, but great at short bursts—they had great endurance.

As expected, they preferred to play and pass to one another, and I was forced to master their staccato passing rhythm. It also helped to learn basic soccer Spanish. A favorite word was "cambio," meaning to switch the point of attack and swing the ball to the other side of the pitch. Not to be confused with Mexicans, who at best were kind of neutral and at their worst a bit surly, were the handful of Colombian guys who showed up. Those guys were there to play some soccer, but even more to fight. Starting with a little foul, an extra chop to the shin there, a push here, and things would escalate to what I would call the "puta" point, when it became personal. The Colombians would square off against anyone and everyone and would bring the game to a complete stop. Leaving, they would throw rocks and invite people to fight. A tough crowd, those Escobar-era Colombians.

Central Park was fascinating. Whether Olmstead and Vaux intended it or not, the park is set up to be explored differently by everyone. For the naturalists (and naturists) there is the bramble, a wild strand of deciduous forest whose concealed trysting spots made for gay cruising heaven for a long time in the '80s and '90s. The bridle paths may seem pastoral until you are jogging or walking on one and a seven-foot, one-ton mare mounted by an overeager student from the Claremont Riding Academy on West 92nd Street comes thundering along, kicking up plumes of brown dust at you.

The reservoir's 1.6-mile path, officially named the Jacqueline Onassis Running Path, is perfect unless you go during the morning rush. With a path that is about twelve feet wide, you are forced into Olympian decisions: when to pass and when to be passed, when to draft and when to be drafted upon. My standard run was an "outside" lap on the bridle path, finished with an inside lap on the Jackie O running path. There is no better way to engage Manhattan than to glimpse the seasons as you jog on the path. I marked the seasons by my runs on the bridle and reservoir paths, noting the shifting winds, the autumnal flush of oak and maple leaves, the oppressive mask of midsummer, and the crunch of packed snow yielding to slippery mud. The undulations of the path take on familiar milestones and markers; rounding the turn at 96th Street, you get a glimpse of the foreboding State Office Building in Harlem, signaling the snakey section of the path leading to the home stretch. I especially liked to go for a jog on the big holidays when it was quiet. This is one of the great benefits of living in New York: the way you can sense the spirit of the place without even seeing anything. If you live long enough in New York, you can begin to discern the different holidays simply by the sound of the city. Christmas has a hush, and Christmas Eve on a snowy Sunday is about as close to silence in Manhattan that you will ever get. During the Jewish holidays, Manhattan has a great processional of temple goers, and there is a quaint nineteenth-century air about town. Despite the quiet, there is always something going on. One person's day of atonement is another's workday. The Cuban-Chinese joint staffed by Ecuadorians does not heed the Hebrew calendar so much. There is always someone eager to scarf down a half roasted chicken with black beans and yellow rice.

One great festive memory was playing in the 83rd Street dust bowl in the summer, late into the evening when Shakespeare in the Park was going on. The Shakespeare Theater, a decent-sized, but still intimate outdoor space, makes tickets available on a first-come, first-served basis, and this policy creates one of New York's basic constructs: the gigantic line that forms twelve hours prior to the event. People take blankets, baskets, the remainder of the Sunday *New York Times*, and whatever distracts them from waiting for hours to snag a couple of free tickets to *Macbeth* or *As You Like It*. The line would form at the edge of the soccer "field," and it made for a gallery of spectators, which was kind of weird at first, but got kind of fun as people would watch and get into it. The collision of street sports and the everyday activity of Manhattan goes on all over the island: cyclists performing lazy eights through traffic, urban joggers threading through the throngs in midtown, skate kids in Union Square, basketball at the fringes of the pocket parks, and soccer at the dusty fringes of the big parks.

South of 96th Street, maybe the biggest street sport spectacle was the West 3rd Street basketball court. The quality of basketball was variable—sometimes amazing, sometimes pure junk, but the entertainment level was consistently high. Games at West 3rd Street looked like a shattered theater of dreams with players who had the tools, the skills, the attitude—everything except the discipline and the breaks. You see the 6'9" guy, built like an extruded Thomas Hearns, dominant under the boards except with a pronounced limp that forces him to trail the play by twenty feet. Quicksilver guards crossover and step back effortlessly, launching fade-away thirty-foot jumpers. But attitude reigns supreme. Winners hold court, and sportsmanship is a distant cousin of bravado.

Always, whether it's Shakespeare in the Park, West 3rd Street, or a crisp November Sunday just cold enough for a wool coat and scarf, Manhattan beckons you to find its white-hot center. For a New Yorker, like the party gal glancing over your shoulder just in case there is a better move to be made, there is always another there there. The center is actually multiple points, say, the café in the basement of Barneys on Madison Avenue, the coffee line at Dean and Deluca on Prince Street, or a gallery opening on Stanton Street. If you are lucky enough to be at one of these places, you have either paid dearly for the privilege, or know someone who has. Anyone who has been out at a great lunch spot during the height of the holidays in Manhattan knows this feeling. The ambient conversation is frothy, pitched just so, and carries you along. People are dressed, and not just dressed well, as they would be in Dallas or Charlotte, but with personality and in keeping with the neighborhood.

Traversing Manhattan on either of its axes reveals a morphing sartorial feast. From 96th on down on the east side, formality and conservatism reigns, whether it is the oxford- and khaki-wearing postfraternity crowd living in "Dormandy Court," the massive rental complex at 96th Street, or the aging prepsters sporting their Gucci loafers and casually draped cardigans lower down on Park and Lex. On the Upper West Side, all things fashion become democratic. Grandparents seem to have been cryogenically frozen, wearing similar polyester separates that came in with the Lindsay administration. My grandmother died in 1995, but I'd have sworn up and down that I saw her several times in the 2000s in the vicinity of Fairway on West 74th Street.

Soccer in New York has had its moments: the Hakoah tour in the '40s, the Cosmos in the late '70s, the World Cup in '94, and Steve Nash hosting a celebrity kick-around in Tompkins Square Park in 2009 with his buddy Thierry Henry. Soccer is the split personality of sports in America: downscale in the cities, with its network of Sunday ethnic leagues and hardscrabble pickup games at the fringes of the city's parks, and decidedly middle class in the suburbs. On Wall Street and in the law and ad corridors of midtown, there does not seem to be as extensive a good ol' boy network of soccer players as there has been for football, hockey, and lacrosse. In keeping with my general lack of social awareness that hit me like a hammer in business school, I never gleaned that playing college, or better yet, pro sports could get you an edge in a lucrative career. Knowing stuff is good, knowing people is a lot better.

Hobey Baker, hockey and football hero for Princeton in the teens, was an early networker, securing a Wall Street sinecure after starring for the St. Nicks pro hockey team. Baker, who was bored by finance and crashed his plane during an aborted mission in France during the First World War, was the archetypal beneficiary of sports largesse: chiseled, blond, smart enough, and famous enough for his charisma to rub off on his friends and colleagues. Baker was a banker's son who was wired into New York privilege when his father sent him off to the St. Paul's school in New Hampshire. Perhaps the least well-known of great American athletes, Baker dazzled his classmates with extraordinary athletic feats at St. Paul's and learned to play hockey in the subarctic winters of New England in the early part of the twentieth century. Before there was such a thing as professional hockey, he played for the semipro New York St. Nick's and introduced New Yorkers to the exotic, whirling dervish spectacle known as ice hockey.

I got an inside look at this life when I met one of my boyhood sports idols in my real estate licensing class in the late '80s. While Littlefield was a real estate developer, we were in the business of leasing office and retail space, and Myron thought that it was important for me to get my license, "just in case anything should go wrong." Myron had a paranoid view of life, everything just a half step away from massive litigation.

On the first day, I scanned the room, and saw the usual array of female residential brokers, a hustler type that is bred in vast numbers in New York. There are, of course, male residential brokers, but women still dominate the profession. They are essentially a facilitator between the iron fist of the typical Manhattan coop board and the powerless (but often rich) prospective purchaser of apartment shares (coops entail the purchase of shares, condos of real property). Among the trussed and dramatically coiffed rank and file, there sat my idol, a Hockey Hall of Famer, completely unnoticed by the room. I was shocked. What was this guy, someone who I had watched on TV for years, who was a dominant player in his sport for a decade and a half, doing in a dopey prep course for real estate salespeople? After ingratiating myself, I learned he was a commercial real estate broker with one of the big houses, and was in there, like everyone else, because he had to be.

One thing the New York State Salesperson's exam is not is an academically rigorous exercise. Sure, there are some tricky terms and a bit of memorization involved, but a casual inspection of some of the course graduates would reveal, in very short order, that this test is nothing to fret over. I was happy to help my new Hall of Fame pal with a little extra tutoring; who wouldn't help one of their childhood idols? After we became friends, I learned that there was a parallel universe of sports stars, whose exalted status conveyed benefits in the clubs, bars, and arenas all over town. I had gotten a taste of the anachronistic life of patrician white men while playing squash and dining in my sweaty gym clothes with Fitz in the locker room of the Union League Club, and now I got a chance to see a couple of the other ones, the University Club and the New York Athletic Club.

There was a formula to these places: neoclassical or Beaux Art brick and limestone facades, officious porters and doormen, and common areas redolent of leather and Barbasol. The whole idea of the men's club was to create a time shift back to one's real or imagined life as a tenth grader at an elite boarding school, ideally as a star athlete. The university clubs, of course, sustained the fantasy of undergraduate life, flaunting school crests and colors like it was pledge week. I had briefly joined the Cornell Club, right after it was built on East 44th Street, in hope of getting some business connections and having the same type of convivial atmosphere as the Yale or Harvard Clubs.

The problem was that the club was new; there was no way around this, no matter how leathery the chairs and how much wainscoting detail was incorporated into the design scheme.

Acquiring a patina was something that took at least fifty years, maybe a hundred. The Cornell Club was an aspirant, an arriviste, a pretender to old money, just as Cornell itself was a perpetual also-ran in the Ivy sweepstakes. You could not possibly get to the top with such a diluted product: too many ag courses, too many students enrolled in the statutory divisions, classes that were too big, and a small town locale too far from a big city.

The Cornell Club, two blocks west of Yale's and a block west of Harvard's, was in the equivalent of upstate midtown Manhattan. To an outsider, all of midtown must seem to consist of dense, packed blocks, some with retail, some with offices, and some mixed. To real estate professionals, midtown reveals a vast number of microturfs, with a taxonomy that cascades as follows: boroughs, neighborhoods, avenues, streets, the sides of streets (north, south, east, and west), and buildings. Factors such as sunshine, ownership, level of maintenance, location of trash pickup, adjacent uses, and proximity to transit stops create a rich broth from which any given use can be a smashing success or abject failure. The traditional clubs were all set up within easy striking distance from Grand Central, where the last bits of a gimlet could be licked from the rim at 5:32 and a man could still get a seat on the 5:47 to New Canaan.

The library of the Cornell Club was indicative of the failure of the whole enterprise. One day it was empty, a long, narrow room, and then one day it was filled with regulation "library" furniture: club chairs, reading tables, and banker's lamps. It was as if Manny's Universe of Library Furniture had backed up a truck and dumped its cargo out. It seemed sad, all this new stuff. The Yale Club, by contrast, was a study in Ralph Lauren patinaed perfection: the burnished leather chairs, scuffed oak floors, and muted Asian rugs exuding patrician calm. My lot was to have gone to a second-tier Ivy League school, which may sound like an absurdity, but in some ways it may have been better to have gone to NYU or Fordham than to Cornell, which always suffers by comparison. Of course all this Ivy League pecking-order bullshit could have been obviated by having a membership at the University or Union League or Cosmopolitan Clubs where social, not academic, affiliation was key.

The club scene in New York was a grand perversion of meritocracy. It plainly exposed the myth of the middle-class childhood: that by studying hard and avoiding trouble, one could overcome the shackles of mediocrity and enjoy the good life. The good life, as evinced by the power brokers at the Yale and Union League and university clubs, was unattainable to the commoner, even one with an Ivy League degree. Working in New York, it was quickly apparent that there was nothing that special about an Ivy League degree. In Ithaca or Hanover or Providence, there is only one Ivy campus, but in New York they all converge. And while Ivy grads are perhaps found in disproportionate numbers at elite law firms and investment banks, it is also quickly apparent that there is another elite club in New York formed by graduates of the rough and tumble commuter colleges, including St. John's, City College, and Pace. These places cranked out smart operators, many of whom were smart enough to go Ivy, but whose working-class or poor parents didn't have the cash to send them or to supplement student loans. Of course there was a much bigger pool of mediocre students at these places, but the top of the class was as good and ambitious as any school's graduates.

Where Ivy and non-Ivy grads mixed in the workplace, which is to say most places in New York, there was a reverse snobbery in effect. If you were Ivy, there was the smugness with, well, having gone to an Ivy League school. If you were St. Johns or City

College, then you could stare the Ivy League sucker straight in the eye and think, "Hey, I am sitting at the same table, making the same salary, working for the same company, and I'm $100k less in debt."

Even the most democratic sounding of all the clubs, the New York Athletic Club, with its Nike-esque winged foot logo, had a secret handshake. One day my friend Bob called me to tell me he was coming up from D.C. with his over-thirty team to play a team from the NYAC. I didn't know that the NYAC fielded a team, but after a bit of research I learned that a big part of the club was like a finishing school for college athletes. I met Bob and his team at a field in New Rochelle, about fifteen miles from midtown, which was part of a waterfront sports retreat, with fields, picnic grounds, and a marina. The NYAC team had a heavily Irish flavor. Who were these guys? They didn't seem like the type who could afford an expensive private club membership in New York. I guessed that they were part of some kind of junior scholarship/subsidy program: you play for us and you can work out for free at the club.

I began to see that New York, for all its ethnic variety, was antisoccer. Central Park was a no-soccer zone with the exception of two dust patches, one at 99th Street on the east side, the other where I played, at 83rd Street on the west side. Flushing Meadow Park in Queens was filled with soccer, but the Central and South American teams there played in leagues, and it was kind of a closed society.

*   *   *

Sniffing around for soccer started to become more chore then delight. The one informal playing surface New York has in abundance is blacktop. In a completely non-soccer-related stroke of luck, I got a call from my friend Doug in the fall of 1990. He told me that he and some friends had started playing pickup hockey on inline skates at a playground on East 67th Street. He said that I should show up Saturday morning. Inline skating was getting big, with a growing group of people circling the park with their first-generation skates: giant booted things that fastened with a modified hose clamp around your ankle. The first wave of skaters took the brunt of the punishment. The sneaky bad injury was a broken wrist, from falling hard and bracing yourself with your hand. Soon they developed those funny wrist guards with a plastic protrusion that really worked but left you unable to hold anything while you skated. Nothing about inline skating appealed to me at first. It seemed kind of dopey, swishing around on the pavement and squealing on your rear breaks every five seconds to dodge something. It was also kind of spandexy in its infancy, attracting more than its fair share of posers. But hockey? Now that was kind of cool. In the '40s, roller hockey on quad skates was a pretty popular sport, especially in Queens, where my dad and his friends played in the street. Nike briefly exploited inline hockey in the mid-to-late 1990s, when it thought that it could be used as a gateway drug for ice hockey. After investing several hundred million to acquire the Bauer hockey brand, and promoting hockey heavily, Nike sold the division. But for a good part of the '90s, inline hockey flourished as a pickup sport, especially in Manhattan and on the parking lots in Venice, California.

Roller hockey on quad skates always hung on in New York. Joey Mullen, a 500-goal scorer in the NHL, grew up playing on quad skates in Clinton (nee Hell's Kitchen) where it was a bucket o' blood kind of affair. If you think about it, hockey on pavement makes about as much sense as basketball on ice; there is no give to tarmac, and because it's not ice hockey, there is kind of a macho refusal to pad up a whole lot. Gloves, shin pads, and maybe a helmet, and you're good to go. Also, the sliding properties of ice work to "cushion" your fall, whereas when you hit pavement that is pretty much a showstopper. Quad skates are not nearly as fast as inline skates but better for getting your weight behind something. When I started playing inline hockey, a couple of guys had not yet switched over to inlines. They were kids who grew up on Long Island playing old-school roller. When we all started to improve, they had to change. The beauty of inline hockey was twofold: you didn't need ice and you could be outside. Ice hockey is thrilling, but getting ice time if you are south of the 26th parallel is a royal pain in the ass and expensive. There's little good to be said about having to get a 5 A.M. rink time and spending ten or twenty bucks every time you want a workout.

East 67th Street had a playground with a chain-link fence running about 300 feet on one side and a brick and concrete wall that bordered a vocational high school on the other side. The surface was mostly slick black asphalt with a couple of rougher concrete patches mixed in. One of my friends bought a cheap orange kids' puck, the hollow kind that can't hurt you. He sliced a narrow slit in the top and stuffed it full of paper clips. It was ingenious, a New York City sports miracle. The orange puck was slippery enough to glide over the rougher, concrete sections, and the paper clips gave it the ballast it needed to sit flat most of the time. It also gave a satisfying thwack when it hit a stick just right.

Where soccer seemed to be an uphill battle in New York, roller hockey was a perfect fit. It was urban. It was gritty. It was played on hard, man-made surfaces. The cacophonous stick and skate clattering was the kind of sound you could have imagined inspiring Gershwin to write a *Symphony on Skates*. It was also smelly, mainly because the ideal roller hockey goal is a garbage can. Not one plucked fresh off the shelf of Target, smelling of new rubber, but a thirty-pound steel can from the playground, preferably empty. The best sound of all was a clean goal that hit the back of the can without touching the sides first. Like the door of a Mercedes closing, it was a very gratifying sound.

Whereas soccer had interloper status in New York, roller hockey—newly incarnated as "inline hockey"—was as much a part of the urban sports fabric of New York as basketball, albeit on a smaller scale. Roller hockey on quad skates was played extensively in Queens from the 1930s on, sometimes in the street, but often in the vest-pocket parks that dot all the boroughs of the city. These parks, almost entirely paved over, are designated as "green" spaces on maps. These parks should no more be designated "green" than the sewer system. A typical New York City pocket park has basketball rims on steel poles, massive concrete walls used for handball, and sometimes a piece or two of primitive children's play sculpture. Like nature, the parks cultivate a cycle of nocturnal and diurnal behavior. Roller hockey, due to the need to commandeer the entire park, demanded that the games start early. In New York, 7:30 or 8 A.M. on a late fall or winter Saturday is early enough to see the remnants of the previous night's activities. In the late '90s, this meant the occasional crack vial, spilt condom, and all kinds of clothing strewn about. With bottles and cans still commanding a nickel rebate from the groceries, the parks were mined by collectors with stolen shopping carts. The more enterprising among the collectors had a half dozen or so giant trash bags lashed to their carts overflowing with bottles and cans. The cart people provided an efficient service to the public.

The dog people were also out in force early. Park people and dog people are old combatants when it comes to dog poop and pee. One person's doggie piddle is another person's "sterile fluid," a phrase one guy used one morning when we complained that his dog was peeing right smack in the middle of the playground. Sterile yes, pleasant no. There are not a lot of places in the country where you can debate the rights of dogs versus roller hockey players in a public park.

Asserting territoriality not only required getting there early, but if there were only a couple of skaters, we had to make big ostentatious loops around the playground. I guess, in our way, we were marking our territory. And if the grand old bunker of a bathroom was closed, we would literally mark our territory. Part of the mystique of the New York City playground is the sporadic access to bathrooms. Beginning in the Olmstead and Vaux era of grand parks, numbers 1 & 2 were granted a rather exalted status, with toilets and urinals housed in fortress-like Beaux Arts structures, many of which survive today. The problem was that the Parks Department maintains and operates the bathrooms with the regularity of snow in Jerusalem. At 67th Street, some mornings the bathroom would be cleaned (sort of) and ready for business, the attendant puttering around and picking up loose trash. Other mornings, the building would be locked, the trash cans overflowing, with no attendant in sight. Learning how to piss in a pocket park smack in the middle of Manhattan with a bunch of hockey gear on and wearing inline skates is, well, an acquired skill. Being on the Upper East Side, the attitude towards human al fresco relief was quite different than that for canines. Below 23rd Street, no one would have looked twice at someone relieving himself or herself in an alley or in the corner of a park, but on East 67th Street, that was not OK.

The total number of players on any given Saturday ranged from eight to sixteen or so, with about ten being the norm. Ten guys with sticks who looked three inches taller than they actually were was generally enough to commandeer the whole park. Even the pickup basketball players, a macho bunch, were pushed to the corner of the playground. The one renegade was a woman, a lonely-heart sort, who showed up every week with an old, Jimmy Connors–style tennis racquet and a little plastic grocery bag filled with old tennis balls. She was about forty, thin, and sort of shapeless and didn't seem to have much strength or tennis ability. But she was always there, plunking the ball against the giant concrete sidewall of the school with a slow, upward sweeping motion that, when I saw it Saturday after Saturday, became an integral part of our roller hockey experience. No matter how the game was going, there was the tennis lady, enduring her athletic regimen. In about ten years of playing roller hockey, none of us spoke a word to this woman, and, assuming we played about forty weeks/year, we saw her 400 or so times.

The tennis lady always seemed a bit sad, her form lackluster and tennis seeming to occupy time. Her form never improved. In a city with eight million people, there is rampant loneliness. Proximity does not mean intimacy. When people are competing for scarce resources like scraps of city parks and a seat on the subway, the opposite is true. There is far more to be gained from creating a conceptual moat than through engagement. Although roller hockey took up the majority of the space at the park, there was lots of other stuff going on—tennis, basketball, kiddie bike riding, even jogging. Every activity had a perimeter, a tacit boundary that defined its natural scope. A breach of the perimeter—a stray puck or ball, or a dog walker getting too close to a game—would draw stern looks and an occasional verbal reprimand.

The New York City subway cars, many of them manufactured by the Japanese firm Kawasaki, were designed for slender Japanese behinds and provided a perfect venue for research into the sociopolitics of scarce resources. Each little plastic indentation on the bench in theory represented a "seat," but these were seats that matched the buttock profile of an average city third grader, not a well-fed denizen of say, the Bronx. Many of New York's more ample residents fit easily into two "seats," one for each buttock, but confusion set in when fractions came into play. I am an average-sized male, and I covered about a seat and a quarter, a real dilemma insofar as another equally sized person would overlap the next seat by 50 percent, and even a smaller person who consumed one seat unit would present only three-quarters of a seat to the next person. Of course, it was rare that there was a whole bank of empty seating, so it was much more common to watch the interplay between the resident seat holders and the would-be sitters, who had to quickly calculate the size of the vacancy relative to the spread factor of their behind. Eye contact, normally the currency of civil discourse, was a surefire deal killer if you wanted to sit. The only tactic was to quickly decide to go and let your bottom drop to create a gravity-assisted space. So it was with standing room in the subway cars, where bags, elbows, and newspapers did the trick of creating the two or three inches of personal space that social scientists suggest is essential to feeling comfortable.

By riding my bike to roller hockey, I got a taste of the life of the bike messenger. I had enough padding—shin pads, gloves, and helmet—to feel falsely secure in traffic. By strategically angling my stick, I created another bit of space that felt almost like a bike lane. Bike riding in Manhattan is very different than in most places. On a bike, you are like water or electricity, a utility of sorts, coursing through the streets in the flow. At the height of the bike messenger era in Manhattan in the mid-1990s, there was a guy who had full-on protection—an amalgam of hockey and motocross gear, including a giant breastplate. Topping it off, he wore a massive steel chain around his torso, a bike lock cum taxicab intimidator. Extreme perhaps, but in a city that relies on visual cues, it was the perfect strategy to carve out a little extra real estate.

I once read a clever aphorism about the distinction between bicycle riders in New York who ride to their livelihood versus those who ride for their livelihood, the point being don't mess with the latter. In my klutzed-up hockey gear and crappy old mountain bike, I could barely chug along at a decent pace, let alone weave majestic lazy eights through traffic like the best messengers. My normal route started at my building at 86th and Amsterdam, from which I headed east on 86th Street into Central Park. There was no bike lane for the 86th Street Transverse, and it mysteriously dumps you on the east side at either East 85th Street or 84th Street.

One day instead of crossing, I decided to head south on Park Drive West, the main north-south route in the park. All padded up with my huge hockey bag slung over my shoulder, I was not a speedster on my old Nishiki mountain bike and was not so fast to begin with. It was a Saturday, about 8 A.M., and it was quiet in the park—eerily quiet. I was coasting down a moderate hill, where at about 79th Street I started hearing some distant shouts.

In New York you don't think a whole lot about people shouting. But the shouts were getting louder and more persistent, and I was worried that someone was in trouble until, in a flash,

I was smothered by a huge peloton. A race! In my lumbering mountain bike prehockey reverie, I had stumbled into the middle of a spandex-clad pack of Tour de France wannabees. They whizzed by me screaming and cursing. The nerve of some fucking guy actually riding his bike through the park during their awesome race! I'm sure they had a permit, but there were no signs or warning when I entered the park. This was part of the social covenant of living in New York. There was a steady demand for privatizing bits of the city at a time. Flea markets, races, parades, and films all shut down public spaces so the Shriners or Robert DeNiro or a bunch of yuppies huffing and puffing can ensure that the unwashed masses didn't encroach on their precious recreational moments.

When the pack passed, I got the park back to myself. I was pissed, but then I thought that taking the park for a private race was pretty much the same as usurping all of a playground to play roller hockey. At least they had a permit. We had to bank on whether the Parks Department flunkie would actually wake up in time to unlock the gate. Occasionally the entire perimeter of the park would be sealed off, and scaling a ten-foot fence in rollerblades was not a picnic. But there was something intoxicating about roller hockey. Unlike playing soccer in New York, where you felt like an interloper, roller hockey felt of New York, part of its urban fabric. Like Parkour, the French-bred amalgam of gymnastics, obstacle course maneuvers, and Capoeira, roller hockey was about the built environment. The poured plastic wheels of an inline skate create a distinctive whirr along smooth pavement and a rougher-sounding noise against concrete. The clatter of sticks and pucks and skates and the triumphant thud of a goal hitting the back of a voided parks trash can were symphonic in their way. Urban too was the way in which you need to work around and with the hardscape. Every corner and wall had its own quirks, and understanding angles of inflection and deflection was essential to success. The playing surface was two-thirds smooth asphalt and one-third rough concrete. The weighted plastic puck glided easily over the asphalt, but the much higher friction of the concrete slowed it dramatically and made for unpredictable bounces and rolls.

One side of the "rink" was a wire fence, the other a concrete wall. Safety was sacrificed for vanity. My choice of headgear for years was a San Francisco Giants baseball cap, the classic 5950 model made out of wool, not from the synthetics they use today. Time and sweat turned the cap into a protean blob of fabric, perfect for molding to my head, but lacking in the protection department. I only had to have one run-in with the steel stanchion of the metal gate to switch to a hockey helmet. It was the first and only time I have been close to blacking out, and not a pleasant experience. Walking around for several weeks with a bandaged head made me thankful I wasn't in the dating pool. I was on the skittering downhill path of a marriage that fell apart when I moved to California to work for a film company, while my wife stayed in New York to work at Morgan Stanley.

When you are in a bad marriage, it's interesting how Manhattan accelerates the end of the process. Every walk, subway ride, or park outing turns into a survey for prospective mates. There they are, supple joggers, budding fashionistas, arty girls downtown, out and about. So what if half of them were taken. There were thousands more in the process of breaking up or single. With a whole lot more free time on my hands, I started to write some freelance pieces and got a gig with *Time Out New York*, writing about the nascent "World Wide Web." My beat was to cover new websites, reviewing content for a short column called "Byte Me." I had a high-energy editor who put me to the task, demanding well-crafted, 500-word pieces that deconstructed content for the emerging New York City technophiles. In the dark ages of dial-up, downloading a website was torture. In the days before I had a decent home connection, I'd have to hump it downtown and pay the hourly rate at an internet café, whose connection was only marginally faster than my home one. Paying the café fees, I pretty much broke even on the articles. Content too was primitive, the equivalent of a page or two of prose. If there was a graphic or photo attached to the site, you may as well have brought your sleeping bag, because you had a good half-day of downloading ahead of you.

Even in the very early days of the Internet, the New York New Media Club held mixers in a Flatiron loft. While people grasped the potential, there was a lot of skepticism about whether the Internet would have a transformational effect on the market or would just be a novelty, a new way of digesting information. For me, hanging out at the cafés was enough of a good thing. For one, it got me out of the smothering Upper West Side Zabars/Fairway/stroller sphere of influence and into the razor's edge of downtown New York. There was something supersexy just rolling up the broad staircase at Union Square, facing the north side of 14th Street at the southern tip of the park. Skaters, dog people, students, and folks whose daily agenda ticked to a sundial instead of a Blackberry staked out their tiny pieces of precious Manhattan turf. The improvement of the park paralleled much of the evolution of city administrations, from the crack-tolerant Dinkins era to the mercenary policies of Giuliani. The vicissitudes of politics: reaction, overreaction, and back, made for interesting happenings on the street. When I first started commuting life from my grandmother's tidy row house on 58th Street in Woodside, Manhattan was pockmarked with danger. In particular, the major crossings, Times Square, Madison Park, Union Square, Washington Square, not to mention the exotic and nefarious spots like Morningside Park and the nether regions of Central Park, were pretty much off limits after dusk. But it is exactly the shifting fortunes of these places that keep people coming back and that keep New York locked in the central narrative of the country. Like an addled boxer, the city fights off the ropes, and with a surge of financial adrenaline, almost always regains control. Parks that were once neglected dark spaces with feral dealers whispering, "Sense, Sense," offering bags of oregano-laced dope with urgency, are today like thematic playgrounds: fun for everyone.

If you spend some time on the *New Yorker*'s cartoon website, you can get an overview of the sociological transformation of Manhattan's neighborhoods in a concise, entertaining fashion. From Getz to Pfeiffer to Sempe, there are constants: the neatly formed swatch of skyline defined by the Sherry Netherland, at the inflection point between midtown and Central Park; Fifth Avenue, defined by teeming masses hoisting umbrellas, hailing taxis, and creating sidewalk logjams. The icons are alluring, but anyone who has lived in Manhattan can tell you that the fragments and little revelations are what make the experience. In a city where so much is familiar, the power of density and the accretive mystery of the built environment yield moments where déjà vu, romance, and harrowing beauty can catch you off guard.

You can go years and years living in Manhattan without setting foot on one of the vestigial cobbled sidewalks in the Meatpacking District, but if you decide to go for brunch on a perfect day in early spring, and you're crossing one of those sidewalks, and the breeze is catching the scent of a dogwood or cherry and you are with someone you really like and there's no line at your favorite restaurant and there's a woman in a diaphanous dress who just may have glanced your way and you are feeling the freshly pressed cotton of your trousers brushing your legs just so and your shoes are just springy enough and your spine is straight and the sky is beckoning, that's a day.

NINE

California Detour

I HAD A FRIEND named Dan who was an architect and a design junkie and had some well-placed friends in L.A. Dan and I met while he was kicking around New York with his other architect buddy, also named Dan. Working for developers made me a bit of an architect wannabe, and unlike a lot of other people working in development, I was actually interested in what they did, how they were influenced, and how they came to their final designs or ideas about a project. The Dans were a wacky pair—Dan 1 kind of tall and languorous, Dan 2 being short, red, and feisty. Neither lacked for self-belief. Both Dans were talented, one of them going on to become one of the world's leading sports facility architects, and the other staying on to run a big architectural shop in New York. Much later, another friend of mine (an architect, of course) who had gone to school with red

Dan, worked with him on a project and we got to calling him Zeus. This came about after Zeus had written a project description for a design he was proposing for my company. As the project executive, I was tasked with editing the thing, which seemed like a cross between a Korean DVD player manual and a third century Danish description of cave paintings. For a graduate trained architect, the prose was astonishingly bad. But his writing was not short of hubris or bombast. He was Zeus, thundering design proclamations from above.

I moved on from real estate after an eye-opening stint working for a chain-smoking douche bag and porn addict who somehow convinced a big Japanese company to hire him to run its real estate portfolio. On the back of the New York City real estate fallout after the crash of '87, I was lured away by the commercial division of a giant civil construction and real estate company called Kajima. I naively accepted an acquisitions job with the guy, only to learn that his previous hire had left after dealing with his freakish behavior for about a month. The first day we went to lunch at his favorite restaurant, a Cantonese place in the low 50s, where he ordered up three or four dishes of seafood. Out of the blue he started talking about his porn collection.

"I have a huge collection of pornography."

I looked at him while I juggled a hot platter of gooey gray shrimp with lobster sauce.

"Yes, wow, huh." I was a day into the job.

"Great stuff," he said.

I wasn't sure whether he was talking about the sauce or the porn. Over the coming weeks, a pattern emerged. He was an apartment investor in a project in Houston and was focusing all our efforts on Houston, primarily to be closer to his personal investment. We wound up buying a shitty suburban office building whose tenants might as well have been staying at a hot sheet motel for all their longevity.

I lasted a year with him, planning my escape from his fat-faced, chain-smoking, bipolar toxicity. It was mutual, of course. He had hired a mild-mannered CPA to run numbers, a guy who wouldn't say boo to anyone. I had already arranged to start a new gig, as a gold options trader on the New York Mercantile Exchange. I later learned that the new hire had a horrific skiing accident, suffering brain trauma that required an extended leave of absence. The boss actually tried to get him fired based on a technicality in the corporate document relating to terms of employment.

Being on a trading floor was not something I ever thought about doing. My dad's cousin, a natural, talented gambler, found his calling as an options trader after a short business career. He was thirteen years older than me, and had set up his own trading firm with one of his stepsons, an MIT engineering grad who loved options and analyzing futures. They knew I had an MBA and a decent understanding of finance, and they offered to sponsor me as a fledgling trader on the "Merc," short for the New York Mercantile Exchange, which was on the fourth floor of the World Trade Center. A bunch of commodities, both futures and options, were traded on the Merc, including all of the precious metals: gold, silver, platinum, palladium, and copper. My cousins (the stepson became a de facto cousin) thought there was relatively more opportunity in gold, so they anointed me gold options trader and I jumped into the business.

Nothing I had ever done prepared me for the gold ring. The options rings, although somewhat civilized compared to the brute scrum atmosphere of the futures pits, were still all about power, fear, and intimidation. From the position you took up in the ring, to whether the key brokers would recognize your bid, to whether you handled the daily hazing as one of the guys or a little bitch, every moment of your time in the ring was tense. Options trading is based on volatility—the more volatility incorporated into the price (and expected future prices) of the underlying commodity, the wider the swings are in option prices, and the greater the opportunity for profits and losses. Traders love "Vol." Without Vol, traders are bored and broke. When the Vol started to move, there was a palpable swell in the ring, voices growing louder, expressions getting more intense, bodies moving closer. On a big day, money flowed like a tsunami. There were about a half-dozen big brokers who doled out contracts to traders screaming bids in the ring. Traders use a shorthand for months, and an offer to sell fifty December contracts would sound like "fifty Dec (pronounced "Deese") at 8." Volume counts. The best traders were physically imposing and street smart and had leather lungs. Guys (women were strictly clerks when I was in the ring) were known by the abbreviated names on their badges. The scariest guy during my fleeting ring time was a guy named Meyer whose badge read "MYR" or something like that. He could always be heard above the din and was known for making a shitload of money year after year. Although Meyer wasn't a broker, he was a fixer; if he liked or tolerated you, the brokers would throw you a bone here and there. Get on Meyer's bad side and he would execute trades just to fuck you over and you were dead.

The strange thing was that my little company was all a bunch of nerdy Jewish guys. None of them were the slightest bit intimidating, but they were all math talents. In addition to "Vol" there was Gamma, or the rate of change of an options price. Making money in options required you to have positions that increased in value depending on how your Gamma interacted with your Vol, but maybe it was the other way around. That confusion led to a short career in the options ring for me. I could never balance the screaming and outright aggression you needed in the ring with the mathematical pyrotechnics you needed to keep your positions profitable. Guys like Gar, a trader who wore skintight polos that displayed his puffy, gym-fed biceps, would stand and shoot the breeze frat-style about needing to eat celery because he needed to take a huge dump and somehow still be getting tons of trades done with an occasional flick of the wrist. The Meyers and the Gars were naturals, like the scratch golfer who hits his drive 320 down the middle without the club registering so much as a "swoosh" when it makes contact with the ball.

I was a sideshow in the options ring, a cubicle jockey without a view. I needed my meetings, my Starbucks, my collegial lunches, my memos. I thanked my cousins profusely for their kindness and support, and called tall Dan.

"I know a guy from L.A. named George who is looking to hire someone for a start-up entertainment company called Iwerks," he told me. From options trading to entertainment in L.A. It was quite the conceptual leap, but yes, I would be more than happy to talk to George when he came to town.

Meeting George was my first exposure to the "Industry." Creative industries in New York are a major part of the social and commercial engine, but the city is driven by the holy trinity of finance, real estate, and law. Media is probably fourth, and I suspect that with the convergence of technology and media, it is probably fair to say that New York now has the big four. George was a different kind of business guy. Casual before it was commonplace, he had the languid, superficial charm of a Southern Californian. His company, a shop called Iwerks Entertainment, was founded by a Stanford hot shot MBA and the grandson of one of the cofounders of Disney named Don Iwerks. The company was involved in the production of special-venue film attractions and large-format (giant screen) film. It was kind of a pre-Internet company, flush with a whole bunch of IPO money. They hunkered down in a couple of old hangar buildings in a desolate spot near the Burbank airport. The summers were blistering hot, and the smog had to be scraped off your windshield at the end of the day. George, Dan, and I had lunch, and George wanted to talk about his real estate strategy for the company.

Moving to California meant one thing—for the first time in my life, I would get to see the World Cup.

* * *

I accepted the Iwerks offer and spent a quick eleven months living in Santa Monica. Iwerks burned through $40 million in IPO money, fired everyone, and I was delighted to head back to Manhattan, albeit without a job and, very shortly thereafter, without a spouse.

After my California hiatus, I found it tough to break back into the New York real estate scene but finally found a home with a company called Summit and was hired as a Director of Marketing and Development for a master-planned project on the Hudson River in Jersey City, on the site of the old Colgate Palmolive manufacturing plant. There were two types of ethnic parts of the New York metro area: interesting ones and desolate ones. Jersey City in the mid to late '90s was in the desolate category. The most excitement that I saw in front of our tower at 101 Hudson Street were the minicyclones that swirled in the barren plaza in front of the building. Once, the vortex was so powerful that a young woman asked me to hold on to her while she went from the lobby door to a waiting car, thirty feet away.

Shifting from a pattern where I was married and led a pretty structured life, I was left with mercurial New York as a partner. With abundant free time, I began to deconstruct things. The commute to work in Jersey City was an epic journey that took me to another state via walking, subway, walking, the Path train, and another walk, a distance of perhaps seven or eight miles that could take up to an hour and a half depending on my connections and luck. New York tends to polarize your tendencies: you become a garrulous and uninhibited extrovert, or you become introspective, along the lines of Ben Katchor's graphic story character Julius Knipl, real estate photographer. A painstaking archivist of recondite New York City, Knipl tours New York with his bulky mechanical gear, documenting its nostalgic and vestigial fragments. Fading signs, crumbling infrastructure, and bedraggled shopkeepers are his stock in trade. Knipl, although thwarted in his personal life, brings inspiration to the proletariat; through him, quotidian routines and habits become the foundation of life in the big city. Without the tailors and street vendors and livery drivers, there would not be the other, dazzling city. The Empire State Building, a monument to technology and a forward-thinking "Empire" when it was built, fell into neglect over time. By the 1990s, the building had passed through a succession of high-profile owners and lawsuits and had become a labyrinthine mess of tiny tenants: dentists, showrooms, travel agents, and bail bond specialists—the connective tissue of Knipl's recondite

New York. While New York had started to boom again in the early '90s, enough of Manhattan languished to serve as a museum of dreary imagery.

Recently I heard the current owner of the Empire State Building speak at a luncheon in Los Angeles, saying that one of the prime motivators for his family to invest in the renovation of the grand tower was that "None of the tenants were people we would want to spend time with socially." Hence, affirmation of Manhattan's great divide, the rich up there, and the rest of us stuck on the metaphorical D train over the East River.

In his introduction to Katchor's Knipl compilation, Michael Chabon describes a form of nostalgia that exists for events and places that never existed. In the time after my separation, I was gripped with a strange sense that I was familiar with the whole of New York. I would get palpitations and fleeting déjà vu going up a flight or two of concrete stairs in Riverside Park and get twitchy at the sight of a gnarled dogwood in Madison Square. People in the street were all, in at least a remote sense, familiar. Grasping and holding on to the familiar with all your life is the great antidote to the fulgent belching of New York. As the philosopher Ortega y Gasset suggested, life cannot exist without your personal circumstances. What is strange and wonderful about New York is that through the noise, there is a ghost-like familiarity in the trees and sharp shadows cast at the penumbral times of the day. It is only when you are alone that you have time to study these things and get a sense of who you are, or who you might have been.

Without overtly realizing it, I think many New Yorkers are drawn to the city by the power of reinvention. There is no more open space in New York City, only the potential for renewal. A building becomes obsolete and is torn down. A park is created from a dilapidated rail line. After a bit, I became part of the context of the neighborhood blocks surrounding my apartment in the Packard on West 86th Street. After feeling disconnected from things for a few months, the feral power of so many New Yorkers and so much history started to become invigorating. Everyone was my friend. I felt ten percent taller and funnier overnight.

Thanks to a pre-Internet bricks and mortar dating site on Amsterdam Avenue called Drip, my friend Kevin and I never lacked for an idea of where to go for a drink. Drip compiled binders full of personal profiles. These made for fantastic reading. Hidden among the sunset-walking, brunch-going, dog-loving blandistablishment were acerbic New York gems. It was hard to think that a date with someone whose favorite moment was "two P.M." would be that boring. But the real function of Drip was to check out the people in the café who were in turn leafing through the profile books. Since most of the people in Drip had profiles already, this was a bit of a circular endeavor: people checking the profiles of people in the café who were in turn checking them out.

Drip was the perfect place for the anti-date, a place to flop down on second-hand furniture and blab with your friend who was setting you up with her friend's cousin's sister. Eventually, as with a broken clock being correct twice a day, anyone could connect through Drip, if not through the bio briefs in the profile books. I also discovered the world's greatest natural dating resource: social work school. Social workers were the opposite of MBA students: nice and almost all women. Through one social worker friend, I got introduced to my second wife, bequeathing Drip back to the throng of Upper West Side lonely hearts I was now free to sidestep on Amsterdam Avenue.

When my wife-to-be moved in with me at the Packard, I started to get the willies. I had lived there with my first wife, and the apartment started feeling claustrophobic. I was ready to consume some suburban living. I had been in Manhattan for over a decade, seeing it transform from a den of urban funk to playground. I had ridden every subway line, braved hurricanes, blackouts, and ice storms, had cabbies brandish tire irons at me driving up Second Avenue, seen fistfights on the street, and watched the procession of misanthropes, bullies, vagrants, poseurs, students, dilettantes, and working stiffs in every borough and just about every neighborhood in the city. Within a year, we bought a house in Nyack, a "starter" suburb thirty minutes up the Hudson from Times Square.

I met a bunch of architects working for Summit, and one of them, a genial Italian guy named Paolo, had an indoor soccer team that played at Chelsea Piers, a private, multisport facility on the west side of Manhattan. After convincing Paolo that I had a reasonable soccer IQ for an American— with foreigners there was always a sniff test involved to see if you actually had a soccer/football pedigree—he asked me if I wanted to play at Chelsea. They had two fields with boards shaped like a hockey rink. The turf was old school, cheap and dangerously hard. Our team was a Euro/Americas blend. The game was five on five, including the goalie. The hyperfast surface and quick boards made for a pass-and-blast style of play, which meant you played five minutes at a time and had to get off for a breather. I played forward and was paired with a ridiculously long-limbed Italian giant named Allesandro, an architect with a cascading plume of curly black hair and poet's eyes. Allesandro was a classic target man, easy to find with a pass.

As always in New York, any kind of sport involved a heap of trash talking and extracurricular nonsense. Pushing, pulling, tripping, and elbowing were standard. During one pretty rough game, I was walking backwards away from the opposing goal when I felt like I had been shot in the back of the ankle. Assuming some moron had come over and deftly kicked me, I turned around to confront him, only to see a vast expanse of field behind me; I had torn my Achilles tendon. Pregnant with my first child, my wife picked me up and took me to the ER. I had surgery the next day and was left to convalesce at my house in Nyack. There was some symmetry there: having recently decamped to the suburbs, I had to rethink the whole city sports thing. When you're young and single in New York, it's like a grown-up sports holiday: soccer, hockey, running, softball are all basically out your front door. In the 'burbs, it was expected that your priorities changed to family and house. Raking, mowing, and child care were on the menu. After I moved, I would stare at the sad pile of skates and hockey sticks and soccer balls in my basement. They seemed tired from the moment I unpacked them.

Paolo's family had deep roots in Piedmont, and he liked to show photographs of the ancestral house, a thirteenth- or fourteenth-century beauty whose rusticated stone walls had elided into its natural surroundings. In high school, the Italians on my team were rough around the edges, the Old World front and center. Their allegiance was to Juventas and Italy, and that was about it. A couple of them barely spoke English and muddled through high school with a few shop courses and a part-time busboy job. Paolo's Italy was Renaissance Italy: stone walls, undulating vineyards, crisp architecture, and elegant soccer. His game was not fast but smart and elegant, a counterattack springing from a stout Cattenaccio defense. Another guy on our team, an architect named Alberto, was Argentine. He wasn't much of an athlete, about 5'6", kind of paunchy, but with a good soccer brain. Out of the blue one day, he came over to me and said, "I love your game," which was kind of strange since I didn't think I had been playing all that well. Something with those Argentines, I suppose. In grad school, the Argentine guys playing on one of the top rival intramural teams were surprised I was American and thought I played more "South American." There it was; my soccer provenance had been sealed. I was actually Argentine, born in Cordoba or Rosario, or maybe Buenos Aires. I can accept that.

After the Achilles injury, I spent a couple of weeks chillaxing at my new house in Upper Grandview, one of the villages that make up the small city of Nyack. Unlike other suburbs, Nyack was only a one-half conceptual leap from Manhattan. If you were to classify New York metro locations in descending order from hip to suburban dork, the list might look like this: Manhattan –> Brooklyn (although in 2011 Brooklyn might be ranked higher than Manhattan) –> Long Island City –> Nyack –> Hoboken/Jersey City –> everyplace else in the metropolitan area. Nyack itself was a strange amalgam of ex-hippies, section 8 tenants, weekenders, and film industry types, all with an aversion to conformity and the constraints imposed by more conventional suburbs. The topography of Nyack and the small towns that made up its ring—Grandview, Upper Grandview, Piermont, Nyack, and South Nyack—created an extruded little place with an eccentric and inbred worldview. My neighbors on one side were a gay couple, arguably one of the most macho in the tristate area. They owned a huge Italianate villa that was one of these forever renovation projects, with pickup trucks coming and going for months. They had plenty of money and brought in crews of Old World Italian plasterers from the Bronx who were recreating the interior period walls. My old house, a craftsman Tudor hybrid, had two nice concrete patios off to the side, offering a nice view of their property and house. For my rehab, I bought a bunch of books on shingle style architecture, including Scully's seminal volume. Organic architecture, appearing to transition from the earth itself, was something I never thought about in the built environment of Manhattan and the boroughs.

The only thing that stood in the way of a contemplative and smooth recovery was the fact that I had a cast on my right foot, and as per doctor's orders I couldn't bear any weight on that leg. With my wife working, I had to fend for myself, hopping from point to point on my left leg or using the crutches. My mother, about fifteen miles east in Stamford, was finally truly sick. But it was impossible to tell just how sick. Her entire adult life had been an unvarnished medical narrative, rife with multiple physical and emotional afflictions.

"I wish I could be there to help you out," she told me on the phone, "but I am just not in any condition to do that."

Over time, her litany of chronic issues had morphed from depression to anxiety to bipolar condition to agoraphobia, and now, it seemed, to full-on delirium. The torpor of forty years in the same little split-level house in a stultifying little community in Stamford, coupled with the trauma of her husband leaving her, had created a very fragile person.

I learned to set up snacks and food to make maximum use of my one-leggedness, and thanks to a friend of mine, learned about Pilates. Once you get into a routine with an injury to a limb (I had my hand in a cast after a classic "bagel" incident—

slicing into the bone of my left middle finger—for a couple of months) it becomes semitolerable. Once I got back to work, my company was very generous, letting me take a car service from 96th Street on the west side to my office at 1 Penn Plaza at 34th Street and 7th Avenue. Ninety-sixth Street was the cross street that my wife used when we came down the West Side Highway and she cut over to her job at Mount Sinai Hospital. Right after I got back to work, I took the subway a couple of times, which was a test of character. Steep in normal times, the multilevel, short-treaded concrete stairs leading in and out of the typical Manhattan subway station become stark death traps on one leg and crutches. And it's not like you have the things all to yourself. Frazzled commuters, feral high school kids, the dazed and confused all share your space and couldn't give a rat's ass about some dude with a boo boo on his leg. I had visions of a Hitchcockesque spiral descent to hell, where I would come to in a state of semiconsciousness surrounded by Tippi Hedren and a bunch of curious onlookers.

Any woman who has been pregnant bristles at the topic of people giving up their seat on the subway. So it goes for crutch users. After a couple of harrowing trips between the busy express stations at 96th and 34th Streets, I yelled virtual "uncle" and started taking black cars (illegal cabs). At my company, we had been going after a big project in San Juan, Puerto Rico, and I was part of the pursuit team. I hadn't thought about it too much, but I wound up having to go down there, cast and all, for a couple of weeks. I stayed at the Caribe Hilton, a beautiful property whose grand expanse of terrazzo lobby glistened with the drippings from the parade of beach-combing guests to and from the bar. If I thought there were hazards in New York, trying to make 200 feet of wet terrazzo crossing through a throng of pina colada–addled hotel guests was the plot line for a reality show about temporary cripples.

I was almost two months into wearing a cast from my Chelsea Piers soccer injury that went from my foot to the bottom of my thigh, and it was now late spring when I moved from the fairly temperate climate of New York to the subtropical heat and humidity of Puerto Rico. The drawbacks of being an aging soccer player were getting more serious. If you are an injured pro, you are coddled like a little baby. If you're an amateur hack, and you get a serious sports injury, you are not. I started to notice that either I was getting fatter or the cast was getting tighter, and as the days wore on I started to feel like cutting the damn thing off myself. One night the air conditioning was cycling on and off, mostly off, and my leg started to feel like an overstuffed Italian sausage.

The next morning I called my surgeon and asked him if I could get the cast cut off in Puerto Rico.

"I wouldn't do that if I were you," and although he didn't elaborate, the meaning was clear: he didn't trust the medical scene in San Juan in case something went wrong.

Between watching everyone coming and going to the beach and having to slog around on my crutches, I was miserable. The workdays were equally strange. We had a toehold on a big development opportunity for a new convention center and related development on a strategic but long-neglected spit of land near downtown. A couple of guys in New York—fixers who had connections in Puerto Rico—were promoting us into the deal, wanting to also carve out a role for themselves. Like Bruce and Big Mike, New York served up a never-ending buffeteria of deal makers, promoters, hustlers, and brokers. I started to distinguish between the different flavors of these guys. At the top of the food chain, you had developers who had actual skin in the game and were looking to bring in a bigger, more credit-worthy entity to assist in running the deal and completing financing. From there, the hill descended sharply, down to the lowest form of life in the New York real estate pantheon, the broker. The guys we were working with on the Puerto Rico deal were somewhere in the middle: they had real connections but no equity invested in the project and no control whatsoever in the process. To a developer, process and control mean everything. Puerto Rico and San Juan were more Central American in terms of culture and business approach compared with the States. Things moved slowly. Very slowly. But the pace of business wasn't nearly the most vexing problem. After a few trips down there I realized that the central problem that San Juan had was that people just flat-out didn't show up to work! Our financial partner, Lehman Brothers, had a small office in a high-rise downtown. On crutches I was forced to go at a slow pace and took in the vast expanse of plaza. It struck me that San Juan was more Brasilia than Manhattan. The buildings were fairly large, but the density must have been a tenth or less than that of Manhattan. Entire floors seemed deserted, and if you met another person in the lobby, it was an event. The office towers there seemed to serve more of a ceremonial purpose than an actual business function.

Up at the Lehman office, no senior people were around, only an intern, an ex-ballerina named Mara whose English was so-so. From this arrangement—an empty office and a couple of speculative government contacts—I was supposed to cobble together a coherent précis for a giant mixed-use convention and office project on one of the most strategic sites in San Juan. Mostly I remember being roasted like a sous-vide lamb chop in the un-air-conditioned Lehman office. Without AC, the lights were dimmed to the point where it seemed like nighttime. My puffed-up leg killed me when I sat upright, but there was no upholstered furniture and I had to go through a bunch of documents. Mara didn't know what to make of me—no one had prepped her or even told her I was going to be in the office. I had no idea what her job function was other than to be a beautiful ex-ballerina decorating a tiny satellite office of one of the most rapacious (and of course now defunct) investment banks ever to disgrace the planet.

I got back to New York with my leg intact but not much in terms of progress on the project. The "Projecto," or descriptive project document, kept getting modified by the governor's office, and the deal dragged into the new administration, which promptly killed our involvement. Back in Nyack, I gradually got my leg back in shape but realized that I had suffered a major suburban casualty: all my city sports were dead. For a bit, I'd make the drive in to East 67th Street on Saturday mornings to play roller hockey—I could blast down the FDR and make it in about a half hour if I left at 7:30. But the original crowd started to thin, mostly by suburban attrition, and since I had to be in the city every day for work, I got sick of going in on Saturdays as well.

Much as it pained me, I got in touch with more pastoral sports—biking, hiking, and running—that were conducive to Upper Grandview. Fifty yards out my front door was a nature trail that paralleled the Hudson, and in the winter the view through the woods was fantastic. I also discovered Tallman State Park, a rustic little gem tucked against the Hudson that had a cool mix of active and passive parkland. Tallman was one of those secret places that you don't know about unless you're a local. It was also not the most groomed or well-maintained place, which gave it a patina. The grass was always a little too high, and the asphalt on the basketball courts had spidery cracks and a weathered sheen to it. Tallman was also usually empty or close to it. It had a whiff of nostalgia, the kind of place that in the '60s was packed on the weekends with families out for a day of fun. That kind of fun, in an era of organized sports, split families, and working parents, had seen its day. On some of the paths that led down to the river banks, there were clusters of tall marsh grass, and it made me think of the Dutch settlers from T.C. Boyle's *World's End*. After all, it was Nyack that he wrote about, and it was plausible that the Dutch settlers in the 1600s walked near the same rushes and looked at the same undulations of shoreline that I did.

On Saturdays, I started doing a mini-triathlon of my own design: bike to and from Tallman, run a couple of miles and play soccer against the wall. One day I heard more noise than usual up from the field, and getting closer, I saw a soccer match with refs, an organized league game. I learned it was a Rockland County rec league, and the level looked decent, certainly not unapproachable. I was at that funny stage transitioning from playing sports, which in New York meant the whole social aspect of hanging out before and going out after and looking forward all week to your big game, to suburban dad and commuter. In a city like New York, where commutes average over an hour one way and are often quite a bit longer, your main sport becomes dodging the type As at Grand Central and trying to squeeze yourself on to the southbound number 4 express. I didn't feel like playing soccer now that I was a suburban guy. Would Cary Grant's Mr. Blanding, in his crisp worsted suit, have been eyeballing pickup soccer in the woods near his house in Connecticut?

There was also a big shift in terms of how I thought in the suburbs versus the city. In New York, despite the fact that I owned my condo (or the bank owned most of it, anyway), I was focused on what I was doing: work, consuming stuff, a date, walking, getting the next event lined up. With the move to Upper Grandview, there was almost an immediate shift to being preoccupied with the one thing that holds every suburban homeowner in its deadly embrace: the value of his or her house. In Manhattan, even if you own an apartment, there are so many of them, and so many similar buildings that real estate is more of a fungible commodity, almost like a paper asset. In the suburbs, where land is extruded and houses are discreet elements, they take on distinct personalities. Like friends and enemies, some you like and some you don't, some change over time, and some become objects of obsession. Nyack's villages were chockfull of splendid Queen Anne and stick-style Victorians, along with a bunch of fantastic shingle-style homes. The latter were what gripped me. Organic by nature—the shingled vernacular grew out of a naturalist imperative, in a line of nature-based design movements that grew out of the design ethos of the Englishman Richard Morris. As fall set in and gold and orange maple and oak leaves swirled in the yards and the early fall sun reflected off the Hudson, I had a sense that I was in a very nice part of the world.

The commute from Nyack to Manhattan, even without my leg in a cast, was ghastly. One of the things that made the place affordable was the absence of a commuter rail line. There once had been one, but it was decommissioned when the spaghetti mess that had been New York's commuter and freight lines was untangled in the 1960s. That left Rockland County as the poor transport stepchild of the region, manifested in lower home prices and generally worse schools than Westchester and Connecticut.

When we moved to Nyack, it was about affordability. We found a beautiful house owned by a photographer in Dobbs

Ferry, but it was about $525k versus the $276k for the house we got in Nyack. Not having grown up in the New York area, my wife's happiness over owning a home vanished the first time we commuted together via the Red and Ten Bus Line. The Red and Ten Coach picked us up at a stop about a five-minute walk from our house, good enough so far, but as it chugged and grunted its way down Route 9W, our gleeful little handholding session and romantic river ride became anguished, as we realized that we would be twenty minutes or more later than our scheduled arrival at the Port Authority Bus Terminal. But it was not the big PA terminal, but the satellite one at 178th and Broadway in Washington Heights. This is probably the least well-known of New York transit terminals, a modernist confection designed by the Italian engineer Pier Luigi-Nervi. The station is an interloper in a sea of gray masonry. Most of upper Manhattan contains Beaux Arts or Art Deco housing. While the George Washington Bus Station has great proximity to the GW Bridge and New Jersey, what it does not have is great proximity to midtown and lower Manhattan. Cruising in our first day after about an hour and forty minutes of herky-jerky bus action, we were dazed and hung over from inhaling the magic elixir of the diesel fumes, which wafted through the cabin with every lurching start. The Red and Ten must have a training center upstate where drivers from Mombasa, Abidjan, and Lagos come to learn how to go from jostling a cab through the Third World to a whole busload of bleary New York commuters. My wife glared at me as we dragged ourselves through Nervi's masterpiece: "I'm not doing this again. You can take the bus, but I'm driving."

It took me almost two full hours to get to 1 Penn Plaza that day. I was gutted. I felt like I had made a massive mistake. It was great to have a charming craftsman house near the Hudson, but if I had to commute four hours a day, inhaling bus fumes for the better part of that time, it was in vain. The subway ride was no picnic either—a half hour from the smelly and cavernous 178th Street stop down to Penn Plaza.

This is the evil New York, the soul-crushing commuter hell where you are only trying to get from point A to point B and things are moving to the beat of a sundial. As intrepid an urban commuter as I was, I also felt defeated. From that point on, my wife and I took our Subaru south down 9W and over the GW Bridge to the West Side Highway. She was the driver, professing to not be bothered by the insane bridge merge and the slow creep down the west side of Manhattan. She dropped me at 96th and Broadway and headed east to Mount Sinai Hospital, and the whole thing would be reversed in the evenings. The difference was that our west side rendezvous point switched to the Starbucks at 86th and Columbus, a block from our old apartment. As much as I love my wife, she too often loses track of time, and I logged a whole bunch of overtime dawdling over tepid cups of Zen tea waiting for my ride.

It was clear that we were biding time in Rockland. As charming as Nyack is, it is a bitch of a commute. Also, all my relatives were on the other side of the river, that is to say, in Westchester, Connecticut, and Queens. Since none of them traveled, we found ourselves back and forth over the Tappan Zee practically every weekend. If you live on the west side of the Hudson River, everyone you know who doesn't considers you to be living "upstate."

TEN

Nomad in New York

AFTER MY DAUGHTER was born and my wife took maternity leave, I was back commuting on my own, and with only one car, I had to start in again with public transportation. After being tortured for a few more months, we decided that we should try to move, and started looking in Westchester County. Priced out of Rye, we looked at the river towns—Tarrytown, Hastings, and Ardsley, along with New Rochelle. More of a small city than a suburb, New Rochelle was a tale of two cities—poorer to the south and Westchester rich to the north. We wound up in the middle, just south of an Orthodox Jewish area called Wykagyl. In a city of distinct neighborhoods, ours was devoid of personality, an older area of decent if unspectacular Tudors, colonials, and Victorians.

We moved in a light snow on a gray day in February 2001. I was immediately relieved. The train from either Pelham or New Rochelle was thirty-five minutes or so, and even if I had to find a way to the Metro North station, I was in a far better place to get to Manhattan. The dirty little secret in Westchester and Connecticut is that you have to wait years for a commuter parking pass. I had to park in a residential area over a mile away from the Pelham station—the neighborhoods close to the station of course have enforced towing to deter people like me.

Another advantage of being in New Rochelle was that we were in an actual neighborhood. Our house, a 1920s Tudor, was surrounded by other homes, and without a fence, we were basically forced to get to know our neighbors. In Nyack, we were far away from the Beaux Arts mansion, and the neighbors downhill from us tried to literally annex some of our yard by planting a hedge about ten feet over our property line. So much for upstate conviviality. New Rochelle was different. The people right to the side of us had two kids, and even though our only child at the time was a baby, there was at least something to talk about.

Bored one day, I took a ball and started to juggle. My neighbor came out and asked me where I played. "Right here, in the backyard." I said. "I know someone at my synagogue that plays soccer. I'll find out where he plays and have him call you." Suddenly, I felt like Max Nordau and Henry Kissinger had sent me a spiritual soccer lifeline. Synagogue? Soccer? Had I struck a rich untapped vein of Jewish soccer? Since seeing that game at Tallman Park in Piermont, I was thinking about playing again. Once I started playing roller hockey in New York, I stopped playing pickup soccer in Central Park. One of my last games at the clearing at 84th Street, a Colombian guy got pissed off and left the game throwing rocks at everyone. I figured that was a good time to take a soccer breather. I did continue to bring a ball to the playground at Columbus and 85th. It made for a good little workout alternating jump rope, push-ups, and kicking the ball off the handball wall. I also half-hoped that other people would see the soccer ball and ask for a game, but no one ever came to even have a kick.

Maybe there was a different vibe in the suburbs. I took the name and number of my neighbor's connection and called. A guy with an English accent answered. He was guarded: there was a game, but they had a lot of players, and I might have to wait and what was my level. I sloughed off the mini-inquisition and showed up that hot July Sunday. After years of pickup soccer, I guess that I've played with people from about seventy different countries. The sport is a simple one and, alone among the major team sports, the only one that does not discriminate for size. Great players are found in all types of physical packages. For a creative player, it may in fact be an advantage to be compactly built, making it easier to shift one's balance and to accelerate quickly. In the U.S., among soccer lovers and haters alike, there is a discussion that goes roughly like this: If the best athletes in the U.S. chose soccer over other sports, this country would be the best soccer nation in the world. I'm not so sure. Given equal opportunity, American black athletes dominate basketball and football and are well represented in baseball of course, and increasingly hockey. Soccer is a much more complex sport to parse. In Africa, the talent has always been there, and Africans are well represented in the top European leagues, but it is certainly not the case that Africans or black soccer players from other parts of the world dominate world soccer. Nor does it seem that there is a pattern of race and field positions in soccer, unlike in American football.

What I saw on the field in New Rochelle was a first for me: a whole group of Jewish soccer players, mostly Israeli. Not since the days of Bi-Cultural Day School had I seen so many Jews on a field at the same time. Since my Bar Mitzvah, the religious aspect of Judaism had slowly trickled out of me, leaving just the chocolatey outer cultural shell. I was the curse of the rabbi: born Jewish, day school educated, not married to a Jew. It wasn't like I adopted anything else—all religions seemed to be kind of a pleasant variation of one another. What struck me at a young age was how polarizing those small differences could be.

New York, as the world capital of Jewish culture, is a giant simulacrum of religion. You can adhere to whatever scraps of Jewish culture that catch your fancy. Food catches most people's fancy at one time or another, and you could say that for some people, food is a form of religion. On the Upper West Side, the streets are redolent with smoked fish and appetizing—appetizing! What a word! My grandmother and her sister used to throw it around when we visited. Appetizing is like a whole bunch of fatty crap that you scarf down before you even start to eat. I never quite got it when I was a kid, but it seemed that appetizing, in fact, was thoroughly unappetizing: smelly herring, gloppy white cheese, and garlicky pucks of something scary called "derma." At the insistence of my grandmother, I would fill a plate full of appetizing and would dutifully scarf it down, and would get wicked stomach cramps. Eating and the fetishization of food are at the foundation of a lot of cultures. My grandmother and aunt, deprived of luxuries and occasionally necessities as children, viewed a moment not eating as a wasted opportunity. When you multiply this by several hundred thousand or so, you have the Upper West Side of Manhattan, a veritable theme park of overindulgence. The few times I allowed myself to eat at Barney Greengrass, the uber appetizorium across from my old apartment on Amsterdam Avenue, I fell right back in the spell of salty fish and heavy cheese, as if my grandmother had been exhumed and was waiting on my table.

Watching two generations of pasty proprietors working the front room at Greengrass, it struck me that this was a Faustian deal—one or two steps removed from the crack dealers at Sabu's two blocks down the street. What was appetizing except for a more benign form of crack? True, appetizing doesn't make you violent or jittery or freaky like crack, just soporific and irritable. But like crack, there was nothing good for you about appetizing, and it made you fat, which like crack, contributed to a health problem that places the economic burden on society at large. Appetizing is also an opiate of sorts; rich, tidbit-sized food that offers a quick fix but leaves you bloated and unhealthy. And I contend that this richness, this insatiable desire for oral satisfaction is what to this day courses up and down Amsterdam Avenue and Broadway and West End Avenue and finds its highest expression in the form of Zabars and Fairway and Barney Greengrass.

Up until the point that I saw a couple of dozen Israeli faces on that field, in the south end of New Rochelle, an area that has a significant black and Hispanic population, I had never quite shaken the antisports sentiment that was prevalent at the Bi-Cultural Day School. Jews were thinkers, scholars, professionals, and . . . eaters. Seeing a whole bunch of Israeli soccer players in the same place was, bizarrely, a moment I had been waiting for since I was a kid. Back in the day, when it was the weeds, that red playground ball, and me, I felt like I was alone. Not only was I a lot better than everyone else, I had a passion for it. Most of the other kids could take it or leave it. I was the kid panting for recess, for a few glorious moments of the fresh air hitting my face and the ball at my feet. Being a poor sport, soccer is filled with the iconography of strivers: doe-eyed African kids flailing away on a dustbowl, Brazilian mixed-race prodigies racing through Favela alleys, Asian kids on deserted tundra. I was that kid, and my kinfolk in 1967 were getting a big jump on me in Tel Aviv and Haifa.

I got lucky and squeaked into the game. When you're new, you always defend. Attacking is for the talented and proven player. I was also pretty damned rusty, not having played since my Achilles tear a few years before. It was also a full-field game, something I had not done since I played in a summer tournament about six or seven years earlier. The full grass field was a wonder, even if it was pretty crabgrassed up. The ball pinged around a bit, and I hunkered down on the left byline, moving here and there to open up for a pass. The first action that came my way was not on the deck, but a fifty-fifty challenge in the air, a hell of a way to start getting into full-field soccer after a six-year hiatus. I went up strong, won the header, and that was it, I was back in the game. I got forward a few times, gradually found my rhythm, and realized that I was among the better guys out there.

There was also Hebrew in the air. Words and phrases I hadn't heard for thirty-five years started to come back to me. The feeling was a cross between being quizzed in Hebrew language class and recess, a weird nostalgic cocktail. A couple of times I heard a word that made me laugh, and I lost concentration, thinking about who said it and where I was when I last heard it. Of course, not everyone out at City Park was Israeli. In fact, there was a real field, with stands and lights and a scoreboard that was used early

Sunday mornings by the Spanish league in Westchester County. Based on what I saw, it was a semipro league. The pace and standard were terrific, and the skill level seemed to be at a Division I college level.

One thing about soccer and sports in general: there is always someone better or bigger or faster. In essence, that is the beauty of team sports, fitting together pieces of disparate skill to achieve something. It is the collective mentality and willingness to subordinate individual glory that made Ajax in the 1970s and Barcelona in the 2010s so remarkable. To be good at a team sport, you need a bunch of good players. To be great, you need those same players who understand how to do the right thing at any given moment. And in soccer, doing the right thing often means to do less, against most players' basic instinct. Every kid wants to dribble, to hold the ball, to be the center of attention, and to get the glory. But most of the time, advancing the ball and gaining an advantage means one-touch passing and understanding how to acquire minute bits of real estate that translate into scoring opportunities. For Barcelona, this means dancing triangles, and a mastery of the concept of playing the ball to the player who played it to you. Making a little return pass creates the opportunity to move just a little bit, and it is that little bit that makes just enough space to get the ball back again, in a better position. Performed with enough frequency, triangle play can kill. Staples High School, with the two Murphys and Phil Moen, triangled us to death. I saw it then, and got it, but my teammates with the exception of the imperial Maurice, did not. We were a collection of foreigners with a case of the dribbles. Jerry "Chooch" Russo, a powerful forward who managed to get to the twelfth grade in Stamford knowing about twenty

English words, routinely gathered the ball and juked two or three defenders before losing the ball. Jerry would rather have watched William F. Buckley interview Henry Kissinger than pass anyone the ball.

With all the Hebrew on the field and being on a field that was more neglected than groomed, I felt a bit like I had taken Michael J. Fox's Delorean back to Colonial Road in Stamford, and that it was 1968, not 2001. I had reached the inflection point in my sports life when adrenaline carries you through during a game, and the pain sets in after. For the next year, while I got back into it, I couldn't figure it out: I felt great while I was playing, but was starting to pop Advil like Mentos. If I didn't have my Advil, sometimes I could barely walk when my feet hit the floor in the morning. I was still doing some gym workouts and other stuff—a little jogging and biking— but the soccer was taking a toll. I also started to wonder about heading. Back in high school, no one ever thought about heading the ball, even though back then soccer balls had the weight and consistency of a shot put. Our drill sergeant coach Vadikos would punt those bad boys 200 feet in the air and make us head them back as far as possible, more artillery training than soccer. We were his raw recruits and he was going to make us men, soccer be damned.

My time capsule soccer trip got weirder as it turned to fall. The Sunday group played indoors at a temple in the south end of New Rochelle. When I first heard about it, I thought it was a modern temple with a big contemporary gym. But the first time I showed up, I was still outside in the dark, walking up a neglected concrete staircase, when I got a creepy déjà vu—my only déjà vu, a weird subset confined to concrete stairways— that I was at my old school. Inside the small temple, it was a complete recreation of Agudath Sholom in Stamford circa 1968, right out of Central Casting. It may well have been used by the Coen Brothers in their shooting of a film that could be my autobiography, *A Serious Man*. The flat Midwestern setting of that small synagogue, with its denuded swath of tarmac-cum-parking lot, was in many ways the perfect evocation of late-1960s/early-1970s sensibility. The low-slung aesthetic formed by the Chevy Impalas and Ford Fairlanes and the curbless, unadorned asphalt formed a bleak wrapper for the interiors of those midcentury synagogues. The first thing I saw when I entered, just like at Agudath Shalom, was the gift shop. I've been to a whole bunch of churches before, and I can't say that I have ever seen a gift shop. Was there a mercantile commandment handed to Moses from above that somehow got lost in the Biblical shuffle? "Thou shalt think about buying stuff immediately upon entering thy holy place of worship."

I suppose selling a lot of stuff eliminates the need for a lot of pesky fundraising and having the rabbis grovel at the end of the service for support. As a kid at Agudath Shalom, I remember enduring three-hour-plus Saturday morning services that were punctuated by our rabbi's extended infomercial about the B'nai Brith club, the Men's Club, and assorted other charitable enterprises connected with the business end of the synagogue. The couple of times I was in church for a hat-passing session, my sense was that it was perhaps a more efficient and direct way of getting things done.

Any thoughts I had about there being some kind of elevated, cerebral aspects to "Jewish" soccer were pretty quickly put to rest after playing with the Israelis for a while. In soccer terms, they were represented by the same assortment of players from other countries. If there was anything that stood out, it was the niggling running critique that went on for the entire game. There was a cynical take on everything. For a lot of these guys, every pass, shot, and decision on the field was subject to verbal critique. "Why? Why?" was a refrain I heard a lot. This must be some Israeli colloquialism. If someone took a shot that was from a little too far out or sprayed a pass or dribbled into traffic, the shouts of "Why? Why?" would come out. I started thinking it was like a baby crying "Waawaa"; that's what "Why? Why?" started to sound like to me.

If anything, there was less joy than I saw in other games dominated by a particular ethnic group. The most fun crowd was the Antiguans in Prospect Park, who played on a grass clearing practically in the woods—I think this was to avoid getting busted for pot. They called me "Danny," and that game had a fast-paced island vibe with lots of banter. There was a lot of slide tackling, but it was pretty good-natured and the guys playing were having fun. The mood running through the game in New Rochelle was one of angst, everything verging on an "Oy Vey" moment. After watching the Israeli national team consistently fail in its attempt to qualify for the European Championships and the World Cup, I think I had established a connection; among Israelis, there was a collective anticipation of failure if it was not a matter of life and death. When you have a military imperative in front of your face at all times, getting a result on the football pitch is not so vital.

The question of soccer-induced schadenfreude suggests that there is an innate sense of not wanting to excel, that failure looms large in achieving acceptance from a wider audience. To deconstruct every play as if it were a theatrical reading is something I have mostly seen from Israelis. It is as if, in their sense of ineluctable failure, they provide a foundation of criticism for everyone to fall back on. "You would have succeeded, tattele, if not for the fact that you shot it over the bar. Why? Why?"

* * *

The 2002 World Cup split between Japan and Korea was great from a commuter's perspective: a lot of the games started at 4 or 5 A.M. Eastern Standard Time, allowing me to catch a game before I went to work. Falling asleep at 8 P.M. wasn't a bad price to pay, and I could even nap on the train on the way home if I could fall asleep before 125th Street, which was key because it was twelve minutes from Grand Central, and if you fell asleep, it meant it was less likely that someone would try to squeeze into the seat next to you. Sleeping people on trains seem to have an invisible force field around them. If you're awake, folks will take a shoehorn out of their bag to squeeze in next to you. But shut your eyes and let your head flop to the side like a rag doll and maybe even let some spittle eddy out of your flapping lips, and, well, you've got yourself a double-wide on the train home.

Japan and Korea coincided with me getting back into playing a regular game. I especially liked the indoor game in the winter because of the intense flashbacks it provided. The dreary brick exterior, little gift shop, and disheveled rabbi's office made me feel right at home. The little synagogue on North Avenue even smelled the same as the one I grew up with in Stamford, kind of a slight whiff of camphor mixed with glue. Maybe it was a dead skin smell, I don't know. When I heard Hebrew spoken outside, it was another retro blast from the past, but inside it was overly familiar, almost creepy. I suppose the creep factor came from the fact that I had consciously rejected structured Judaism, having blown it off pretty much immediately after my Bar Mitzvah, and now I had come back to it in a back-channel sort of way. Of course, things like this are not coincidental. I had clearly chosen to come back to it, to reengage with soccer, with Jews playing soccer, and ultimately to come back to a plaintive little synagogue in New Rochelle.

One of the great things about meeting some Israeli friends was that they had Israeli cable. This meant that I'd finally get a steady diet of seeing the Israeli national team labor through the Euro and World Cup qualifiers. The quixotic path to adopting a national team of a foreign country 5,000 miles away from where I grew up was perplexing even to Israelis, who themselves did not quite grasp the modern role (or lack thereof) of the Jewish athlete in America. There simply was not much for a Jewish kid in the '60s and '70s to get worked up about. Koufax's best years were behind him, and with the exception of a few of baseball players—Ken Holtzman, Ron Blomberg, and Art Shamsky—there wasn't anything much in the way of ethnic sports identity for Jewish kids. After forty-five years, I had finally found a link to that little cartoon with the 8-0 score line and the Hebrew caption without vowels that I was unable to translate.

Israel's men's national team was as perplexing as the nation itself. On my honeymoon in Cyprus in 2000, I coordinated our trip to precisely coincide with an important qualification match. The two national teams, separated by a short flight across the sea, met in the then-aging Cypriot National Stadium in Limassol, a strange city that seems to specialize in stores that sell fur coats in a subtropical climate to Russian mobsters and their consorts.

Armed with tickets sourced by Cypriot friends, I convinced Melissa to head to the stadium early; I wanted to soak in the atmosphere of a European international match. We got there about an hour and a half early. The only fans there were about three busloads of Israelis. They stood on one big line and were all kitted out—a typical bunch of traveling supporters. They had Israeli flags and wore team shirts from the big Israeli clubs— the optic yellow and blue of Maccabi Tel-Aviv, Maccabi Haifa green, and Hapoel Tel-Aviv red. They were singing the national anthem, chanting Israeli chants, and getting rowdy. Not thinking that much about it, we got on line. It was the only line, so there wasn't really a choice. We waited an hour or so—not the honeymoon my wife was expecting—and finally the local constabulary force started to move the line forward. We got to the front, presented our tickets, and the grim-faced cop took a look and waved us away like a French Maître dismissing a bus boy.

"What?" I said to Melissa in a panic.

I asked the cop what was wrong. He simply looked at the tickets and shook his head. His English was too limited to explain the situation. His boss was close by, and seeing that there was a problem, came over.

"These are not for the visitors," he said, meaning that there was a special ticket for the traveling Israelis, to make sure that they were penned off from the home fans. I asked the boss what to do.

"Not this line," he said.

"What then? What line is good?"

He shrugged. He pointed to the other line. "For Cyprus," he said.

It was apparent to me that having played the Israeli card meant that we couldn't just jump over to the Cyprus side. We could have been hatching a nefarious plot. Without hope of getting in with the traveling contingent, I grabbed Melissa and we headed to the Cypriot side. Another cop looked at us, looked at our tickets, and shook his head no.

"We're Americans," I said, "Here's my passport."

He mumbled and pointed over to the Israeli line.

"We just came from there, they wouldn't let us in."

He shrugged in an insouciant way that suggested it wasn't his problem.

I was desperate at that point. "Please, I am a big soccer fan and have no rooting interest. Surely this is a good ticket."

That moment was soccer at its nationalistic worst. Here I was, a fan, thousands of miles away, caught in a Gordian soccer twist. Without a declared allegiance and the proper credentials, I was a soccer traveler without fellows, a minister without portfolio, and close to being up Shit Creek, denied entrance to a game I was desperate to see. I took a deep breath and pointed to Melissa. Perhaps a plea involving a fair-skinned blond woman who had pretty much had it with soccer politics would make them relent.

The Carabiniere pushed his cap to the side. He licked his fingers and checked out the tickets one more time. He beckoned over the boss, the same guy who bounced us from the other line. They went back and forth in Greek, and at last looked at me with pity. We were waved into the Cypriot side, not the side I wanted to be on, but at least we were in. I thought about how strange it was having a ticket for a sporting event and almost being denied access. There is no other sport where this would even be a remote possibility. Soccer is sometimes not a sport but a proxy for nationalism. The literature documenting this is abundant, and you see it mostly in the supporters' clubs, where there is a thin—at times nonexistent—veil between gangs and fans. An unemployed twenty-year-old Czech or Croat or Italian guy can always have his club and sit among the fireworks at the local derby match. Likely, his father and grandfather and uncles did the same.

I sat through the game with the somewhat restrained Cypriot fans. Cyprus won, 3-2, a decent game, but played in the old national stadium (since replaced by a modern one near the airport in Larnaca) that had a track ringing the field. It seems these were a pretty common European design that accommodated track and field plus soccer, but for fans, this means you are very far away from the action. The players become insect-like, disappearing into the whirlpool before the goal. After a while, I found I had to stare into the goal behind the keeper to see if the ball made it in.

The only other European game I saw was in Portugal in 1992, at a tiny concrete bunker of a stadium in Faro, on the southern coast. Sporting Lisbon was visiting the then small First Division side F.C. Farense. Sporting featured a nineteen-year-old wunderkind, Luis Figo, a powerful central midfielder with iron-black curly hair. I had never heard of Figo, but within minutes, my view of soccer was transformed. Our seats were close—it was only about a 3,000 seat capacity, in a brutalist masonry style that looked like the brainchild of a Fascist Portuguese general. But moments into the game, everyone was mesmerized by Figo. He looked jet propelled, exploding one way then the other with feral force, either shooting or pushing the ball into exquisite spaces that were often unnoticed by his teammates. For the first time, I had a chance to see ethereal soccer up close. A young Figo was the ultimate soccer dervish with his wind-whipped mane of black hair, kelly green striped sporting kit, and mastery of that tiny seaside stadium.

As anemic as the Israeli national team was, at least I had a chance to watch them on cable in New Rochelle. Not growing up with a team meant that you were consigned to soccer purgatory. I was not a "supporter" in the true sense of having a team passed on to me by birthright. If my German grandfather supported a team when he was a boy in Frankfurt, he certainly did not pass that on to my dad, who, although he clearly loved soccer, did not really evince a rooting interest for any particular club. The Cosmos in their early days were kind of cute and cuddly, and perhaps they were a team we could have rooted for if they grew organically. Once Ross turned them into a marketing juggernaut, the club seemed more like the Yankees and less like the Cosmos. The weirdness of the turf at Giants Stadium also made the brand of soccer played there a little like another '70s sports fad, jai alai. A Catalan import, jai alai was like squash on steroids, with players launching a rock-hard ball from a slingshot-like basket. Turf soccer—old-school turf—was to grass soccer as jai alai is to squash: faster, bigger, less nuanced.

When I went over to my Israeli friends' homes, usually there was hummus, pita, and Israeli products. I suppose I had at last found my club. After wondering as a kid whether there actually was a Jewish/Israeli soccer fraternity somewhere in the world, I finally discovered it forty years later. What is interesting is how and why Jewish soccer faded in New York, while other ethnic pockets thrived. Greeks, Croatians, Salvadorans, and Italians continue to hold the flag high. The Prospect Unity Club lasted past the founding of Israel, but it seems that conflating religion and national identity just doesn't work outside the motherland. Even Israel itself, as a democracy with non-Jews composing a significant proportion of its population, has non-Jewish Arabs and Druze on its national team. Stalwart Arab players like Walid Badir stand awkwardly during "Hatikvah," the Israeli national anthem, a strange sight that I don't think is seen in any other country.

New York is an extraordinary place if you are a dilettante, a bohemian, a financier, a philanthropist, a freegan, or a single guy with an apartment in Manhattan. If you are a family man, the reality of the city as an adult playground starts to gradually fade and, within a year or two, disappears entirely. If you're single, even if you don't have money or haven't had a date in months, every new block holds promise—a chance encounter by the cheese display at Zabars, a new shop or restaurant, meeting an old friend on the street. As a married guy with kids in the suburbs, your perspective is defined by the grim Bronx landscape. When I worked for Littlefield at 100 Park Avenue, my commute was a forty-three-minute walk through the Central Park Sheep Meadow and Grand Army Plaza at the southern end of the park. The morning stillness and cool of the park yielded to the pedestrian swell and rising tide of traffic on 7th Avenue. There was an oceanic feeling to that walk; the park part was like paddling out, and where the park elided into Manhattan itself, it was like catching a wave.

Coming into Manhattan from Westchester by train takes you through the Bronx, an antediluvian world of fading courthouses and hospitals, once-grand apartment houses in a gradual state of decline, and businesses too prosaic for Manhattan. The Bronx isn't even quite Julius Knipl territory. Where Knipl traverses the realm of the obscure and obsolete, the Bronx is the realm of the bulk transaction: mattresses, auto parts, scaffolding. The Bronx provides a lot of the staging for Manhattan. If something needs to be transported, held in place, or demolished, the process often originates in the Bronx. And then there is the zoo, a natural (albeit man-made) marvel that abuts a real river in the middle of the borough. The collision of hip-hop and primate research is no more evident anywhere on the planet than in the Bronx. Parts of the borough are a mirage. There is quite a bit of grass, and the terraced trails and parkland adjoining the Grand Concourse are reminiscent of Riverside Park. But it is rare that you are that far from blight in the borough. And the swaths of newly created affordable and low-income housing are equally strange: garden apartments in a thoroughly urban borough.

Traversing the Bronx to get into Manhattan, as opposed to living in Manhattan and making an intraborough commute, made me feel like a stranger in my own homeland. I had been Mr. Manhattan for a long time, the guy with the inside dope on the restaurants, shops, and trends. Even among the other New Yorkers at Summit, I was considered the New York guy, a New Yorker's New Yorker. Suddenly I was another schmo on the 6:10, a bleary dude with a deadline and a schedule to juggle. The city was still there in all its glory. I was working for a union-sponsored pension fund that invested primarily in housing through government or GSE-guaranteed paper. It was a complicated way to invest in new housing in New York, especially in a market where developers had pretty easy access to debt and equity without having to jump through the regulatory hoops that our funds required.

Our little office was at 31 West 15th Street, in a building owned by the Needleworker's Union. With its elaborately embroidered pennants and black and white documentary photos, the building could have served as Julius Knipl's studio. Just off Union Square, the location was fantastic. It was near several schools: NYU, the New School, and Cooper Union. Union

Square is one of the great creative clusters in the country. In fact, with the Farmer's Market anchoring Union Square Park three times a week, the neighborhood becomes a movable feast of food, fashion, music, and creative commerce. It is one of the great urban places in the world.

The problem was I felt like an interloper. For more than ten years I lived on the Upper West Side. When it was time to go anywhere, the choices of how to do it were abundant; foot, subway, cab, bus, bike. The suburban guy marches to the beat of the train schedule. Your life is suddenly parsed by the departing times of your trains. Numbers like 5:36, 6:10, and 6:36 become ingrained in your brain. Every day I saw lushness in Union Square. Every day I hustled to and from the subway station and hoped that the swelling crowd for the 2 uptown express wouldn't box me out of getting a seat on my train. Behind me were the real people: the yoga girls toting their mats and sipping tea, lamenting that all the cute boys didn't have money and that the old rich guys were, well, old; the digital designers brilliantly reimagining a campaign for an old-line German camera company; the wiry wheatgrass vendor with his back-to-the-land rap and veggie-oil-powered school bus; the teamsters blowing cigar smoke and bellowing greetings out front of the Hall at 31 West 15th Street; the students, throngs of them, fretting and flirting over nothing, buying lattes and Japanese pastries. I lamented that my creative days were behind me. I went from having a café life to a train life. When you move to the suburbs of a great city, the change from being of a place to being in a place is abrupt. People look at you differently. My hair seemed grayer, my clothes frumpier, and my attitude lamer. The high school kids seemed like grade school kids and the college students like prepsters.

My priorities, of course, had shifted from being an urban consumer to being a dad. The things that were always out of reach—the top restaurants, Barneys, the Hamptons, the squash clubs—were now convincingly out of reach. I had all I could do to get to Trader Joe's and keep the tab under $200. It was getting weird in the sense that all of the things that I used to spend money on in Manhattan had shifted to the suburbs. It was the proverbial carrot on a string. I'd pass restaurants and shops that I used to go to without flinching that had become strictly verboten. My office was also strange. Small to begin with, my coworkers would disappear for weeks at a time on sabbatical or personal leave. That left me fending for myself in a superquiet office. We were like the English in Burma—out of the mainstream but with a mandate to get things done. I had to answer phones, source deals, manage deals, do marketing, analyze projects, and provide regular internal reporting. Oh, and keep the unions happy. The office itself, while in a great location, had a view of the side of the building next door and very little natural light. Winter days were dreary and lonely, and I had to get out of the office as often as I could.

The problem with leaving the office is that in neighborhoods like Union Square, everyone is recreating all the time. Even people who are "at work" are working at coffee shops and networking on the street and strolling the Farmers Market and having lunch at the Coffee Shop, the Brazilian-influenced comfort-food palace at the southwest corner of 14th and Broadway and social safety net for the MAWS (model-actress-wannabes) of Manhattan. The flaneur in me had a lot to choose from: points north headed to the Ladies Mile retail district, colonized by bigger-box-type retailers on 6th Avenue, but still retaining a lot of smaller shops on the side streets. Edging northwest became core Chelsea, gay and stylish, with lots of not-for-profit dance consortiums and new condo product. Straight north led to the increasingly mall-like feel of lower Fifth Avenue, but then the relief of Madison Square Park: urban, but more tailored than its cousin, Union Square Park, seven blocks south. Madison Square Park is a great inflection point, a demarcation between uptown and downtown, bourgeoisie and bohemian, orthogonal and unplanned. More than any park in the city, Madison beckons you to sit down with a magazine and enjoy its mannered take on life.

Over a short period of time—from about 2001 when we moved to New Rochelle to about 2005—the conceptual gulf between suburban and city life became a chasm. Rattle through the Bronx, swim upstream through Grand Central, spend the day in the city as a voyeur, and backtrack in the evening. Telltale signs of weary commuters grew as the months descended into winter. In 2003, there were multiple ice storms that created havoc for the external motors used at that time by most of the Metro North train cars. This created massive delays for the system, to the point where the train schedule might as well have been a kindergartner's doodle pad. It was brutal. I thought that I had endured some pretty god-awful commuting in my Brooklyn days with the heat and the homeless, but the winter of '03 was worse. The signature theme was a packed train crawling into the Pelham station at about three miles per hour. The train would coast in, stop, and sit with its doors closed for five or so minutes, leaving the frozen commuters on the platform wondering when and if the doors would ever open. If—and "if" is the correct word as many of the trains simply glided away—the doors actually opened, what you saw was a solid rear view of thermal commuter mass. No way, no how was there room for anyone except perhaps an attractive petite woman who by dint of Lilliputian dimensions and pert appearance would be graced with a few precious centimeters of access.

This pattern went on for weeks. So many motors had to be sent for refurbishment that the Metro North schedule was in shambles for weeks at a time. I was getting to work at nine, ten, ten-thirty, with one-way commute times approaching three hours. Getting back was a smidgen better. Compounding the problem was that the only other person in my office lived about two blocks away. She was my manager and "ran" the New York office, if running a two-person office was anything to crow about. Living in Manhattan gives folks license to haze suburbanites about their commute. After my three-hour journey, Mindy would give me the half evil eye: "So the trains were late again, huh?"

"Yep, almost three hours in today."

"I hope they straighten it out soon."

I could have answered that I was just a guy who bought a house in a lower-echelon town in Westchester County so my kids might have the privilege of going to an underfunded public school with a dodgy student body because I never got in a career groove after business school and mistimed a whole bunch of bonus events that would have put me on a different trajectory and enabled me to keep a pied-a-terre in the city for complications like the Metro North debacle while having my family safely ensconced in a comfortably renovated shingled masterpiece in an exceptional school district like Rye in order to ameliorate any potential fallouts with my supervisor, except for the fact that had those bonus events fallen for me I wouldn't have had to have finessed my way into a job that really was just window dressing and a palliative for an institutional investor that demanded a New York presence, despite the facts that the corporate charter obviated our ability to fund the vast majority of debt investment opportunities in New York and that notwithstanding my late arrival to work, enduring an hour wait on an ice-covered commuter platform with a thirty-mile-an-hour wind whipping my face and having to let six trains go by before I mustered the temerity to squeeze my way into a packed, overheated sardine can of a car and standing up for two hours while the conductor kept making the same announcement that due to weather conditions, our train would not be arriving on schedule and to please be patient, I did not enjoy being late to work.

With our move to Westchester, we lived a lot closer to my parents. My dad and his wife lived in Rye, and my mother still lived at the ancestral home in Stamford. In Nyack, we had the Tappan Zee Bridge as a built-in excuse to not to visit people; in many ways Nyack relates more to Manhattan than to the suburbs in Westchester and Connecticut. But from New Rochelle, we were on a regular circuit up and back to Stamford and Rye. Stamford was weird, weirder than it was when I was a kid. Colonized by Credit Suisse and other investment banks, Stamford has been admitted to the Fairfield County gold coast but remains fragmented and without a spiritual center. One could argue that the center of the city is an intersection at the corner of Washington and Tresser Boulevards. What comes to mind when people mention Stamford, Connecticut? Beaches? Parks? A charming downtown? Usually it is that there are a bunch of corporate headquarters there. As far as Buckingham Drive went, it was a bit of a time capsule. There were a few minor remodels and even an added room here and there, but for the most part, the micro split levels and high ranches that were there in the 1960s were still intact. Not that they were decrepit or neglected, but shockingly not a lot had changed. Castlewood Park and its sister neighborhood of Three Lakes were at the pinnacle of mediocrity. The topography of the neighborhood was interesting enough, rolling and wooded. In the Westport neighborhood of Compo Hill, the lots are pretty small, perhaps one-eighth to one-quarter of an acre, but the houses are charming and inventively reimagined. No such aesthetic or creative force has emerged in most of Stamford. And Connecticut is not alone in this regard. My aunt has lived in Dix Hills, in mid–Long Island, for about fifty years, and it has the same dug-in, settled feel that many parts of Stamford have. Despite pockets of money, both towns lack a creative dynamic.

My Compo Hill dream died before it started. My wife wanted to go back to San Diego, and we were waiting for the right time to move. When my mother died in late 2005, we sold the house, packed, and switched coasts. It came together quickly, and with the kids all six and under, it seemed more like a big adventure than a strenuous relocation. The saddest part for me was leaving my Sunday soccer crew. Rusty to begin with, over the four years that I started playing outdoors again, I had found my soccer chops—in fact, I can say that I had improved, and by a lot. I was consistently in the middle of the pitch, running the show as it was. After my Achilles injury, I had converted to shooting left footed, and now that my right leg had healed, I was fully two-footed and could blast away with either foot. But what had really improved was my soccer brain. I suppose the thousands of hours I had logged watching every form of pro soccer imaginable, from the old Cosmos on WOR to Mexican league games broadcast on the old channel 41 in Spanish, games that were played in such stultifying heat that the players could barely manage a lope, let alone a sprint, had tweaked my synapses to recognize the difference between success and failure on the field with increased refinement. My soccer palette had emerged. As with artists, who over time develop their relationship with brush and paper and create a distinctive repertoire of strokes and detail that immediately reveal their creator, so it is on the soccer field. Over time, you lose speed but gain an understanding of movement. With nine other field players to share the ball, you have lots of options to create opportunities for others.

ELEVEN

Cali and the Battling Rabbis

ALMOST AS SMOOTHLY as switching the ball cross-field, we sold our house in New Rochelle and packed up to move to San Diego. Before we left, I met a few of my soccer friends at the new Buffalo Wild Wings in the weird downtown renewal project called "New Roc City." The project is a mixed-use high rise with an elevated plaza that violates the most basic tenet of good urban development. Instead of a "street wall," an inviting façade that is accessible at grade that draws pedestrian interest, there was an elevated plaza. After years of zoning policy that incentivized huge, windswept plazas, New York City shifted course in the 1990s, reverting to code that required street walls for new projects. New Rochelle was not so quick on the uptake, and the New Roc Project makes you either climb a whole bunch of ugly stairs or enter the project through a bleak parking garage. Anyhow, the draft beer at the Wild Wing was decent, and after an hour of semi-awkward chit-chat, I said goodbye to the park soccer crowd.

I had been trying to get a transfer with my company for a year or so but didn't have the clout. Through a friend, a well-connected retail real estate broker, I met an entrepreneur who owned a New England–based real estate company. He was a cross between Doc in *Back to the Future* and a finance professor and was enamored with a niche acquisition strategy that focused on buying fee (land) positions with high-value office buildings on long-term ground leases. These would be aggregated and resold, earning a spread in the process. We hit it off, and soon I was designated the West Coast guy. That facilitated our move, and off we went.

I had lived in California for a year in '94–'95, but moving a family of five versus just me had a lot more gravitas for obvious reasons. Before our Jet Blue flight out of JFK, we bunked at the airport Doubletree, which was just dirty enough to make me happy to be moving. When we decided to move, the slow process of my alienation from Manhattan was accelerated. But it would be great for the kids to have the sun in their faces and the sand between their toes. And the weather would have benefits for me as well. I heard that sports were big in San Diego.

In New Rochelle, I had dipped my toe into kid-sport water with a run-around soccer program for three-year-olds. It was an excuse for parents to schmooze on a crisp fall morning while the precious spawn ambled around a field. Nice enough. But soon we were in California, living in the overgrown surf town of Encinitas. All of San Diego is sports crazy. The temperature is nearly perfect year round, and with the exception of a week or two in the winter, there are no rainouts. We put my daughter, six at the time, in the Y program, and I volunteered to coach. It was sweet, coaching the six-year-old girls. They chugged up and down the plastic turf of the converted hockey rinks, the ball rounding the boards like a pinball vectoring towards a hole. I had never really coached before. I had done it on a lark, thinking that it would be a casual thing, getting across the simple points of trapping, passing, and shooting.

One girl had parents who were Division I athletes, the dad a hockey player, and the mom a soccer player. One day I was chatting with the dad, and I was talking about how the girls were having fun and how they had improved. His daughter was a nice little player, good but probably short of gifted. Without a hint of irony he looked at me and said, "Well, hopefully they get a scholarship out of it, that's the whole point, isn't it?" After a half a lifetime of nibbling at the edges of soccer, playing on makeshift club teams, on the fringes of urban parks on patches of dust, watching World Cup qualifiers between obscure South American and Caribbean nations, and behaving like a voracious soccer bottom feeder, I had to think to myself that, no, getting a scholarship was emphatically not the point.

But in the bright sun on an early Saturday morning at a California Y overlooking the Pacific Ocean, there is a bit of logic to the view that with the right inputs and DNA, you could envision your kid playing at a high level. In fact, the list of pros coming out of San Diego is pretty impressive: Frankie Hejduk, Steve Cherundolo, Sal Zisso, and a bunch of others in the national team mix come from the area.

That a lot of pros come out of San Diego (in a lot of sports, not just soccer) is a major contributor to the phenomenon of the Soccer Industrial Complex. The paradox of the SIC is that the

American compulsion to organize and structure is in complete opposition to the essence of soccer, which is improvisation. Structure, planning, preparation, and tactics are at the core of football. George Carlin famously contrasted the pastoral qualities of baseball with the militarism of football. Soccer perhaps occupies the middle zone, far too frenetic and active to be pastoral, but with possession continuously contested between two sides, there is precious little opportunity for scripted plays, with the exception of set pieces. If you watch the Premiership and other high-level soccer, there seems to be an increasing reliance on set pieces to settle games and create scoring chances. Goals from set pieces constitute a significant portion of total scoring in soccer. This should please the American sports fan, since set pieces can be practiced and run from a clipboard, just like football. The cult of Beckham is built around the set piece. His size twelve boot has been trained to strike the ball at an extremely acute angle, which imparts a severe downward rotation. When struck with just the right amount of power, this technique gets the ball up and over the wall quickly and on the frame of the goal. Cristiano Ronaldo has expanded this technique to being able to do this while addressing the ball straight on, essentially the up-and-over without movement in the horizontal plane.

But the prevalent status of soccer is that the more it grows, the more it is administered, overseen, and coopted by commercial interests. For a huge country, I'm not sure there is any other way. There seems to be three models of soccer development in the world. The first is the most organic and relies on sheer serendipity. This is the model used by poor countries with no choice and larger, richer countries that rely on their poor areas to incubate talent born of desperation. Brazil and Argentina can create massive numbers of talented kids because the talent emerges in the face of all obstacles. A kid with talent will take a bus three hours each way to find a decent trainer or club team in those countries. The second model, the academy model, is the choice for top European model and is used by Ajax, Barcelona, and many English teams. There, talent is identified at an early age and brought into soccer-specific training where academics are a secondary concern. Soccer is a business and is taught in a highly structured manner intended to prepare players for professional careers. The third model is the U.S. model that uses the NCAA as a de facto amateur development league. For a player it is like kissing your sister: pleasant but not great. You can learn the sport pretty well, maybe go pro, but you are not likely to get a shot at the top leagues until you apprentice for awhile in Norway or Bulgaria.

Without a strong tradition of soccer in the U.S.—and I think it is important to contrast history with tradition, insofar as there is a long history of soccer here, with only fragments of tradition—there is a profoundly diluted pool of soccer management. By default, parents, many of them well-meaning, have stepped in to fill the soccer void and have deployed their vestigial knowledge of Little League and Pop Warner to soccer. "Move here, Johnny, go there, Suzie!" Ouch! To coach is to love.

One day before one of our girls' games at the outdoor rink, I grabbed a few old tennis balls. I took all of the regular balls off the field and tossed out one of the little fuzzy ones. The kids stood around, flummoxed. The parents watching on the side were agitated: was there a kook in their midst? I told the girls to scrimmage with the tennis ball. They were a little tentative but gradually got into it. I noticed that they were concentrating more with the little ball—they had to, it was a lot harder to track and control. The extra attention forced them to focus on their footwork and close control. The best part was that it was extemporaneous fun, something not in the script.

And fun seems to be at the heart of the kid sports debate. Moving into league soccer, I was asked to be the assistant coach for my daughter's U-9 team. We practiced twice a week and played on Saturdays. It was scary. The trappings were beautiful: a cluster of real grass fields in Carlsbad, gently perched next to an office park. The fields were shaded by mature, broadleaf coral trees. Our Uber Mom, Andrea, came to the games early, armed with clipboard, snacks, and inspirational banners. Teams set up encampments, and the coaches put the girls through warm-ups.

Although the proverbial bad sports parent is well documented in the press, nothing quite prepared me for my first real encounter. An opposing coach, with leather lungs and a bad attitude, spent an entire game shouting at his team: "C'mon Lacey, GET THERE. Brittany, THAT'S YOUR BALL. Alex, DIG IN." A full hour of merciless hounding to the point where it was torture, like listening to secret Guantanamo tapes. Was this coaching or a sordid form of sports exorcism? The man was literally handing out a verbal beating to his girls. Part of the problem is that with a "coach" like that, his recriminations and bellowing are heard by all the girls, not just his charges. That the ranting was directed towards his team became moot after the first ten minutes or so. It assumed a larger context and enveloped the whole game with a twisted reality: what was supposed to be a fun day for a bunch of little girls turned into a forum for a frustrated and maniacal adult to vent his emotions.

And the adults who played in California were worse. Through our real estate agent's girlfriend, an Israeli, I learned about a game a lot like the one I left in New Rochelle. One Sunday, I met up with an Israeli guy named Teddy and followed him to a pristine field next to a superfancy grammar school in Del Mar Heights. One thing California is not short on is beautiful fields. Where in New York the fields range from dust bowls to crabgrass with every variation of lumpy weed and encrusted muddy tundra in between, California's twelve-month growing season and fanatical army of landscapers makes for really nice playing surfaces.

It was love all over again. I was energized by the short, groomed grass, the sea air, and a different crowd. You always have something to prove when you join a different group. Like in a marriage, playing week after week with the same bunch of people habituates you to their style but doesn't always make for that frisson that sparks your passion. Of course they are watching you too. Is this guy a star or a dud or something most likely in between?

I did decently, spraying a few passes, but also connecting on some beauties. I didn't score but pushed forward enough to prove that I had some skill going forward. There was some Hebrew spoken on the field. If it wasn't for the dry Santa Ana wind and powerful California sun, I could have sworn that I had imported my old game all the way from New Rochelle.

But there was something a bit different from this crowd. The New Rochelle Israelis were animated and obviously yelled in Hebrew on the pitch, but the Californians kept up with Hebrew, even in the presence of non-Hebrew speakers. It was clear that there was a crowd within a crowd. You were welcome to play, but not welcome to be part of the conversation. Four years into playing in this game, and the situation hasn't changed. And it's not that a lot of them aren't friendly; when I initiate a conversation in English, they are more than welcoming, but they revert to all Hebrew when there is a kaffeklatch.

Not long after starting in Del Mar, a guy showed up with a skullcap and a beard. A rabbi. In New York, I had never seen a rabbi anywhere near a sports field since my days at Bi-Cultural Day School, and that memory was of my Hebrew Studies teacher, Rabbi Kosowski, swinging a baseball bat so awkwardly that his yarmulke went one way and his portly body the other. I had read *The Chosen* as a kid, finding the baseball scenes with the orthodox guys only semibelievable. There were, of course, whole Yeshivas, including Yeshiva University, that fielded NCAA teams, but for me, with the whole antisports scene that I dealt with in grade school, Orthodox Judaism and sports never really mixed. This particular rabbi did not have a whole bunch of skill but had the tenacity of a badger. Squat and determined, he had tremendous endurance and a reputation for fouling.

Two other rabbis were regular players, and they had much more skill. They were younger guys, in their twenties and thirties, and foreign born, but they were damn good players. Their clerical calling did not exactly translate to a higher standard of sporting behavior. One time I came in late on one of the rabbis and clipped his ankle pretty hard. It was definitely a foul, but nothing intentional or especially dirty. He was on the ground, holding his ankle and wincing. After about ten seconds or so, I went over to help him up and he looked at me and snarled. Something about the way he looked at me set me off—he had fouled me a whole bunch of times before, and I called a foul and got on with it. No need to make these things personal. For once I had gotten him, and now he was making a big deal of it.

"I don't think I got you all that badly," I said after he refused my helping hand.

Again, he glared: "You know what I think? I think you're a low-life."

With that comment, I had reached the pinnacle, or depending on how you think about it, the nadir of my sports career. In a sense it was pretty cool being cursed out by a rabbi. Doesn't happen every day. It also seemed like a real California thing. The sun, the babes, the beach eventually get to everyone out here. They make you dreamy and mushy and rob you of the clarity that you need to survive, say, in New York. Maybe I'm wrong, but I couldn't imagine doing anything to piss off a New York rabbi enough for him or her to call someone a low-life, let alone a fairly harmless soccer foul. In grade school, all I saw of rabbis was an endless recitation of Jewish lore, customs, laws, and ethical dilemmas. A lot of it seemed to center around oxen goring one another, or at least that's how my hormone-addled seventh grade brain parsed it.

So there he sat, writhing, or at least pretending to writhe. As much as I thought he was being a petulant little whiny baby, I had extended my hand to help him up and he had declined. Empowered, I told him he was a piece of work and deserved his fate. Callous? Sacrilegious? I think not. He had felt free to express himself, and in the grand scheme of things, he was just another soccer player on the field, covenant with god or not. Soccer is a level playing field, and once you start, whether it is a World Cup final or a pickup game with a bunch of Advil-popping geriatrics, there is an elemental form of striving that comes out in ways that are sometimes beautiful and sometimes ugly. Everyone is welcome to join the party.

DANIEL LILIE is a freelance author and occasional radio personality who has an abiding interest in the intersection between amateur sport and urban culture. He has been a regular columnist for *Time Out New York* and *Inline Hockey News* and has contributed feature pieces to *Inline Magazine*. Dan has also appeared as a guest on *World Football Daily,* the largest subscription-based podcast of its kind.

Made in the USA
Middletown, DE
14 November 2017